INDUSTRIAL BIOGRAPHY

INDUSTRIAL
BIOGRAPHY

EARLY IRON-MAKERS.

INDUSTRIAL BIOGRAPHY

Iron Workers and Tool Makers

by

Samuel Smiles

A reprint of the 1863 edition with
additional illustrations and a new introduction by

L. T. C. ROLT

DAVID & CHARLES : NEWTON ABBOT

7153 4208 8

This work was first published by John Murray of Albemarle Street in November 1863. The copy from which this edition has been produced was marked 1863 and 'Fifteenth Thousand', showing that the book met with immediate success. It was reprinted, using the same type, in January 1874, November 1876, April 1879, January 1882, October 1883, September 1886, September 1889 and March 1895. There was then a Popular Edition, but again using the same type, issued in November 1897, reprinted one month later and again in August 1902 and July 1908, since when the book has become increasingly scarce. A few minor corrections made in later reprints of the first edition are not included here since the first edition has been chosen for reproduction due to the clarity of the type.

New introduction and illustrations

© L. T. C. Rolt 1967

Printed in Great Britain
by Latimer Trend & Co Ltd Whitstable
for David & Charles (Publishers) Ltd
Newton Abbot Devon

INTRODUCTION TO 1967 EDITION

'Kings, warriors and statesmen have heretofore mono-
polised not only the pages of history, but almost those of
biography. Surely some niche ought to be found for the
Mechanic, without whose skill and labour society, as it is,
could not exist.'

In his Preface to this book, Samuel Smiles quotes this
comment, made to him by 'a distinguished living mechanic'
and for over eighty years its validity would stand. Only
recently has the rapid growth of interest in the history of
technology done something towards restoring the engineer
to his rightful place in our social history. Yet the attitude
which the distinguished mechanic complained about in
1875 still exists in 1967. It may be found entrenched in the
literary columns of the Sunday newspapers, for example,
where reviewers betray an archaic attitude towards anything to do with technology similar to that of the Victorian
landed gentleman's towards 'trade'.

But whether this beleaguered ivory tower of literature
can hold out very much longer against a growing assault
is doubtful, for if we compare the between-wars years with
today, particularly in the sphere of education, a significant
change is apparent. As a child who grew up during those
years I could not fail to become aware of the immense
changes in our society that developments in our technology
had brought about. The process filled me with curiosity.
I passionately sought to know how this Industrial Revolution, as it was called, had come about and what manner of
men had led it. My historical education at a public school
left this very natural curiosity totally unsatisfied. It was
wholly concerned with those kings, warriors and statesmen
and if the Industrial Revolution was mentioned at all it
was solely as an impersonal phenomenon, presenting these
eminent gentlemen with novel social problems which they
attempted to solve—or more often failed to solve—by

traditional means. It became clear even to my childish mind that the Industrial Revolution had created a situation in which the figureheads of the history books were no longer in control of events as was comfortably assumed, but of the forces responsible for this situation I could learn nothing.

It was not until I was nearing the end of my engineering apprenticeship, six years after I had left school, that I was enlightened. I picked up the three volumes of Samuel Smiles' *Lives of the Engineers,* 1862 edition, for 7s 6d and my education began.

Recent research has revealed Smiles' defects as an historian. To conform with his ideas of self-help, his engineers appear as scarcely human paragons of industry and virtue while, because he lived much closed to the events he describes, he was apt to rely too heavily upon hearsay; upon the fallible recollections of elderly men. Again, although Smiles' secretaryship of the Leeds & Thirsk and the South Eastern railways proved valuable to him in writing of the railway revolution wrought by the two Stephensons, he was not himself an engineer and was thus not fully competent to assess the technical achievements of his characters. However, in his day (and the same is true today) very few engineers possesed the gift of writing about their profession in a manner which would interest the layman. Smiles had this gift and on this account we should not presume to judge his work by too narrowly academic a standard. In its scope and range, the sum of Smiles writing on the history of the Industrial Revolution is a masterly achievement and any detail errors pale into insignificance beside the graphic picture he presents of the transformation of society under the impact of technology change. How many of us would be in a position to prove Smiles wrong in detail had our imaginations not been quickened and our interest fired by his own writing?

In his *Lives of the Engineers* Smiles dealt almost exclusively with the revolution of transportation brought about by the great pioneer builders of roads, canals and railways. This choice of subject for his first major work in this field was doubtless deliberate. First, it was of vital importance. Without improved means of transport technological change was impossible. Secondly, the work of great civil engineers like Brindley, Rennie and Telford has an overtly dramatic quality which appeals to the layman and, for a writer like Smiles, it has the advantage that, unlike the work of mechanical engineers, it can be more readily described in non-technical terms. But the improvement in transportation, though essential, was only one of the vigorously interacting and potent forces that generated the Industrial Revolution. The development of steam power and the improvement in methods of iron production and engineering workshop practice were equally important.

For this reason, *Lives of the Engineers* has been criticised as presenting a one-sided view of the Revolution by overemphasising the part played by improved communications. Because *Lives of the Engineers* was the author's first, most weighty and best-known contribution to this field, such a criticism was perhaps inevitable, but it is hardly fair to Smiles. He was clearly aware that there were other forces at work; that, for example, the success of the railway revolution depended not only upon the development of steam power but upon those improvements in metal production and metal working which made that development a practical possibility. He dealt with the development of steam power in his *Lives of Boulton and Watt* and with the contribution of the iron workers and tool makers in *Industrial Biography*. Moreover, one chapter in the latter book was later greatly expanded into the *Autobiography* of James Nasmyth of which Smiles modestly styled himself editor, although he wrote the book with Nasmyth's notes and diaries as his primary source.

It is unfair, therefore, to judge Smiles' achievement as a

historian on his *Lives of the Engineers* alone. It is essential to read his other three books, and particularly *Industrial Biography,* in order fairly to assess his achievement. *Industrial Biography* was first published in November 1863 and by 1908, when Smiles' works fell into eclipse, it had been reprinted twelve times. Nevertheless, it never enjoyed the popularity of the *Lives* and today it remains the least-known of his historical writings and the hardest to obtain. This comparative lack of popularity is understandable. From the point of view of the layman, the lives of the great iron-masters and mechanics with whom the book deals lack the drama and romance which surround the achievements of Rennie, Telford or the Stephensons. Inevitably, great works such as the Menai suspension bridge or the first trunk railways captured the imagination of the public who were thus eager to learn more of the men responsible for them. Ironmasters and 'ingenious mechanics', on the other hand, were the 'back-room boys' of the Industrial Revolution. Their furnaces and machine shops and the feats they performed therein were unknown and unintelligible to the public. Yet the parts they played were vital to the success of the revolution and the fact that so little would otherwise be known about them makes this book particularly valuable.

On some details the book is untrustworthy. For instance, in Chapter 3 Smiles accepts Dud Dudley's own claim in *Metallum Martis* that he succeeded in smelting iron with pit coal whereas modern historians of the iron industry agree that he could not have done so with success and unanimously award the palm for this vastly significant innovation to Abraham Darby I of Coalbrookdale. Again on page 205, Smiles accepts Nasmyth's story that it was Henry Maudslay's invention of a self-sealing leather collar that made Joseph Bramah's hydraulic press workable, yet recent research into the life and work of Bramah has shown this to be a groundless legend. On such points of detail,

Smiles' statements should be accepted with reserve but they should not be allowed to blind us to the book's merits. We should be surprised, not that Smiles erred occasionally, but that he erred so seldom. The total picture he presents of a period of great technological endeavour and innovation is masterly. Indeed, Smiles' supreme gift for organising a mass of historical material and presenting it in a concise and highly readable form is nowhere better displayed than in this book.

Like the great civil engineers described in the *Lives*, the ironmasters and mechanics of *Industrial Biography* display those qualities which Smiles most admired: self-help, self-discipline and a single-minded devotion to their work. For them, work was their life. The works of Smiles became unpopular in the new century because an egalitarian and socialistic current of thought considered his philsophy old-fashioned and the qualities he admired in the pioneer engineers no longer admirable. Such a devotion to work was considered puritanical and inimicable to the full flowering of the human spirit, a criticism which at first thought seems valid but which overlooks the great change that has taken place in the nature of work since the period of which Smiles writes. For the technological revolution has reached a stage in which it allows too little scope for creative living. The majority of jobs are too specialised, too repetitive and too boring to be regarded as other than an irksome means of earning a livelihood, of buying the maximum freedom from work's stress and tedium. In such a pass we should not condemn Smiles' heroes as so many grim-faced puritans but rather envy them their creative freedom. The smaller, simpler, slower-paced world that Smiles describes was the engineer's oyster and it was his work that made his life infinitely exciting and challenging.

We are still living in the Industrial Revolution; indeed in the last twenty years its tempo has accelerated prodigiously. If we are to learn how to live with it and how to control it, a knowledge of how it all began is essential. The books of Samuel Smiles still provide the most comprehensive picture we have of that momentous beginning and the publishers are to be commended for their enterprise in re-issuing a little-known book which deserves to be far more widely read.

L.T.C.R.

PREFACE.

~~~~~~~~~

THE Author offers the following book as a continuation, in a more generally accessible form, of the Series of Memoirs of Industrial Men introduced in his *Lives of the Engineers.* While preparing that work he frequently came across the tracks of celebrated inventors, mechanics, and iron-workers —the founders, in a great measure, of the modern industry of Britain—whose labours seemed to him well worthy of being traced out and placed on record, and the more so as their lives presented many points of curious and original interest. Having been encouraged to prosecute the subject by offers of assistance from some of the most eminent living mechanical engineers, he is now enabled to present the following further series of memoirs to the public.

Without exaggerating the importance of this class of biography, it may at least be averred that it has not yet received its due share of attention. While commemorating the labours and honouring the names of those who have striven to elevate man above the material and mechanical, the labours of the important industrial class to whom society owes so much of its comfort and well-being are also entitled to consideration. Without derogating from the biographic claims of those who minister to intellect and taste, those who minister to utility need not be overlooked. When a Frenchman was praising to Sir John Sinclair the artist who invented ruffles, the Baronet shrewdly remarked that some merit was also due to the man who added the shirt.

A distinguished living mechanic thus expresses himself to the Author on this point :—" Kings, warriors, and statesmen have heretofore monopolized not only the pages of history, but almost those of biography. Surely some niche ought to be found for the Mechanic, without whose skill and labour society, as it is, could not exist. I do not begrudge destructive heroes their fame, but the constructive ones ought not to be forgotten ; and there *is* a heroism of skill and toil belonging to the latter class, worthy of as grateful record,—less perilous and romantic, it may be, than that of the other, but not less full of the results of human energy, bravery, and character. The lot of labour is indeed often a dull one; and it is doing a public service to endeavour to lighten it up by records of the struggles and triumphs of our more illustrious workers, and the results of their labours in the cause of human advancement."

As respects the preparation of the following memoirs, the Author's principal task has consisted in selecting and arranging the materials so liberally placed at his disposal by gentlemen for the most part personally acquainted with the subjects of them, and but for whose assistance the book could not have been written. The materials for the biography of Henry Maudslay, for instance, have been partly supplied by the late Mr. Joshua Field, F.R.S. (his partner), but principally by Mr. James Nasmyth, C.E., his distinguished pupil. In like manner Mr. John Penn, C.E., has supplied the chief materials for the memoir of Joseph Clement, assisted by Mr. Wilkinson, Clement's nephew. The Author has also had the valuable assistance of Mr. William Fairbairn, F.R.S., Mr. J. O. March, tool manufacturer (Mayor of Leeds), Mr. Richard Roberts, C.E., Mr. Henry Maudslay, C.E., and Mr. J. Kitson, Jun., iron manufacturer, Leeds, in the preparation of the other memoirs of mechanical engineers included in this volume.

The materials for the memoirs of the early iron-workers have in like manner been obtained for the most part from original sources; those of the Darbys and Reynoldses from Mr. Dickinson of Coalbrookdale, Mr. William Reynolds of Coed-dû, and Mr. William G. Norris of the former place, as well as from Mr. Anstice of Madeley Wood, who has kindly supplied the original records of the firm. The substance of the biography of Benjamin Huntsman, the inventor of cast-steel, has been furnished by his lineal representatives; and the facts embodied in the memoirs of Henry Cort and David Mushet have been supplied by the sons of those inventors. To Mr. Anderson Kirkwood of Glasgow the Author is indebted for the memoir of James Beaumont Neilson, inventor of the hot blast; and to Mr.

Ralph Moore, Inspector of Mines in Scotland, for various information relative to the progress of the Scotch iron manufacture.

The memoirs of Dud Dudley and Andrew Yarranton are almost the only ones of the series in preparing which material assistance has been derived from books; but these have been largely illustrated by facts contained in original documents preserved in the State Paper Office, the careful examination of which has been conducted by Mr. W. Walker Wilkins.

It will thus be observed that most of the information embodied in this volume, more especially that relating to the inventors of tools and machines, has heretofore existed only in the memories of the eminent mechanical engineers from whom it has been collected. The estimable Joshua Field has died since the date at which he communicated his recollections; and in a few more years many of the facts which have been caught and are here placed on record would, probably, in the ordinary course of things, have passed into oblivion. As it is, the Author feels that there are many gaps yet to be filled up; but the field of Industrial Biography is a wide one, and is open to all who will labour in it.

London, October, 1863.

CONTENTS.

CHAPTER I.

IRON AND CIVILIZATION.

CHAPTER II.

BEGINNINGS OF THE IRON-MANUFACTURE IN BRITAIN.

CHAPTER III.

IRON SMELTING BY PIT-COAL — DUD DUDLEY.

CHAPTER IV.

ANDREW YARRANTON.

CHAPTER V.

COALBROOKDALE IRON WORKS — THE DARBYS AND REYNOLDSES.

CHAPTER VI.

CHAPTER VII.

CHAPTER VIII.

CHAPTER IX.

INVENTION OF THE HOT BLAST — JAMES BEAUMONT
NEILSON.

CHAPTER X.

MECHANICAL INVENTIONS AND INVENTORS.

CHAPTER XI.

Joseph Bramah.

CHAPTER XII.

Henry Maudslay.

CHAPTER XIII.

JOSEPH CLEMENT.

CHAPTER XIV.

FOX OF DERBY — MURRAY OF LEEDS — ROBERTS AND WHITWORTH OF MANCHESTER.

CHAPTER XV.

James Nasmyth.

CHAPTER XVI.

William Fairbairn.

INDUSTRIAL BIOGRAPHY.

CHAPTER I.

IRON AND CIVILIZATION.

" Iron is not only the soul of every other manufacture, but the mainspring perhaps of civilized society."—FRANCIS HORNER.

" Were the use of iron lost among us, we should in a few ages be unavoidably reduced to the wants and ignorance of the ancient savage Americans ; so that he who first made known the use of that contemptible mineral may be truly styled the father of Arts and the author of Plenty." —JOHN LOCKE.

WHEN Captain Cook and the early navigators first sailed into the South Seas on their voyages of discovery, one of the things that struck them with most surprise was the avidity which the natives displayed for iron. " Nothing would go down with our visitors," says Cook, " but metal; and iron was their beloved article." A nail would buy a good-sized pig ; and on one occasion the navigator bought some four hundred pounds weight of fish for a few wretched knives improvised out of an old hoop.

" For iron tools," says Captain Carteret, " we might have purchased everything upon the Freewill Islands that we could have brought away. A few pieces of old iron hoop presented to one of the natives threw him into an ecstasy little short of distraction." At Otaheite the people were found generally well-behaved and honest; but they were not proof against the fascinations of iron. Captain Cook says that one of them, after resisting all other temptations, " was at length ensnared by the charms of a basket of nails." Another lurked about for several days, watching the opportunity to steal a coal-rake.

The navigators found they could pay their way from island to island merely with scraps of iron, which were as useful for the purpose as gold coins would have been in Europe. The drain, however, being continuous, Captain Cook became alarmed at finding his currency almost exhausted; and he relates his joy on recovering an old anchor which the French Captain Bougainville had lost at Bolabola, on which he felt as an English banker would do after a severe run upon him for gold, when suddenly placed in possession of a fresh store of bullion.

The avidity for iron displayed by these poor islanders will not be wondered at when we consider that whoever among them was so fortunate as to obtain possession of an old nail, immediately became a man of greater power than his fellows, and assumed the rank of a capitalist. " An Otaheitan chief," says Cook, "who had got two nails in his possession, received no small emolument by letting out the use of them to his neighbours for the purpose of boring holes when their own methods failed, or were thought too tedious."

The native methods referred to by Cook were of a very clumsy sort; the principal tools of the Otaheitans being of wood, stone, and flint. Their adzes and axes were of stone. The gouge most commonly used by them was made out of the bone of the human forearm. Their substitute for a knife was a shell, or a bit of flint or jasper. A shark's tooth, fixed to a piece of wood, served for an auger; a piece of coral for a file; and the skin of a sting-ray for a polisher. Their saw was made of jagged fishes' teeth fixed on the convex edge of a piece of hard wood. Their weapons were of a similarly rude description; their clubs and axes were headed with stone, and their lances and arrows were tipped with flint. Fire was another agency employed by them, usually in boat-building. Thus, the New Zealanders, whose tools were also of stone, wood, or bone, made their boats of the trunks of trees hollowed out by fire.

The stone implements were fashioned, Captain Cook says, by rubbing one stone upon another until brought to the required shape; but, after all, they were found very inefficient for their purpose. They soon became blunted and useless; and the laborious process of making new tools had to be begun again. The delight of the islanders at being put in possession of a material which was capable of taking a comparatively sharp edge and keeping it, may therefore readily be imagined; and hence the remarkable incidents to which we have referred in the experience of the early voyagers. In the minds of the natives, iron became the representative of power, efficiency, and wealth; and they were ready almost to fall down and worship their new tools, esteeming the axe as a deity, offering sacrifices to the saw, and holding the knife in especial veneration.

In the infancy of all nations the same difficulties must have been experienced for want of tools, before the arts of smelting and working in metals had become known; and it is not improbable that the Phœnician navigators who first frequented our coasts found the same avidity for bronze and iron existing among the poor woad-stained Britons who flocked down to the shore to see their ships and exchange food and skins with them, that Captain Cook discovered more than two thousand years later among the natives of Otaheite and New Zealand. For, the tools and weapons found in ancient burying-places in all parts of Britain clearly show that these islands also have passed through the epoch of stone and flint.

There was recently exhibited at the Crystal Palace a collection of ancient European weapons and implements placed alongside a similar collection of articles brought from the South Seas; and they were in most respects so much alike that it was difficult to believe that they did not belong to the same race and period, instead of being the implements of races sundered by half the globe, and living at periods more than two thousand years apart. Nearly every weapon in the one collection had its counterpart in the other,

—the mauls or celts of stone, the spearheads of flint or jasper, the arrowheads of flint or bone, and the saws of jagged stone, showing how human ingenuity, under like circumstances, had resorted to like expedients. It would also appear that the ancient tribes in these islands, like the New Zealanders, used fire to hollow out their larger boats; several specimens of this kind of vessel having recently been dug up in the valleys of the Witham and the Clyde, some of the latter from under the very streets of modern Glasgow.* Their smaller boats, or coracles, were made of osiers interwoven, covered with hides, and rigged with leathern sails and thong tackle.

It will readily be imagined that anything like civilization, as at present understood, must have been next to impossible under such circumstances. " Miserable indeed," says Carlyle, " was the condition of the aboriginal savage, glaring fiercely from under his fleece of hair, which with the beard reached down to his loins, and hung round them like a matted cloak; the rest of his body sheeted in its thick natural fell. He loitered in the sunny glades of the forest, living on wild fruits; or, as the ancient Caledonians, squatted himself in morasses, lurking for his bestial or human prey; without implements, without arms, save the ball of heavy flint, to which, that his sole possession and defence might not be lost, he had attached a long cord of

---

* " Mr. John Buchanan, a zealous antiquary, writing in 1855, informs us that in the course of the eighty years preceding that date, no less than seventeen canoes had been dug out of this estuarine silt [of the valley of the Clyde], and that he had personally inspected a large number of them before they were exhumed. Five of them lay buried in silt under the streets of Glasgow, one in a vertical position with the prow uppermost, as if it had sunk in a storm. . . . Almost every one of these ancient boats was formed out of a single oak-stem, hollowed out by blunt tools, probably stone axes, aided by the action of fire; a few were cut beautifully smooth, evidently with metallic tools. Hence a gradation could be traced from a pattern of extreme rudeness to one showing great mechanical ingenuity. . . . In one of the canoes a beautifully polished celt or axe of greenstone was found; in the bottom of another a plug of cork, which, as Mr. Geikie remarks, ' could only have come from the latitudes of Spain, Southern France, or Italy.' " —Sir C. LYELL, Antiquity of Man, 48-9.

plaited thongs; thereby recovering as well as hurling it with deadly, unerring skill."

The injunction given to man to "replenish the earth and subdue it" could not possibly be fulfilled with implements of stone. To fell a tree with a flint hatchet would occupy the labour of a month, and to clear a small patch of ground for purposes of culture would require the combined efforts of a tribe. For the same reason, dwellings could not be erected; and without dwellings domestic tranquillity, security, culture, and refinement, especially in a rude climate, were all but impossible. Mr. Emerson well observes, that "the effect of a house is immense on human tranquillity, power, and refinement. A man in a cave or a camp—a nomad—dies with no more estate than the wolf or the horse leaves. But so simple a labour as a house being achieved, his chief enemies are kept at bay. He is safe from the teeth of wild animals, from frost, sunstroke, and weather; and fine faculties begin to yield their fine harvest. Inventions and arts are born, manners, and social beauty and delight." But to build a house which should serve for shelter, for safety, and for comfort—in a word, as a home for the family, which is the nucleus of society—better tools than those of stone were absolutely indispensable.

Hence most of the early European tribes were nomadic: first hunters, wandering about from place to place like the American Indians, after the game; then shepherds, following the herds of animals which they had learnt to tame, from one grazing-ground to another, living upon their milk and flesh, and clothing themselves in their skins held together by leathern thongs. It was only when implements of metal had been invented that it was possible to practise the art of agriculture with any considerable success. Then tribes would cease from their wanderings, and begin to form settlements, homesteads, villages, and towns. An old Scandinavian legend thus curiously illustrates this last period:—There was a giantess whose daughter one day saw a husbandman ploughing in the field. She ran and picked him up with her finger and thumb, put him and his plough and oxen into her apron, and carried them to her mother, saying, " Mother, what sort of beetle is this that I have found wriggling in the sand?" But the mother said, " Put it away, my child; we must begone out of this land, for these people will dwell in it."

M. Worsaae of Copenhagen, who has been followed by other antiquaries, has even gone so far as to divide the natural history of civilization into three epochs, according to the character of the tools used in each. The first was the Stone period, in which the implements chiefly used were sticks, bones, stones, and flints. The next was the Bronze period, distinguished by the introduction and general use of a metal composed of copper and tin, requiring a comparatively low degree of temperature to smelt it, and render it capable of being fashioned into weapons, tools, and implements; to make which, however, indicated a great advance in experience, sagacity, and skill in the manipulation of metals. With tools of bronze, to which considerable hardness could be given, trees were felled, stones hewn, houses and ships built, and agriculture practised with comparative facility. Last of all came the Iron period, when the art of smelting and working that most difficult but widely diffused of the minerals was discovered; from which point the progress made in all the arts of life has been of the most remarkable character.

Although Mr. Wright rejects this classification as empirical, because the periods are not capable of being clearly defined, and all the three kinds of implements are found to have been in use at or about the same time,* there is, nevertheless, reason to believe that it is, on the whole, well founded. It is doubtless true that implements of stone continued in use long after those of bronze and iron had been invented, arising most probably from the dear-

---

* THOMAS WRIGHT, F.S.A., *The Celt, The Roman, and The Saxon*, ed. 1861.

ness and scarcity of articles of metal; but when the art of smelting and working in iron and steel had sufficiently advanced, the use of stone, and afterwards of bronze tools and weapons, altogether ceased.

The views of M. Worsaae, and the other Continental antiquarians who follow his classification, have indeed received remarkable confirmation of late years, by the discoveries which have been made in the beds of most of the Swiss lakes.*   It appears that a subsidence took place in the waters of the Lake of Zurich in the year 1854, laying bare considerable portions of its bed.   The adjoining proprietors proceeded to enclose the new land, and began by erecting permanent dykes to prevent the return of the waters.   While carrying on the works, several rows of stakes were exposed; and on digging down, the labourers turned up a number of pieces of charred wood, stones blackened by fire, utensils, bones, and other articles, showing that at some remote period, a number of human beings had lived over the spot, in dwellings supported by stakes driven into the bed of the lake.

The discovery having attracted attention, explorations were made at other places, and it was shortly found that there was scarcely a lake in Switzerland which did not yield similar evidence of the existence of an ancient Lacustrine or Lake-dwelling population.   Numbers of their tools and implements were brought to light—stone axes and saws, flint arrowheads, bone needles, and such like— mixed with the bones of wild animals slain in the chase; pieces of old boats, portions of twisted branches, bark, and rough planking, of which their dwellings had been formed, the latter still bearing the marks of the rude tools by which they had been laboriously cut.   In the most ancient, or lowest series of deposits, no traces of metal, either of bronze or iron, were discovered; and it is most probable that these lake-dwellers lived in as primi-

---

* Referred to at length in the *Antiquity of Man*, by Sir C. Lyell, who adopts M. Worsaae's classification.

tive a state as the South Sea islanders discovered by Captain Cook, and that the huts over the water in which they lived resembled those found in Papua and Borneo, and the islands of the Salomon group, to this day.

These aboriginal Swiss lake-dwellers seem to have been succeeded by a race of men using tools, implements, and ornaments of bronze. In some places the remains of this bronze period directly overlay those of the stone period, showing the latter to have been the most ancient; but in others, the village sites are altogether distinct. The articles with which the metal implements are intermixed, show that considerable progress had been made in the useful arts. The potter's wheel had been introduced. Agriculture had begun, and wild animals had given place to tame ones. The abundance of bronze also shows that commerce must have existed to a certain extent; for tin, which enters into its composition, is a comparatively rare metal, and must necessarily have been imported from other European countries.

The Swiss antiquarians are of opinion that the men of bronze suddenly invaded and extirpated the men of flint; and that at some still later period, another stronger and more skilful race, supposed to have been Celts from Gaul, came armed with iron weapons, to whom the men of bronze succumbed, or with whom, more probably, they gradually intermingled. When iron, or rather steel, came into use, its superiority in affording a cutting edge was so decisive that it seems to have supplanted bronze almost at once; *

---

* Mr. Mushet, however, observes that "the general use of hardened copper by the ancients for edge-tools and warlike instruments, does not preclude the supposition that iron was then comparatively plentiful, though it is probable that it was confined to the ruder arts of life. A knowledge of the mixture of copper, tin, and zinc, seems to have been among the first discoveries of the metallurgist. Instruments fabricated from these alloys, recommended by the use of ages, the perfection of the art, the splendour and polish of their surfaces, not easily injured by time and weather, would not soon be superseded by the invention of simple iron, inferior in edge and polish, at all times easily injured by rust, and in the early stages of its manufacture converted with difficulty into forms that required proportion or elegance." — (*Papers on Iron and Steel*, 365-6.) By some secret method that has been

the latter metal continuing to be employed only for the purpose of making scabbards or sword-handles. Shortly after the commencement of the iron age, the lake-habitations were abandoned, the only settlement of this later epoch yet discovered being that at Téne, on Lake Neufchatel : and it is a remarkable circumstance, showing the great antiquity of the lake-dwellings, that they are not mentioned by any of the Roman historians.

That iron should have been one of the last of the metals to come into general use, is partly accounted for by the circumstance that iron, though one of the most generally diffused of minerals, never presents itself in a natural state, except in meteorites ; and that to recognise its ores, and then to separate the metal from its matrix, demands the exercise of no small amount of observation and invention. Persons unacquainted with minerals would be unable to discover the slightest affinity between the rough ironstone as brought up from the mine, and the iron or steel of commerce. To unpractised eyes they would seem to possess no properties in common, and it is only after subjecting the stone to severe processes of manufacture that usable metal can be obtained from it. The effectual reduction of the ore requires an intense heat, maintained by artificial methods, such as furnaces and blowing apparatus.* But it is principally in combination with other elements that iron is so valuable when compared with other metals. Thus, when combined with carbon, in varying proportions, substances are produced, so different, but each so valuable, that they might almost be regarded in the light of distinct metals,—such, for example, as cast-iron, and cast and bar-

lost, perhaps because no longer needed since the invention of steel, the ancients manufactured bronze tools capable of taking a fine edge. In our own time, Chantrey the sculptor, in his reverence for classic metallurgy, had a bronze razor made with which he martyred himself in shaving ; but none were found so hardy and devoted as to follow his example.

* It may be mentioned in passing, that while Zinc is fusible at 3° of Wedgwood's pyrometer, Silver at 22°, Copper at 27°, and Gold at 32°, Cast Iron is only fusible at 130°. Tin (one of the constituents of the ancient bronze) and Lead are fusible at much lower degrees than zinc.

steel; the various qualities of iron enabling it to be used for purposes so opposite as a steel pen and a railroad, the needle of a mariner's compass and an Armstrong gun, a surgeon's lancet and a steam engine, the mainspring of a watch and an iron ship, a pair of scissors and a Nasmyth hammer, a lady's earrings and a tubular bridge.

The variety of purposes to which iron is thus capable of being applied, renders it of more use to mankind than all the other metals combined. Unlike iron, gold is found pure, and in an almost workable state; and at an early period in history, it seems to have been much more plentiful than iron or steel. But gold was unsuited for the purposes of tools, and would serve for neither a saw, a chisel, an axe, nor a sword; whilst tempered steel could answer all these purposes. Hence we find the early warlike nations making the backs of their swords of gold or copper, and economizing their steel to form the cutting edge. This is illustrated by many ancient Scandinavian weapons in the museum at Copenhagen, which indicate the greatest parsimony in the use of steel at a period when both gold and copper appear to have been comparatively abundant.

The knowledge of smelting and working in iron, like most other arts, came from the East. Iron was especially valued for purposes of war, of which indeed it was regarded as the symbol, being called "Mars" by the Romans.* We find frequent mention of it in the Bible. One of the earliest notices of the metal is in connexion with the conquest of Judea by the Philistines. To complete the subjection of the Israelites, their conquerors made captive all the smiths of the land, and carried them away. The Philistines felt that their hold of the country was insecure so long as the inhabitants possessed the means of forging weapons. Hence "there was no smith found throughout all the land

---

* The Romans named the other metals after the gods. Thus Quicksilver was called *Mercury*, Lead *Saturn*, Tin *Jupiter*, Copper *Venus*, Silver *Luna*, and so on; and our own language has received a colouring from the Roman nomenclature, which it continues to retain.

of Israel; for the Philistines said, Lest the Hebrews make them swords or spears. But the Israelites went down to the Philistines, to sharpen every man his share, and his coulter, and his axe, and his mattock."* At a later period, when Jerusalem was taken by the Babylonians, one of their first acts was to carry the smiths and other craftsmen captives to Babylon.† Deprived of their armourers, the Jews were rendered comparatively powerless.

It was the knowledge of the art of iron-forging which laid the foundation of the once great empire of the Turks. Gibbon relates that these people were originally the despised slaves of the powerful Khan of the Geougen. They occupied certain districts of the mountain-ridge in the centre of Asia, called Imaus, Caf, and Altai, which yielded iron in large quantities. This metal the Turks were employed by the Khan to forge for his use in war. A bold leader arose among them, who persuaded the iron-workers that the arms which they forged for their masters might in their own hands become the instruments of freedom. Sallying forth from their mountains, they set up their standard, and their weapons soon freed them. For centuries after, the Turkish nation continued to celebrate the event of their liberation by an annual ceremony, in which a piece of iron was heated in the fire, and a smith's hammer was successively handled by the prince and his nobles.

We can only conjecture how the art of smelting iron was discovered. Who first applied fire to the ore, and made it plastic; who discovered fire itself, and its uses in metallurgy? No one can tell. Tradition says that the metal was discovered through the accidental burning of a wood in Greece. Mr. Mushet thinks it more probable that the discovery was made on the conversion of wood into charcoal for culinary or chamber purposes. "If a mass of ore," he says, "accidentally dropped into the middle of the

---

* I. Samuel xiii. 19, 20.   † II. Kings xxiv. 16.

burning pile during a period of neglect, or during the existence of a thorough draught, a mixed mass, partly earthy and partly metallic, would be obtained, possessing ductility and extension under pressure. But if the conjecture is pushed still further, and we suppose that the ore was not an oxide, but rich in iron, magnetic or spicular, the result would in all probability be a mass of perfectly malleable iron. I have seen this fact illustrated in the roasting of a species of iron-stone, which was united with a considerable mass of bituminous matter. After a high temperature had been excited in the interior of the pile, plates of malleable iron of a tough and flexible nature were formed, and under circumstances where there was no fuel but that furnished by the ore itself." *

The metal once discovered, many attempts would be made to give to that which had been the effect of accident a more unerring result. The smelting of ore in an open heap of wood or charcoal being found tedious and wasteful, as well as uncertain, would naturally lead to the invention of a furnace, with the object of keeping the ore surrounded as much as possible with fuel while the process of conversion into iron was going forward. The low conical furnaces employed at this day by some of the tribes of Central and Southern Africa, are perhaps very much the same in character as those adopted by the early tribes of all countries where iron was first made. Small openings at the lower end of the cone to admit the air, and a larger orifice at the top, would, with charcoal, be sufficient to produce the requisite degree of heat for the reduction of the ore. To this the foot-blast was added, as still used in Ceylon and in India; and afterwards the water-blast, as employed in Spain (where it is known as the Catalan forge), along the coasts of the Mediterranean, and in some parts of America.

It is worthy of remark, that the ruder the method em-

---

* *Papers on Iron and Steel*, 363-4.

ployed for the reduction of the ore, the better the quality of the iron usually is.   Where the art is little
advanced, only the most tractable ores are selected ; and as
charcoal is the only fuel used, the quality of the metal is
almost invariably excellent.   The ore being long exposed
to the charcoal fire, and the quantity made small, the
result is a metal having many of the qualities of steel,
capable of being used for weapons or tools after a comparatively small amount of forging.   Dr. Livingstone
speaks of the excellent quality of the iron made by the
African tribes on the Zambesi, who refuse to use ordinary
English iron, which they consider "rotten." *   Du Chaillu
also says of the Fans, that, in making their best knives
and arrow-heads, they will not use European or American
iron, greatly preferring their own.   The celebrated *wootz*
or steel of India, made in little cakes of only about two
pounds weight, possesses qualities which no European steel
can surpass.   Out of this material the famous Damascus
sword-blades were made ; and its use for so long a period is
perhaps one of the most striking proofs of the ancient
civilization of India.

The early history of iron in Britain is necessarily very
obscure.   When the Romans invaded the country, the
metal seems to have been already known to the tribes along
the coast.   The natives had probably smelted it themselves
in their rude bloomeries, or obtained it from the Phœni-
cians in small quantities in exchange for skins and food, or
tin.   We must, however, regard the stories told of the
ancient British chariots armed with swords or scythes as
altogether apocryphal.   The existence of iron in sufficient
quantity to be used for such a purpose is incompatible
with contemporary facts, and unsupported by a single

* Dr. Livingstone brought with him
to England a piece of the Zambesi iron,
which he sent to a skilled Birmingham
blacksmith to test.   The result was,
that he pronounced the metal as
strongly resembling Swedish or Russian ; both of which kinds are smelted
with charcoal.   The African iron
was found " highly carbonized," and
" when chilled it possessed the properties of steel."

vestige remaining to our time. The country was then mostly forest, and the roads did not as yet exist upon which chariots could be used; whilst iron was too scarce to be mounted as scythes upon chariots, when the warriors themselves wanted it for swords. The orator Cicero, in a letter to Trebatius, then serving with the army in Britain, sarcastically advised him to capture and convey one of these vehicles to Italy for exhibition; but we do not hear that any specimen of the British war-chariot was ever seen in Rome.

It is only in the tumuli along the coast, or in those of the Romano-British period, that iron implements are ever found; whilst in the ancient burying places of the interior of the country they are altogether wanting. Herodian says of the British pursued by Severus through the fens and marshes of the east coast, that they wore iron hoops round their middles and their necks, esteeming them as ornaments and tokens of riches, in like manner as other barbarous people then esteemed ornaments of silver and gold. Their only money, according to Cæsar, consisted of pieces of brass or iron, reduced to a certain standard weight.* It is particularly important to observe, says M. Worsaae, that all the antiquities which have hitherto been found in the large burying places of the Iron period, in Switzerland, Bavaria, Baden, France, England, and the North, exhibit traces more or less of Roman influence.†

The Romans themselves used weapons of bronze when they could not obtain iron in sufficient quantity, and many of the Roman weapons dug out of the ancient tumuli are of that metal. They possessed the art of tempering and hardening bronze to such a degree as to enable them to

---

* HOLINSHED, i. 517. Iron was also the currency of the Spartans, but it has been used as such in much more recent times. Adam Smith, in his *Wealth of Nations* (Book I. ch. 4, published in 1776), says, " there is at this day a village in Scotland where it is not uncommon, I am told, for a workman to carry nails, instead of money, to the baker's shop or the alehouse."

† *Primeval Antiquities of Denmark*. London, 1849, p. 140.

manufacture swords with it of a pretty good edge; and in those countries which they penetrated, their bronze implements gradually supplanted those which had been previously fashioned of stone. Great quantities of bronze tools have been found in different parts of England,—sometimes in heaps, as if they had been thrown away in basketfuls as things of little value. It has been conjectured that when the Romans came into Britain they found the inhabitants, especially those to the northward, in very nearly the same state as Captain Cook and other voyagers found the inhabitants of the South Sea Islands; that the Britons parted with their food and valuables for tools of inferior metal made in imitation of their stone ones; but finding themselves cheated by the Romans, as the natives of Otaheite have been cheated by Europeans, the Britons relinquished the bad tools when they became acquainted with articles made of better metal.*

The Roman colonists were the first makers of iron in Britain on any large scale. They availed themselves of the mineral riches of the country wherever they went. Every year brings their extraordinary industrial activity more clearly to light. They not only occupied the best sites for trade, intersected the land with a complete system of well-constructed roads, studded our hills and valleys with towns, villages, and pleasure-houses, and availed themselves of our medicinal springs for purposes of baths to an extent not even exceeded at this day, but they explored our mines and quarries, and carried on the smelting and manufacture of metals in nearly all parts of the island. The heaps of mining refuse left by them in the valleys and along the hill-sides of North Derbyshire are still spoken of by the country people as " old man," or the " old man's work." Year by year, from Dartmoor to the Moray Firth, the plough turns up fresh traces of their

---

* See Dr. Pearson's paper in the *Philosophical Transactions*, 1796, relative to certain ancient arms and utensils found in the river Witham between Kirkstead and Lincoln.

indefatigable industry and enterprise, in pigs of lead, implements of iron and bronze, vessels of pottery, coins, and sculpture ; and it is a remarkable circumstance that in several districts where the existence of extensive iron beds had not been dreamt of until within the last twenty years, as in Northamptonshire and North Yorkshire, the remains of ancient workings recently discovered show that the Roman colonists were fully acquainted with them.

But the principal iron mines worked by that people were those which were most conveniently situated for purposes of exportation, more especially in the southern counties and on the borders of Wales. The extensive cinder heaps found in the Forest of Dean—which formed the readiest resource of the modern iron-smelter when improved processes enabled him to reduce them—show that their principal iron manufactures were carried on in that quarter.* It is indeed matter of history, that about seventeen hundred years since (A.D. 120) the Romans had forges in the West of England, both in the Forest of Dean and in South Wales ; and that they sent the metal from thence to Bristol, where it was forged and made into weapons for the use of the troops. Along the banks of the Wye, the ground is in many places a continuous bed of iron cinders, in which numerous remains have been found, furnishing unmistakeable proofs of the Roman furnaces. At the same time, the iron ores of Sussex were extensively worked, as appears from the cinder heaps found at Maresfield and

---

* "In the Forest of Dean and thereabouts the iron is made at this day of cinders, being the rough and offal thrown by in the Roman time ; they then having only foot-blasts to melt the ironstone ; but now, by the force of a great wheel that drives a pair of bellows twenty feet long, all that iron is extracted out of the cinders which could not be forced from it by the Roman foot-blast. And in the Forest of Dean and thereabouts, and as high as Worcester, there are great and infinite quantities of these cinders ; some in vast mounts above ground, some under ground, which will supply the iron works some hundreds of years; and these cinders are they which make the prime and best iron, and with much less charcoal than doth the ironstone."—A. Yarranton, *England's Improvement by Sea and Land.* London, 1677.

several places in that county, intermixed with Roman pottery, coins, and other remains. In a bed of scoriæ several acres in extent, at Old Land Farm in Maresfield, the Rev. Mr. Turner found the remains of Roman pottery so numerous that scarcely a barrow-load of cinders was removed that did not contain several fragments, together with coins of the reigns of Nero, Vespasian, and Dioclesian.*

In the turbulent infancy of nations it is to be expected that we should hear more of the Smith, or worker in iron, in connexion with war, than with more peaceful pursuits. Although he was a nail-maker and a horse-shoer—made axes, chisels, saws, and hammers for the artificer—spades and hoes for the farmer—bolts and fastenings for the lord's castle-gates, and chains for his draw-bridge—it was principally because of his skill in armour-work that he was esteemed. He made and mended the weapons used in the chase and in war—the gavelocs, bills, and battle-axes; he tipped the bowmen's arrows, and furnished spear-heads for the men-at-arms; but, above all, he forged the mail-coats and cuirasses of the chiefs, and welded their swords, on the temper and quality of which, life, honour, and victory in battle depended. Hence the great estimation in which the smith was held in the Anglo-Saxon times. His person was protected by a double penalty. He was treated as an officer of the highest rank, and awarded the first place in precedency. After him ranked the maker of mead, and then the physician. In the royal court of Wales he sat in the great hall with the king and queen, next to the domestic chaplain; and even at that early day there seems to have been a hot spark in the smith's throat which needed much quenching; for he was " entitled to a draught of every kind of liquor that was brought into the hall."

The smith was thus a mighty man. The Saxon Chronicle

---

* M. A. Lower, *Contributions to Literature, Historical, Antiquarian, and Metrical.* London, 1854, pp. 88-9.

describes the valiant knight himself as a "mighty war-smith." But the smith was greatest of all in his forging of swords; and the bards were wont to sing the praises of the knight's "good sword" and of the smith who made it, as well as of the knight himself who wielded it in battle. The most extraordinary powers were attributed to the weapon of steel when first invented. Its sharpness seemed so marvellous when compared with one of bronze, that with the vulgar nothing but magic could account for it. Traditions, enshrined in fairy tales, still survive in most countries, illustrative of its magical properties. The weapon of bronze was dull; but that of steel was bright— the "white sword of light," one touch of which broke spells, liberated enchanted princesses, and froze giants' marrow. King Arthur's magic sword "Excalibur" was regarded as almost heroic in the romance of chivalry.* So were the swords "Galatin" of Sir Gawain, and "Joyeuse" of Charlemagne, both of which were reputed to be the work of Weland the Smith, about whose name clusters so much traditional glory as an ancient worker in metals.† The heroes of the Northmen in like manner wielded magic swords. Olave the Norwegian possessed the sword "Maca-buin," forged by the dark smith of Drontheim, whose feats are recorded in the tales of the Scalds. And so, in like manner, traditions of the supernatural power of the black-smith are found existing to this day all over the Scottish Highlands.‡

When William the Norman invaded Britain, he was well

---

* This famous sword was after-wards sent by Richard I. as a present to Tancred; and the value attached to the weapon may be estimated by the fact that the Crusader sent the English monarch, in return for it, "four great ships and fifteen galleys."

† Weland was the Saxon Vulcan. The name of Weland's or Wayland's Smithy is still given to a monument on Lambourn Downs in Wiltshire. The place is also known as Wayland Smith's Cave. It consists of a rude gallery of stones.

‡ Among the Scythians the iron sword was a god. It was the image of Mars, and sacrifices were made to it. "An iron sword," says Mr. Camp-bell, "really was once worshipped by a people with whom iron was rare. Iron is rare, while stone and bronze weapons are common, in British tombs,

supplied with smiths. His followers were clad in armour of steel, and furnished with the best weapons of the time. Indeed, their superiority in this respect is supposed to have been the principal cause of William's victory over Harold; for the men of both armies were equal in point of bravery. The Normans had not only smiths to attend to the arms of the knights, but farriers to shoe their horses. Henry de Ferrariis, or Ferrers, "prefectus fabrorum," was one of the principal officers entrusted with the supervision of the Conqueror's ferriery department; and long after the earldom was founded his descendants continued to bear on their coat of arms the six horse-shoes indicative of their origin.* William also gave the town of Northampton, with the hundred of Fackley, as a fief to Simon St. Liz, in consideration of his providing shoes for his horses.† But though the practice of horse-shoeing is said to have been introduced to this country at the time of the Conquest, it

---

and the sword of these stories is a personage. It shines, it cries out—the lives of men are bound up in it. And so this mystic sword may, perhaps, have been a god amongst the Celts, or the god of the people with whom the Celts contended somewhere on their long journey to the west. It is a fiction now, but it may be founded on fact, and that fact probably was the first use of iron." To this day an old horse-shoe is considered a potent spell in some districts against the powers of evil; and for want of a horse-shoe a bit of a rusty reaping-hook is supposed to have equal power. "Who were these powers of evil who could not resist iron—these fairies who shoot *stone* arrows, and are of the foes to the human race? Is all this but a dim, hazy recollection of war between a people who had iron weapons and a race who had not—the race whose remains are found all over Europe? If these were wandering tribes, they had leaders; if they were warlike, they had weapons. There is a smith in the Pantheon of many nations. Vulcan was a smith; Thor wielded a hammer; even Fionn had a hammer, which was heard in Lochlann when struck in Eirinn. Fionn may have borrowed his hammer from Thor long ago, or both may have got theirs from Vulcan, or all three may have brought hammers with them from the land where some primeval smith wielded the first sledge-hammer; but may not all these 'smith-gods be the smiths who made iron weapons for those who fought with the skin-clad warriors who shot flint-arrows, and who are now bogles, fairies, and demons? In any case, tales about smiths seem to belong to mythology, and to be common property."—CAMPBELL, *Popular Tales of the West Highlands*, Preface, 74-6.

* BROOK, *Discovery of Errors in the Catalogue of the Nobility*, 198.

† MEYRICK, i. 11.

is probably of an earlier date; as, according to Dugdale, an old Saxon tenant in capite of Welbeck in Nottingham-shire, named Gamelbere, held two carucates of land by the service of shoeing the king's palfrey on all four feet with the king's nails, as oft as the king should lie at the neighbouring manor of Mansfield.

Although we hear of the smith mostly in connexion with the fabrication of instruments of war in the Middle Ages, his importance was no less recognized in the ordinary affairs of rural and industrial life. He was, as it were, the rivet that held society together. Nothing could be done without him. Wherever tools or implements were wanted for building, for trade, or for husbandry, his skill was called into requisition. In remote places he was often the sole mechanic of his district; and, besides being a tool-maker, a farrier, and agricultural implement maker, he doctored cattle, drew teeth, practised phlebotomy, and sometimes officiated as parish clerk and general news-monger; for the smithy was the very eye and tongue of the village. Hence Shakespeare's picture of the smith in King John:—

> " I saw a smith stand with his hammer, thus,
> The whilst his iron did on the anvil cool,
> With open mouth swallowing a tailor's news."

The smith's tools were of many sorts; but the chief were his hammer, pincers, chisel, tongs, and anvil. It is astonishing what a variety of articles he turned out of his smithy by the help of these rude implements. In the tooling, chasing, and consummate knowledge of the capa-bilities of iron, he greatly surpassed the modern workman; for the mediæval blacksmith was an artist as well as a workman. The numerous exquisite specimens of his handi-craft which exist in our old gateways, church doors, altar railings, and ornamented dogs and andirons, still serve as types for continual reproduction. He was, indeed, the most " cunninge workman" of his time. But besides all this, he was an engineer. If a road had to be made, or a stream embanked, or a trench dug, he was invariably called upon to provide the tools, and often to direct the work. He was also the military engineer of his day, and as late as the reign of Edward III. we find the king repeatedly sending for smiths from the Forest of Dean to act as engineers for the royal army at the siege of Berwick.

The smith being thus the earliest and most important of mechanics, it will readily be understood how, at the time when surnames were adopted, his name should have been so common in all European countries.

> " From whence came Smith, all be he knight or squire,
> But from the smith that forgeth in the fire?" *

Hence the multitudinous family of Smiths in England, in some cases vainly disguised under the " Smythe " or " De Smijthe ;" in Germany, the Schmidts ; in Italy, the Fabri, Fabricii, or Fabbroni ; in France, the Le Febres or Lefevres ; in Scotland, the Gows, Gowans, or Cowans. We have also among us the Brownsmiths, or makers of brown bills ; the Nasmyths, or nailsmiths ; the Arrowsmiths, or makers of arrowheads ; the Spearsmiths, or spear makers ; the Shoosmiths, or horse shoers ; the Goldsmiths, or workers in gold ; and many more. The Smith proper was, however, the worker in iron—the maker of iron tools, implements, and arms—and hence this name exceeds in number that of all the others combined.

In course of time the smiths of particular districts began to distinguish themselves for their excellence in particular branches of iron-work. From being merely the retainer of some lordly or religious establishment, the smith worked to supply the general demand, and gradually became a manufacturer. Thus the makers of swords, tools, bits, and nails, congregated at Birmingham ; and the makers of knives and arrowheads at Sheffield. Chaucer speaks of

---

* GILBERT, *Cornwall.*

the Miller of Trompington as provided with a Sheffield whittle :—

  " A Shefeld thwytel bare he in his hose."*

The common English arrowheads manufactured at Sheffield were long celebrated for their excellent temper, as Sheffield iron and steel plates are now. The battle of Hamildon, fought in Scotland in 1402, was won mainly through their excellence. The historian records that they penetrated the armour of the Earl of Douglas, which had been three years in making; and they were " so sharp and strong that no armour could repel them." The same arrowheads were found equally efficient against French armour on the fields of Crecy and Agincourt.

Although Scotland is now one of the principal sources from which our supplies of iron are drawn, it was in ancient times greatly distressed for want of the metal. The people were as yet too little skilled to be able to turn their great mineral wealth to account. Even in the time of Wallace, they had scarcely emerged from the Stone period, and were under the necessity of resisting their iron-armed English adversaries by means of rude weapons of that material. To supply themselves with swords and spearheads, they imported steel from Flanders, and the rest they obtained by marauding incursions into England. The district of Furness in Lancashire—then as now an iron-producing district —was frequently ravaged with that object; and on such occasions the Scotch seized and carried off all the manufactured iron they could find, preferring it, though so heavy, to every other kind of plunder.† About the same period, however, iron must have been regarded as almost a precious

---

* Before table-knives were invented, in the sixteenth century, the knife was a very important article; each guest at table bearing his own, and sharpening it at the whetstone hung up in the passage, before sitting down to dinner. Some even carried a whet-stone as well as a knife; and one of Queen Elizabeth's presents to the Earl of Leicester was a whetstone tipped with gold.

† The early scarcity of iron in Scotland is confirmed by Froissart, who says,—" In Scotland you will

metal even in England itself; for we find that in Edward the Third's reign, the pots, spits, and frying-pans of the royal kitchen were classed among his Majesty's jewels.*

The same famine of iron prevailed to a still greater extent. in the Highlands, where it was even more valued, as the clans lived chiefly by hunting, and were in an almost constant state of feud. Hence the smith was a man of indispensable importance among the Highlanders, and the possession of a skilful armourer was greatly valued by the chiefs. The story is told of some delinquency having been committed by a Highland smith, on whom justice must be done; but as the chief could not dispense with the smith, he generously offered to hang two weavers in his stead!

At length a great armourer arose in the Highlands, who was able to forge armour that would resist the best Sheffield arrow-heads, and to make swords that would vie with the best weapons of Toledo and Milan. This was the famous Andrea de Ferrara, whose swords still maintain their ancient reputation. This workman is supposed to have learnt his art in the Italian city after which he was called, and returned to practise it in secrecy among the Highland hills. Before him, no man in Great Britain is said to have known how to temper a sword in such a way as to bend so that the point should touch the hilt and spring back uninjured. The swords of Andrea de Ferrara did this, and were accordingly in great request; for it was of every importance to the warrior that his weapon should be strong and sharp without being unwieldy, and that it

---

never find a man of worth; they are like savages, who wish not to be acquainted with any one, are envious of the good fortune of others, and suspicious of losing anything themselves; for their country is very poor. When the English make inroads thither, as they have very frequently done, they order their provisions, if they wish to live, to follow close at their backs; for nothing is to be had in that country without great difficulty. There is neither iron to shoe horses, nor leather to make harness, saddles, or bridles: all these things come ready made from Flanders by sea; and should these fail, there is none to be had in the country.'

* Parker's *English Home*, 77.

should not be liable to snap in the act of combat. This celebrated smith, whose personal identity* has become merged in the Andrea de Ferrara swords of his manufacture, pursued his craft in the Highlands, where he employed a number of skilled workmen in forging weapons, devoting his own time principally to giving them their required temper. He is said to have worked in a dark cellar, the better to enable him to perceive the effect of the heat upon the metal, and to watch the nicety of the operation of tempering, as well as possibly to serve as a screen to his secret method of working.†

Long after Andrea de Ferrara's time, the Scotch swords were famous for their temper; Judge Marshal Patten, who accompanied the Protector's expedition into Scotland in 1547, observing that " the Scots came with swords all broad and thin, of exceeding good temper, and universally so made to slice that I never saw none so good, so I think it hard to devise a better." The quality of the steel used for weapons of war was indeed of no less importance for the effectual defence of a country then than it is now. The courage of the attacking and defending forces being equal, the victory would necessarily rest with the party in possession of the best weapons.

England herself has on more than one occasion been supposed to be in serious peril because of the decay of her iron manufactures. Before the Spanish Armada, the

---

* The precise time at which Andrea de Ferrara flourished cannot be fixed with accuracy; but Sir Walter Scott, in one of the notes to *Waverley*, says he is believed to have been a foreign artist brought over by James IV. or V. of Scotland to instruct the Scots in the manufacture of sword-blades. The genuine weapons have a crown marked on the blades.

† Mr. Parkes, in his *Essay on the Manufacture of Edge Tools*, says, " Had this ingenious artist thought of a bath of oil, he might have heated this by means of a furnace underneath it, and by the use of a thermometer, to the exact point which he found necessary; though it is inconvenient to have to employ a thermometer for every distinct operation. Or, if he had been in the possession of a proper bath of fusible metal, he would have attained the necessary certainty in his process, and need not have immured himself in a subterranean apartment."
—Parkes' *Essays*, 1841, p. 495.

production of iron had been greatly discouraged because of the destruction of timber in the smelting of the ore— the art of reducing it with pit coal not having yet been invented ; and we were consequently mainly dependent upon foreign countries for our supplies of the material out of which arms were made. The best iron came from Spain itself, then the most powerful nation in Europe, and as celebrated for the excellence of its weapons as for the discipline and valour of its troops. The Spaniards prided themselves upon the superiority of their iron, and regarded its scarcity in England as an important element in their calculations of the conquest of the country by their famous Armada. "I have heard," says Harrison, "that when one of the greatest peers of Spain espied our nakedness in this behalf, and did solemnly utter in no obscure place, that it would be an easy matter in short time to conquer England because it wanted armour, his words were not so rashly uttered as politely noted." The vigour of Queen Elizabeth promptly supplied a remedy by the large impor- tations of iron which she caused to be made, principally from Sweden, as well as by the increased activity of the forges in Sussex and the Forest of Dean; "whereby," adds Harrison, "England obtained rest, that otherwise might have been sure of sharp and cruel wars. Thus a Spanish word uttered by one man at one time, overthrew, or at the leastwise hindered sundry privy practices of many at another." *

Nor has the subject which occupied the earnest at- tention of politicians in Queen Elizabeth's time ceased to be of interest; for, after the lapse of nearly three hundred

---

* HOLINSHED, *History of England.* It was even said to have been one of the objects of the Spanish Armada to get the oaks of the Forest of Dean destroyed, in order to prevent further smelting of the iron. Thus Evelyn, in his *Sylva*, says, " I have heard that in the great expedition of 1588 it was expressly enjoined the Spanish Armada that if, when landed, they should not be able to subdue our nation and make good their conquest, they should yet be sure not to leave a tree standing in the Forest of Dean."—NICHOLS, *History of the Forest of Dean*, p. 22.

years, we find the smith and the iron manufacturer still uppermost in public discussions. It has of late years been felt that our much-prized " hearts of oak " are no more able to stand against the prows of mail which were supposed to threaten them, than the sticks and stones of the ancient tribes were able to resist the men armed with weapons of bronze or steel. What Solon said to Crœsus, when the latter was displaying his great treasures of gold, still holds true :—" If another comes that hath better iron than you, he will be master of all that gold." So, when an alchemist waited upon the Duke of Brunswick during the Seven Years' War, and offered to communicate the secret of converting iron into gold, the Duke replied :—" By no means : I want all the iron I can find to resist my enemies : as for gold, I get it from England." Thus the strength and wealth of nations depend upon coal and iron, not forgetting Men, far more than upon gold.

Thanks to our Armstrongs and Whitworths, our Browns and our Smiths, the iron defences of England, manned by our soldiers and our sailors, furnish the assurance of continued security for our gold and our wealth, and, what is infinitely more precious, for our industry and our liberty.

COAL BURNING

heap before turfing
ourtesy of the Science
um)

ng the vent holes
ourtesy of the Science
um)

CHAPTER II.

Early English Iron Manufacture.

———

" He that well observes it, and hath known the welds of Sussex, Surry, and Kent, the grand nursery especially of oake and beech, shal find such an alteration, within lesse than 30 yeeres, as may well strike a feare, lest few yeeres more, as pestilent as the former, will leave fewe good trees standing in those welds. Such a heate issueth out of the many forges and furnaces for the making of iron, and out of the glasse kilnes, as hath devoured many famous woods within the welds." — John Norden, *Surveyors' Dialogue* (1607).

———

Few records exist of the manufacture of iron in England in early times. After the Romans left the island, the British, or more probably the Teutonic tribes settled along the south coast, continued the smelting and manufacture of the metal after the methods taught them by the colonists. In the midst of the insecurity, however, engendered by civil war and social changes, the pursuits of industry must necessarily have been considerably interfered with, and the art of iron-forging became neglected. No notice of iron being made in Sussex occurs in Domesday Book, from which it would appear that the manufacture had in a great measure ceased in that county at the time of the Conquest, though it was continued in the iron-producing districts bordering on Wales. In many of the Anglo-Saxon graves which have been opened, long iron swords have been found, showing that weapons of that metal were in common use. But it is probable that iron was still scarce, as ploughs and other agricultural implements continued to be made of wood,—one of the Anglo-Saxon laws enacting that no man should undertake to guide a plough who could not make one; and that the cords with which it was bound should be of twisted willows. The metal was held in esteem principally as the material of war.   All male adults were required to be provided with weapons, and honour was awarded to such artificers as excelled in the fabrication of swords, arms, and defensive armour.[*]

Camden incidentally states that the manufacture of iron was continued in the western counties during the Saxon era, more particularly in the Forest of Dean, and that in the time of Edward the Confessor the tribute paid by the city of Gloucester consisted almost entirely of iron rods wrought to a size fit for making nails for the king's ships. An old religious writer speaks of the ironworkers of that day as heathenish in their manners, puffed up with pride, and inflated with worldly prosperity.   On the occasion of St. Egwin's visit to the smiths of Alcester, as we are told in the legend, he found them given up to every kind of luxury; and when he proceeded to preach unto them, they beat upon their anvils in contempt of his doctrine so as completely to deafen him; upon which he addressed his prayers to heaven, and the town was immediately destroyed.[†]   But the first reception given to John Wesley by the miners of the Forest of Dean, more than a thousand years later, was perhaps scarcely more gratifying than that given to St. Egwin.

That working in iron was regarded as an honourable and useful calling in the Middle Ages, is apparent from the extent to which it was followed by the monks, some of whom were excellent craftsmen.   Thus St. Dunstan, who governed England in the time of Edwy the Fair, was a skilled blacksmith and metallurgist.   He is said to have had a forge even in his bedroom, and it was there that his reputed encounter with Satan occurred, in which of course the saint came off the victor.

---

[*] Wilkins, *Leges Sax.* 25.

[†] Life of St. Egwin, in Capgrave's *Nova Legenda Angliæ.*   Alcester was, as its name indicates, an old Roman settlement (situated on the Icknild Street), where the art of working in iron was practised from an early period. It was originally called Alauna, being situated on the river Alne in Warwickshire.   It is still a seat of the needle manufacture.

There was another monk of St. Alban's, called Anketil, who flourished in the twelfth century, so famous for his skill as a worker in iron, silver, gold, jewelry, and gilding, that he was invited by the king of Denmark to be his goldsmith and banker. A pair of gold and silver candlesticks of his manufacture, presented by the abbot of St. Alban's to Pope Adrian IV., were so much esteemed for their exquisite workmanship that they were consecrated to St. Peter, and were the means of obtaining high ecclesiastical distinction for the abbey.

We also find that the abbots of monasteries situated in the iron districts, among their other labours, devoted themselves to the manufacture of iron from the ore. The extensive beds of cinders still found in the immediate neighbourhood of Rievaulx and Hackness, in Yorkshire, show that the monks were well acquainted with the art of forging, and early turned to account the riches of the Cleveland ironstone. In the Forest of Dean also, the abbot of Flaxley was possessed of one stationary and one itinerant forge, by grant from Henry II., and he was allowed two oaks weekly for fuel,—a privilege afterwards commuted, in 1258, for Abbot's Wood of 872 acres, which was held by the abbey until its dissolution in the reign of Henry VIII. At the same time the Earl of Warwick had forges at work in his woods at Lydney; and in 1282, as many as 72 forges were leased from the Crown by various iron-smelters in the same Forest of Dean.

There are numerous indications of iron-smelting having been conducted on a considerable scale at some remote period in the neighbourhood of Leeds, in Yorkshire. In digging out the foundations of houses in Briggate, the principal street of that town, many " bell pits " have been brought to light, from which ironstone has been removed. The new cemetery at Burmandtofts, in the same town, was in like manner found pitted over with these ancient holes. The miner seems to have dug a well about 6 feet in diameter, and so soon as he reached the mineral, he worked it away all round, leaving the bell-shaped cavities in question. He did not attempt any gallery excavations, but when the pit was exhausted, a fresh one was sunk. The ore, when dug, was transported, most probably on horses' backs, to the adjacent districts for the convenience of fuel. For it was easier to carry the mineral to the wood—then exclusively used for smelting,—than to bring the wood to the mineral. Hence the numerous heaps of scoriæ found in the neighbourhood of Leeds,—at Middleton, Whitkirk, and Horsforth—all within the borough. At Horsforth, they are found in conglomerated masses from 30 to 40 yards long, and of considerable width and depth. The remains of these cinder-beds in various positions, some of them near the summit of the hill, tend to show, that as the trees were consumed, a new wind furnace was erected in another situation, in order to lessen the labour of carrying the fuel. There are also deposits of a similar kind at Kirkby Overblow, a village a few miles to the north-east of Leeds; and Thoresby states that the place was so called because it was the village of the "Ore blowers,"—hence the corruption of "Overblow." A discovery has recently been made among the papers of the Wentworth family, of a contract for supplying wood and ore for iron "blomes" at Kirskill near Otley, in the fourteenth century;* though the manufacture near that place has long since ceased.

Although the making of iron was thus carried on in various parts of England in the Middle Ages, the quantity produced was altogether insufficient to meet the ordinary demand, as it appears from our early records to have long continued one of the principal articles imported from

---

* The following is an extract of this curious document, which is dated the 26th Dec. 1352:—

"Ceste endenture fait entre monsire Richard de Goldesburghe, chivaler, dune part, et Robert Totte, seignour, dautre part, tesmoigne qe le dit monsire Richard ad graunte et lesse al dit Robert deuz Olyveres contenaunz vynt quatre blomes de la feste seynt Piere ad vincula lan du regne le Roi Edward tierce apres le conqueste vynt sysme, en sun parke de Creskelde, rendant al dit monsire Richard chesqune semayn quatorzse soutz dargent duraunt les deux Olyvers avaunt dist; a tenir et

foreign countries. English iron was not only dearer, but
it was much inferior in quality to that manufactured
abroad; and hence all the best arms and tools continued to
be made of foreign iron. Indeed the scarcity of this metal
occasionally led to great inconvenience, and to prevent its
rising in price Parliament enacted, in 1354, that no iron,
either wrought or unwrought, should be exported, under
heavy penalties. For nearly two hundred years—that is,
throughout the fourteenth and fifteenth centuries—the
English market was principally supplied with iron and steel
from Spain and Germany; the foreign merchants of the Steelyard doing a large and profitable trade in those commodities.
While the woollen and other branches of trade were making
considerable progress, the manufacture of iron stood still.
Among the lists of articles, the importation of which was
prohibited in Edward IV.'s reign, with a view to the protection of domestic manufactures, we find no mention of
iron, which was still, as a matter of necessity, allowed
to come freely from abroad.

The first indications of revival in the iron manufacture
showed themselves in Sussex, a district in which the
Romans had established extensive works, and where smelting operations were carried on to a partial extent in
the neighbourhood of Lewes, in the thirteenth and fourteenth centuries, where the iron was principally made into
nails and horse-shoes. The county abounds in ironstone,

---

avoir al avaunt dit Robert del avaunt
dit monsire Richard de la feste seynt
Piere avaunt dist, taunque le bois soit
ars du dit parke a la volunte le dit
monsire Richard saunz interrupcione
[e le dicte monsieur Richard trovera
a dit Robert urre suffisaunt pur lez
ditz Olyvers pur le son donaunt: *these
words are interlined*]. Et fait a savoir
qe le dit Robert ne nule de soens cou-
pard ne abatera nule manere darbre ne
de boys pur les deuz olyvers avaunt ditz
mes par la veu et la lyvere le dit monsire Richard, ou par ascun autre par le

dit monsire Richard assigne. En tes-
moigaunz (sic) de quenx choses a cestes
presentes endentures les parties enter-
chaungablement ount mys lour seals.
Escript a Creskelde le meskerdy en le
semayn de Pasque lan avaunt diste."

It is probable that the "blomes"
referred to in this agreement were the
bloomeries or fires in which the iron
was made; and that the "olyveres"
were forges or erections, each of which
contained so many bloomeries, but were
of limited durability, and probably
perished in the using.

which is contained in the sandstone beds of the Forest
ridge, lying between the chalk and oolite of the district,
called by geologists the Hastings sand.   The beds run in
a north-westerly direction, by Ashburnham and Heath-
field, to Crowborough and thereabouts.   In early times
the region was covered with wood, and was known as the
Great Forest of Anderida.   The Weald, or wild wood,
abounded in oaks of great size, suitable for smelting ore ;
and the proximity of the mineral to the timber, as well
as the situation of the district in the neighbourhood of the
capital, sufficiently account for the Sussex iron-works being
among the most important which existed in England previous to the discovery of smelting by pit-coal.

The iron manufacturers of the south were especially
busy during the fifteenth and sixteenth centuries.   Their
works were established near to the beds of ore, and in
places where water-power existed, or could be provided
by artificial means.   Hence the numerous artificial ponds
which are still to be found all over the Sussex iron
district.   Dams of earth, called " pond-bays," were thrown
across watercourses, with convenient outlets built of
masonry, wherein was set the great wheel which worked
the hammer or blew the furnace.   Portions of the adjoining forest-land were granted or leased to the iron-
smelters ; and the many places still known by the name
of " Chart " in the Weald, probably mark the lands char-
tered for the purpose of supplying the iron-works with
their necessary fuel.   The cast-iron tombstones and slabs in
many Sussex churchyards, — the andirons and chimney
backs* still found in old Sussex mansions and farm-houses,
and such names as Furnace Place, Cinder Hill, Forge Farm,
and Hammer Pond, which are of very frequent occurrence

---

* The back of a grate has recently been found, cast by Richard Leonard at Brede Furnace in 1636.   It is curious as containing a representation of the founder with his dog and cups ; a drawing of the furnace, with the wheelbarrow and other implements for the casting, and on a shield the pincers and other marks of the blacksmith. Leonard was tenant of the Sackville furnace at Little Udimore.—*Sussex Archæological Collections*, vol. xii.

throughout the county, clearly mark the extent and activity of this ancient branch of industry.*   Steel was also manufactured at several places in the county, more particularly at Steel-Forge Land, Warbleton, and at Robertsbridge.   The steel was said to be of good quality, resembling Swedish— both alike depending for their excellence on the exclusive use of charcoal in smelting the ore,—iron so produced maintaining its superiority over coal-smelted iron to this day.

When cannon came to be employed in war, the nearness of Sussex to London and the Cinque Ports gave it a great advantage over the remoter iron-producing districts in the north and west of England, and for a long time the iron-works of this county enjoyed almost a monopoly of the manufacture.   The metal was still too precious to be used for cannon balls, which were hewn of stone from quarries on Maidstone Heath.   Iron was only available, and that in limited quantities, for the fabrication of the cannon themselves, and wrought-iron was chiefly used for the purpose. An old mortar which formerly lay on Eridge Green, near Frant, is said to have been the first mortar made in England;† only the chamber was cast, while the tube consisted of bars strongly hooped together.   Although the local distich says that

> " Master Huggett and his man John
> They did cast the first cannon,"

there is every reason to believe that both cannons and mortars were made in Sussex before Huggett's time; the old hooped guns in the Tower being of the date of Henry VI. The first cast-iron cannons of English manufacture were made at Buxtead, in Sussex, in 1543, by Ralph Hogge, master founder, who employed as his principal assistant

---

* For an interesting account of the early iron industry of Sussex see M. A. LOWER'S *Contributions to* *Literature, Historical, Antiquarian, and Metrical.*   London, 1854.
† *Archæologia*, vol. x. 472.

one Peter Baude, a Frenchman. Gun-founding was a French invention, and Mr. Lower supposes that Hogge brought over Baude from France to teach his workmen the method of casting the guns. About the same time Hogge employed a skilled Flemish gunsmith named Peter Van Collet, who, according to Stowe, "devised or caused to be made certain mortar pieces, being at the mouth from eleven to nine inches wide, for the use whereof the said Peter caused to be made certain hollow shot of cast-iron to be stuffed with fyrework, whereof the bigger sort for the same has screws of iron to receive a match to carry fyre for to break in small pieces the said hollow shot, whereof the smallest piece hitting a man would kill or spoil him." In short, Peter Van Collet here introduced the manufacture of the explosive shell in the form in which it continued to be used down to our own day.

Baude, the Frenchman, afterwards set up business on his own account, making many guns, both of brass and iron, some of which are still preserved in the Tower.* Other workmen, learning the trade from him, also began to manufacture on their own account; one of Baude's servants, named John Johnson, and after him his son Thomas, becoming famous for the excellence of their cast-iron guns. The Hogges continued the business for several generations, and became a wealthy county family. Huggett was another cannon maker of repute; and Owen became celebrated for his brass culverins. Mr. Lower mentions, as a curious instance of the tenacity with which families continue to follow a particular vocation, that many persons of the name of Huggett still carry on the trade of blacksmith in East Sussex. But most of the early workmen at the Sussex iron-works, as in other branches of skilled industry in England during the sixteenth century, were foreigners—Flemish and French—many of whom had

---

* One of these, 6½ feet long, and of | bears the cast inscription of *Petrus* 2½ inches bore, manufactured in 1543, | *Baude Gallus operis artifex.*

taken refuge in this country from the religious persecutions then raging abroad, while others, of special skill, were invited over by the iron manufacturers to instruct their workmen in the art of metal-founding.*

As much wealth was gained by the pursuit of the revived iron manufacture in Sussex, iron-mills rapidly extended over the ore-yielding district.   The landed proprietors entered with zeal into this new branch of industry, and when wood ran short, they did not hesitate to sacrifice their ancestral oaks to provide fuel for the furnaces.   Mr. Lower says even the most ancient families, such as the Nevilles, Howards, Percys, Stanleys, Montagues, Pelhams, Ashburnhams, Sidneys, Sackvilles, Dacres, and Finches, prosecuted the manufacture with all the apparent ardour of Birmingham and Wolverhampton men in modern times. William Penn, the courtier Quaker, had iron-furnaces at Hawkhurst and other places in Sussex.   The ruins of the Ashburnham forge, situated a few miles to the north-east of Battle, still serve to indicate the extent of the manufacture. At the upper part of the valley in which the works were situated, an artificial lake was formed by constructing an embankment across the watercourse descending from the higher ground,† and thus a sufficient fall of water was procured for the purpose of blowing the furnaces, the site of which is still marked by surrounding mounds of iron cinders and charcoal waste.   Three quarters of a mile lower down the valley stood the forge, also provided with water-power for working the hammer; and some of the old build-ings are still standing, among others the boring-house, of small size, now used as an ordinary labourer's cottage,

---

* Mr. Lower says, " Many foreigners were brought over to carry on the works; which perhaps may account for the number of Frenchmen and Germans whose names appear in our parish registers about the middle of the sixteenth century."—*Contributions to Literature*, 108.

† The embankment and sluices of the furnace-pond at the upper part of the valley continue to be maintained, the lake being used by the present Lord Ashburnham as a preserve for fish and water-fowl.

where the guns were bored. The machine was a mere upright drill worked by the water-wheel, which was only eighteen inches across the breast. The property belonged, as it still does, to the Ashburnham family, who are said to have derived great wealth from the manufacture of guns at their works, which were among the last carried on in Sussex. The Ashburnham iron was distinguished for its toughness, and was said to be equal to the best Spanish or Swedish iron.

Many new men also became enriched, and founded county families; the Fuller family frankly avowing their origin in the singular motto of *Carbone et forcipibus*—literally, by charcoal and tongs.* Men then went into Sussex to push their fortunes at the forges, as they now do in Wales or Staffordshire; and they succeeded then, as they do now, by dint of application, industry, and energy. The Sussex Archæological Papers for 1860 contain a curious record of such an adventurer, in the history of the founder of the Gale family. Leonard Gale was born in 1620 at Riverhead, near Sevenoaks, where his father pursued the trade of a blacksmith. When the youth had reached his seventeenth year, his father and mother, with five of their sons and daughters, died of the plague, Leonard and his brother being the only members of the family that survived. The patrimony of 200*l.* left them was soon spent; after which Leonard paid off his servants, and took to work diligently at his father's trade. Saving a little money, he determined to go down into Sussex, where we shortly find

---

* Reminding one of the odd motto assumed by Gillespie, the tobacconist of Edinburgh, founder of Gillespie's Hospital, on whose carriage-panels was emblazoned a Scotch mull, with the motto,

    "Wha wad ha' thocht it,
      That noses could ha' bought it!"

It is just possible that the Fullers may have taken their motto from the words employed by Juvenal in describing the father of Demosthenes, who was a blacksmith and a sword-cutler—

   "Quem pater ardentis massæ fuligine lippus,
   A *carbone et forcipibus* gladiosque parante
   Incude et luteo Vulcano ad rhetora misit."

him working the St. Leonard's Forge, and afterwards the
Tensley Forge near Crawley, and the Cowden Iron-works,
which then bore a high reputation.   After forty years'
labour, he accumulated a good fortune, which he left to his
son of the same name, who went on iron-forging, and
eventually became a county gentleman, owner of the house
and estate of Crabbett near Worth, and Member of Parliament for East Grinstead.

Several of the new families, however, after occupying a
high position in the county, again subsided into the
labouring class, illustrating the Lancashire proverb of
" Twice clogs, once boots," the sons squandering what the
fathers had gathered, and falling back into the ranks again.
Thus the great Fowles family of Riverhall disappeared
altogether from Sussex.   One of them built the fine mansion of Riverhall, noble even in decay.   Another had a
grant of free warren from King James over his estates
in Wadhurst, Frant, Rotherfield, and Mayfield.   Mr. Lower
says the fourth in descent from this person kept the turnpike-gate at Wadhurst, and that the last of the family,
a day-labourer, emigrated to America in 1839, carrying
with him, as the sole relic of his family greatness, the royal
grant of free warren given to his ancestor.   The Barhams
and Mansers were also great iron-men, officiating as high
sheriffs of the county at different times, and occupying
spacious mansions.   One branch of these families terminated,
Mr. Lower says, with Nicholas Barham, who died in the
workhouse at Wadhurst in 1788; and another continues
to be represented by a wheelwright at Wadhurst of the
same name.

The iron manufacture of Sussex reached its height
towards the close of the reign of Elizabeth, when the
trade became so prosperous that, instead of importing iron,
England began to export it in considerable quantities, in
the shape of iron ordnance.   Sir Thomas Leighton and Sir
Henry Neville had obtained patents from the queen, which
enabled them to send their ordnance abroad, the conse-

quence of which was that the Spaniards were found arming
their ships and fighting us with guns of our own manufacture. Sir Walter Raleigh, calling attention to the
subject in the House of Commons, said, " I am sure heretofore one ship of Her Majesty's was able to beat ten
Spaniards, but now, by reason of our own ordnance, we
are hardly matcht one to one." Proclamations were issued
forbidding the export of iron and brass ordnance, and a
bill was brought into Parliament to put a stop to the
trade; but, notwithstanding these prohibitions, the Sussex
guns long continued to be smuggled out of the country in
considerable numbers. " It is almost incredible," says
Camden, " how many guns are made of the iron in this
county. Count Gondomar (the Spanish ambassador) well
knew their goodness when he so often begged of King
James the boon to export them." Though the king refused
his sanction, it appears that Sir Anthony Shirley of Weston,
an extensive iron-master, succeeded in forwarding to the
King of Spain a hundred pieces of cannon.

So active were the Sussex manufacturers, and so brisk
was the trade they carried on, that during the reign of
James I. it is supposed one-half of the whole quantity
of iron produced in England was made there. Simon
Sturtevant, in his 'Treatise of Metallica,' published in
1612, estimates the whole number of iron-mills in England
and Wales at 800, of which, he says, " there are foure
hundred milnes in Surry, Kent, and Sussex, as the townsmen of Haslemere have testified and numbered unto me."
But the townsmen of Haslemere must certainly have been
exaggerating, unless they counted smiths' and farriers'
shops in the number of iron-mills. About the same time
that Sturtevant's treatise was published, there appeared a
treatise entitled the 'Surveyor's Dialogue,' by one John
Norden, the object of which was to make out a case
against the iron-works and their being allowed to burn
up the timber of the country for fuel. Yet Norden does
not make the number of iron-works much more than

a third of Sturtevant's estimate. He says, "I have heard that there are or lately were in Sussex neere 140 hammers and furnaces for iron, and in it and Surrey adjoining three or four glasse-houses." Even the smaller number stated by Norden, however, shows that Sussex was then regarded as the principal seat of the iron-trade. Camden vividly describes the noise and bustle of the manufacture—the working of the heavy hammers, which, "beating upon the iron, fill the neighbourhood round about, day and night, with continual noise." These hammers were for the most part worked by the power of water, carefully stored in the artificial "Hammer-ponds" above described. The hammer-shaft was usually of ash, about 9 feet long, clamped at intervals with iron hoops. It was worked by the revolutions of the water-wheel, furnished with projecting arms or knobs to raise the hammer, which fell as each knob passed, the rapidity of its action of course depending on the velocity with which the water-wheel revolved. The forge-blast was also worked for the most part by water-power. Where the furnaces were small, the blast was produced by leather bellows worked by hand, or by a horse walking in a gin. The foot-blasts of the earlier iron-smelters were so imperfect that but a small proportion of the ore was reduced, so that the iron-makers of later times, more particularly in the Forest of Dean, instead of digging for iron-stone, resorted to the beds of ancient scoriæ for their principal supply of the mineral.

Notwithstanding the large number of furnaces in blast throughout the county of Sussex at the period we refer to, their produce was comparatively small, and must not be measured by the enormous produce of modern iron-works ; for while an iron-furnace of the present day will easily turn out 150 tons of pig per week, the best of the older furnaces did not produce more than from three to four tons. One of the last extensive contracts executed in Sussex was the casting of the iron rails which enclose St. Paul's Cathedral. The contract was thought too large for one iron-master to undertake, and it was consequently distributed amongst several contractors, though the principal part of the work was executed at Lamberhurst, near Tunbridge Wells.   But to produce the comparatively small quantity of iron turned out by the old works, the consumption of timber was enormous; for the making of every ton of pig-iron required four loads of timber converted into charcoal fuel, and the making of every ton of bar-iron required three additional loads.   Thus, notwithstanding the indispensable need of iron, the extension of the manufacture, by threatening the destruction of the timber of the southern counties, came to be regarded in the light of a national calamity.   Up to a certain point, the clearing of the Weald of its dense growth of underwood had been of advantage, by affording better opportunities for the operations of agriculture.   But the "voragious iron-mills" were proceeding to swallow up everything that would burn, and the old forest growths were rapidly disappearing.   An entire wood was soon exhausted, and long time was needed before it grew again.   At Lamberhurst alone, though the produce was only about five tons of iron a-week, the annual consumption of wood was about 200,000 cords!   Wood continued to be the only material used for fuel generally—a strong prejudice existing against the use of sea-coal for domestic purposes.*   It therefore began to be feared that there would be no available fuel left within practicable reach of the metropolis; and the contingency of having to face the rigorous cold of an English winter without fuel naturally occasioning much alarm, the action of the Government was deemed necessary to remedy the apprehended evil.

---

* It was then believed that sea or pit-coal was poisonous when burnt in dwellings, and that it was especially injurious to the human complexion. All sorts of diseases were attributed to its use, and at one time it was even penal to burn it.   The Londoners only began to reconcile themselves to the use of coal when the wood within reach of the metropolis had been nearly all burnt up, and no other fuel was to be had.

To check the destruction of wood near London, an Act was passed in 1581 prohibiting its conversion into fuel for the making of iron within fourteen miles of the Thames, forbidding the erection of new ironworks within twenty-two miles of London, and restricting the number of works in Kent, Surrey, and Sussex, beyond the above limits. Similar enactments were made in future Parliaments with the same object, which had the effect of checking the trade, and several of the Sussex ironmasters were under the necessity of removing their works elsewhere. Some of them migrated to Glamorganshire, in South Wales, because of the abundance of timber as well as ironstone in that quarter, and there set up their forges, more particularly at Aberdare and Merthyr Tydvil. Mr. Llewellin has recently published an interesting account of their proceedings, with descriptions of their works,* remains of which still exist at Llwydcoed, Pontyryns, and other places in the Aberdare valley. Among the Sussex masters who settled in Glamorganshire for the purpose of carrying on the iron manufacture, were Walter Burrell, the friend of John Ray, the naturalist, one of the Morleys of Glynde in Sussex, the Relfes from Mayfield, and the Cheneys from Crawley.

Notwithstanding these migrations of enterprising manufacturers, the iron trade of Sussex continued to exist until the middle of the seventeenth century, when the waste of timber was again urged upon the attention of Parliament, and the penalties for infringing the statutes seem to have been more rigorously enforced. The trade then suffered a more serious check; and during the civil wars, a heavy blow was given to it by the destruction of the works belonging to all royalists, which was accomplished by a division of the army under Sir William Waller. Most of the Welsh ironworks were razed to the ground about

---

* *Archæologia Cambrensis*, 3rd Series, No. 34, April, 1863.   Art. " Sussex Ironmasters in Glamorganshire."

the same time, and were not again rebuilt. And after the Restoration, in 1674, all the royal ironworks in the Forest of Dean were demolished, leaving only such to be supplied with ore as were beyond the forest limits; the reason alleged for this measure being lest the iron manufacture should endanger the supply of timber required for ship-building and other necessary purposes.

From this time the iron manufacture of Sussex, as of England generally, rapidly declined. In 1740 there were only fifty-nine furnaces in all England, of which ten were in Sussex; and in 1788 there were only two. A few years later, and the Sussex iron furnaces were blown out altogether. Farnhurst, in western, and Ashburnham, in eastern Sussex, witnessed the total extinction of the manufacture. The din of the iron hammer was hushed, the glare of the furnace faded, the last blast of the bellows was blown, and the district returned to its original rural solitude. Some of the furnace-ponds were drained and planted with hops or willows; others formed beautiful lakes in retired pleasure-grounds; while the remainder were used to drive flour-mills, as the streams in North Kent, instead of driving fulling-mills, were employed to work paper-mills. All that now remains of the old iron-works are the extensive beds of cinders from which material is occasionally taken to mend the Sussex roads, and the numerous furnace-ponds, hammer-posts, forges, and cinder places, which mark the seats of the ancient manufacture.

Coalbrookdale Ironworks, 1805, an aquatint by William Pickett after a drawing by Phillip James de Loutherbourg

Cast-iron rails and sleepers cast at Coalbrookdale, c 1770 (*by courtesy of the Science Museum*)

6 Interior of Smelting House, Broseley, 1788, engraved by Wilson Lowry (from a pai
by George Robertson)

7 The Iron Bridge, Coalbrookdale, in 1788, engraved by James Fittle (from a painti
George Robertson)

CHAPTER III.

Iron-smelting by Pit-Coal — Dud Dudley.

" God of his Infinite goodness (if we will but take notice of his goodness unto this Nation) hath made this Country a very Granary for the supply-ing of Smiths with Iron, Cole, and Lime made with cole, which hath much supplied these men with Corn also of late ; and from these men a great part, not only of this Island, but also of his Majestie's other Kingdoms and Territories, with Iron wares have their supply, and Wood in these parts almost exhausted, although it were of late a mighty wood-land country."—Dudley's *Metallum Martis*, 1665.

THE severe restrictions enforced by the legislature against the use of wood in iron-smelting had the effect of almost extinguishing the manufacture.   New furnaces ceased to be erected, and many of the old ones were allowed to fall into decay, until it began to be feared that this important branch of industry would become completely lost.   The same restrictions alike affected the operations of the glass manufacture, which, with the aid of foreign artisans, had been gradually established in England, and was becoming a thriving branch of trade.   It was even proposed that the smelting of iron should be absolutely prohibited : " many think," said a contemporary writer, " that there should be *no works anywhere*—they do so devour the woods."

The use of iron, however, could not be dispensed with. The very foundations of society rested upon an abundant supply of it, for tools and implements of peace, as well as for weapons of war.   In the dearth of the article at home, a supply of it was therefore sought for abroad ; and both iron and steel came to be imported in largely-increased quantities.   This branch of trade was principally in the hands of the Steelyard Company of Foreign Merchants, established in Upper Thames Street, a little above London Bridge; and they imported large quantities of iron and steel from foreign countries, principally from Sweden, Germany, and Spain. The best iron came from Spain, though the Spaniards on their part coveted our English made cannons, which were better manufactured than theirs; while the best steel came from Germany and Sweden.*

Under these circumstances, it was natural that persons interested in the English iron manufacture should turn their attention to some other description of fuel which should serve as a substitute for the prohibited article. There was known to be an abundance of coal in the northern and midland counties, and it occurred to some speculators more than usually daring, to propose it as a substitute for the charcoal fuel made from wood. But the same popular prejudice which existed against the use of coal for domestic purposes, prevented its being employed for purposes of manufacture; and they were thought very foolish persons indeed who first promulgated the idea of smelting iron by means of pit-coal. The old manufacturers held it to be impossible to reduce the ore in any other way than by means of charcoal of wood. It was only when the wood in the neighbourhood of the ironworks had been almost entirely burnt up, that the manufacturers were driven to entertain the idea of using coal as a substitute; but more than a hundred years passed before the practice of smelting iron by its means became general.

The first who took out a patent for the purpose was one Simon Sturtevant, a German skilled in mining operations; the professed object of his invention being "to neale, melt, and worke all kind of metal oares, irons, and steeles with

---

* As late as 1790, long after the monopoly of the foreign merchants had been abolished, Pennant says, " The present Steelyard is the great repository of imported iron, which furnishes our metropolis with that neces-sary material. The quantity of bars that fills the yards and warehouses of this quarter strikes with astonishment the most indifferent beholder."—PEN-NANT, *Account of London*, 309.

sea-coale, pit-coale, earth-coale, and brush fewell." The
principal end of his invention, he states in his *Treatise of
Metallica*,* is to save the consumption and waste of the
woods and timber of the country; and, should his design
succeed, he holds that it "will prove to be the best and
most profitable business and invention that ever was known
or invented in England these many yeares." He says he
has already made trial of the process on a small scale, and
is confident that it will prove equally successful on a large
one. Sturtevant was not very specific as to his process;
but it incidentally appears to have been his purpose to
reduce the coal by an imperfect combustion to the condition of coke, thereby ridding it of "those malignant
proprieties which are averse to the nature of metallique
substances." The subject was treated by him, as was
customary in those days, as a great mystery, made still
more mysterious by the multitude of learned words under
which he undertook to describe his "Ignick Invention."
All the operations of industry were then treated as secrets.
Each trade was a craft, and those who followed it were
called craftsmen. Even the common carpenter was a handicraftsman; and skilled artisans were "cunning men." But
the higher branches of work were mysteries, the communication of which to others was carefully guarded by
the regulations of the trades guilds. Although the early
patents are called specifications, they in reality specify
nothing. They are for the most part but a mere haze
of words, from which very little definite information can
be gleaned as to the processes patented. It may be that
Sturtevant had not yet reduced his idea to any practicable
method, and therefore could not definitely explain it.
However that may be, it is certain that his process failed
when tried on a large scale, and Sturtevant's patent was
accordingly cancelled at the end of a year.

---

* STURTEVANT'S *Metallica; briefly
comprehending the Doctrine of Diverse
New Metallical Inventions, &c.* Re- | printed and published at the Great
Seal Patent Office, 1858.

The idea, however, had been fairly born, and repeated patents were taken out with the same object from time to time. Thus, immediately on Sturtevant's failure becoming known, one John Rovenzon, who had been mixed up with the other's adventure, applied for a patent for making iron by the same process, which was granted him in 1613. His 'Treatise of Metallica'* shows that Rovenzon had a true conception of the method of manufacture. Nevertheless he, too, failed in carrying out the invention in practice, and his patent was also cancelled. Though these failures were very discouraging, like experiments continued to be made and patents taken out,—principally by Dutchmen and Germans,†—but no decided success seems to have attended their efforts until the year 1620, when Lord Dudley took out his patent "for melting iron ore, making bar-iron, &c., with coal, in furnaces, with bellows." This patent was taken out at the instance of his son Dud Dudley, whose story we gather partly from his treatise entitled 'Metallum Martis,' and partly from various petitions presented by him to the king, which are preserved in the State Paper Office, and it runs as follows:—

Dud Dudley was born in 1599, the natural son of Edward Lord Dudley of Dudley Castle in the county of Worcester. He was the fourth of eleven children by the same mother, who is described in the pedigree of the family given in the Herald's visitation of the county of Stafford in the year 1663, signed by Dud Dudley himself, as "Elizabeth, daughter of William Tomlinson of Dudley, concubine of Edward Lord Dudley." Dud's eldest brother is described in the same pedigree as Robert Dudley, Squire, of Netherton Hall; and as his sisters mostly married well, several of them county gentlemen, it is obvious that the

* Reprinted and published at the Great Seal Patent Office, 1858.

† Among the early patentees, besides the names of Sturtevant and Rovenzon, we find those of Jordens, Francke, Sir Phillibert Vernatt, and other foreigners of the above nations.

family, notwithstanding that the children were born out of wedlock, held a good position in their neighbourhood, and were regarded with respect. Lord Dudley, though married and having legitimate heirs at the time, seems to have attended to the up-bringing of his natural children; educating them carefully, and afterwards employing them in confidential offices connected with the management of his extensive property. Dud describes himself as taking great delight, when a youth, in his father's iron-works near Dudley, where he obtained considerable knowledge of the various processes of the manufacture.

The town of Dudley was already a centre of the iron manufacture, though chiefly of small wares, such as nails, horse-shoes, keys, locks, and common agricultural tools; and it was estimated that there were about 20,000 smiths and workers in iron of various kinds living within a circuit of ten miles of Dudley Castle. But, as in the southern counties, the production of iron had suffered great diminution from the want of fuel in the district, " though formerly a mighty woodland country;" and many important branches of the local trade were brought almost to a stand-still. Yet there was an extraordinary abundance of coal to be met with in the neighbourhood—coal in some places lying in seams ten feet thick—ironstone four feet thick immediately under the coal, with limestone conveniently adjacent to both. The conjunction seemed almost providential—" as if," observes Dud, " God had decreed the time when and how these smiths should be supplied, and this island also, with iron, and most especially that this cole and ironstone should give the first and just occasion for the invention of smelting iron with pit-cole;" though, as we have already seen, all attempts heretofore made with that object had practically failed.

Dud was a special favourite of the Earl his father, who encouraged his speculations with reference to the improvement of the iron manufacture, and gave him an education calculated to enable him to turn his excellent practical abilities to account. He was studying at Baliol College, Oxford, in the year 1619, when the Earl sent for him to take charge of an iron furnace and two forges in the chase of Pensnet in Worcestershire. He was no sooner installed manager of the works, than, feeling hampered by the want of wood for fuel, his attention was directed to the employment of pit-coal as a substitute. He altered his furnace accordingly, so as to adapt it to the new process, and the result of the first trial was such as to induce him to persevere. It is nowhere stated in Dud Dudley's Treatise what was the precise nature of the method adopted by him; but it is most probable that, in endeavouring to substitute coal for wood as fuel, he would subject the coal to a process similar to that of charcoal-burning. The result would be what is called Coke; and as Dudley informs us that he followed up his first experiment with a second blast, by means of which he was enabled to produce good marketable iron, the presumption is that his success was also due to an improvement of the blast which he contrived for the purpose of keeping up the active combustion of the fuel. Though the quantity produced by the new process was comparatively small—not more than three tons a week from each furnace—Dudley anticipated that greater experience would enable him to increase the quantity; and at all events he had succeeded in proving the practicability of smelting iron with fuel made from pit-coal, which so many before him had tried in vain.

Immediately after the second trial had been made with such good issue, Dud wrote to his father the Earl, then in London, informing him what he had done, and desiring him at once to obtain a patent for the invention from King James. This was readily granted, and the patent (No. 18), dated the 22nd February, 1620, was taken out in the name of Lord Dudley himself.

Dud proceeded with the manufacture of iron at Pensnet, and also at Cradley in Staffordshire, where he erected

another furnace; and a year after the patent was granted
he was enabled to send up to the Tower, by the King's
command, a considerable quantity of the new iron for trial.
Many experiments were made with it : its qualities were
fairly tested, and it was pronounced " good merchantable
iron." Dud adds, in his Treatise, that his brother-in-law,
Richard Parkshouse, of Sedgeley,* " had a fowling-gun
there made of the Pit-cole iron," which was " well approved." There was therefore every prospect of the new
method of manufacture becoming fairly established, and
with greater experience further improvements might with
confidence be anticipated, when a succession of calamities
occurred to the inventor which involved him in difficulties
and put an effectual stop to the progress of his enterprise.

The new works had been in successful operation little
more than a year, when a flood, long after known as
the " Great May-day Flood," swept away Dudley's principal works at Cradley, and otherwise inflicted much
damage throughout the district. " At the market town
called Stourbridge," says Dud, in the course of his curious
narrative, " although the author sent with speed to preserve the people from drowning, and one resolute man was
carried from the bridge there in the day-time, the nether
part of the town was so deep in water that the people had
much ado to preserve their lives in the uppermost rooms of
their houses." Dudley himself received very little sym-
pathy for his losses. On the contrary, the iron-smelters of
the district rejoiced exceedingly at the destruction of his
works by the flood. They had seen him making good iron
by his new patent process, and selling it cheaper than they

---

* Mr. Parkshouse was one of the
esquires to Sir Ferdinando Dudley (the
legitimate son of the Earl of Dudley)
when he was made Knight of the Bath.
Sir Ferdinando's only daughter Frances
married Humble Ward, son and heir of
William Ward, goldsmith and jeweller
to Charles the First's queen. Her
husband having been created a baron by
the title of Baron Ward of Birmingham,
and Frances becoming Baroness of
Dudley in her own right on the
demise of her father, the baronies of
Dudley and Ward thus became united
in their eldest son Edward in the year
1697.

could afford to do. They accordingly put in circulation all manner of disparaging reports about his iron. It was bad iron, not fit to be used; indeed no iron, except what was smelted with charcoal of wood, could be good. To smelt it with coal was a dangerous innovation, and could only result in some great public calamity. The ironmasters even appealed to King James to put a stop to Dud's manufacture, alleging that his iron was not merchantable. And then came the great flood, which swept away his works; the hostile ironmasters now hoping that there was an end for ever of Dudley's pit-coal iron.

But Dud, with his wonted energy, forthwith set to work and repaired his furnaces and forges, though at great cost; and in the course of a short time the new manufacture was again in full progress. The ironmasters raised a fresh outcry against him, and addressed another strong memorial against Dud and his iron to King James. This seems to have taken effect; and in order to ascertain the quality of the article by testing it upon a large scale, the King commanded Dudley to send up to the Tower of London, with every possible speed, quantities of all the sorts of bar-iron made by him, fit for the " making of muskets, carbines, and iron for great bolts for shipping; which iron," continues Dud, " being so tried by artists and smiths, the ironmasters and iron-mongers were all silenced until the 21st year of King James's reign." The ironmasters then endeavoured to get the Dudley patent included in the monopolies to be abolished by the statute of that year; but all they could accomplish was the limitation of the patent to fourteen years instead of thirty-one; the special exemption of the patent from the operation of the statute affording a sufficient indication of the importance already attached to the invention. After that time Dudley " went on with his invention cheerfully, and made annually great store of iron, good and merchantable, and sold it unto diverse men at twelve pounds per ton." " I also," said he, " made all sorts of cast-iron wares, as brewing cisterns, pots, mortars,

&c., better and cheaper than any yet made in these nations with charcoal, some of which are yet to be seen by any man (at the author's house in the city of Worcester) that desires to be satisfied of the truth of the invention."

Notwithstanding this decided success, Dudley encountered nothing but trouble and misfortune. The ironmasters combined to resist his invention; they fastened lawsuits upon him, and succeeded in getting him ousted from his works at Cradley. From thence he removed to Himley in the county of Stafford, where he set up a pitcoal furnace; but being without the means of forging the iron into bars, he was constrained to sell the pig-iron to the charcoal-ironmasters, " who did him much prejudice, not only by detaining his stock, but also by disparaging his iron." He next proceeded to erect a large new furnace at Hasco Bridge, near Sedgeley, in the same county, for the purpose of carrying out the manufacture on the most improved principles. This furnace was of stone, twenty-seven feet square, provided with unusually large bellows; and when in full work he says he was enabled to turn out seven tons of iron per week, " the greatest quantity of pit-coal iron ever yet made in Great Britain." At the same place he discovered and opened out new workings of coal ten feet thick, lying immediately over the ironstone, and he prepared to carry on his operations on a large scale ; but the new works were scarcely finished when a mob of rioters, instigated by the charcoal-ironmasters, broke in upon them, cut in pieces the new bellows, destroyed the machinery, and laid the results of all his deep-laid ingenuity and persevering industry in ruins. From that time forward Dudley was allowed no rest nor peace : he was attacked by mobs, worried by lawsuits, and eventually overwhelmed by debts. He was then seized by his creditors and sent up to London, where he was held a prisoner in the Comptoir for several thousand pounds. The charcoal-iron men thus for a time remained masters of the field.

Charles I. seems to have taken pity on the suffering inventor; and on his earnest petition, setting forth the great advantages to the nation of his invention, from which he had as yet derived no advantage, but only losses, sufferings, and persecution, the King granted him a renewal of his patent * in the year 1638; three other gentlemen joining him as partners, and doubtless providing the requisite capital for carrying on the manufacture after the plans of the inventor. But Dud's evil fortune continued to pursue him. The patent had scarcely been secured ere the Civil War broke out, and the arts of peace must at once perforce give place to the arts of war. Dud's nature would not suffer him to be neutral at such a time; and when the nation divided itself into two hostile camps, his predilections being strongly loyalist, he took the side of the King with his father. It would appear from a petition presented by him to Charles II. in 1660, setting forth his sufferings in the royal cause, and praying for restoral to certain offices which he had enjoyed under Charles I., that as early as the year 1637 he had been employed by the King on a mission into Scotland,† in the train of the Marquis of Hamilton, the King's Commissioner. Again in 1639, leaving his ironworks and partners, he accompanied Charles on his expedition across the Scotch border, and was present with the army until its discomfiture at Newburn near Newcastle in the following year.

The sword was now fairly drawn, and Dud seems for a time to have abandoned his iron-works and followed

---

* Patent No. 117, Old Series, granted in 1638, to Sir George Horsey, David Ramsey, Roger Foulke, and Dudd Dudley.

† By his own account, given in *Metallum Martis*, while in Scotland in 1637, he visited the Highlands as well as the Lowlands, spending the whole summer of that year " in opening of mines and making of discoveries;" spending part of the time with Sir James Hope of Lead Hills, near where,

he says, " he got gold." It does not appear, however, that any iron forges existed in Scotland at the time: indeed Dudley expressly says that " Scotland maketh no iron;" and in his treatise of 1665 he urges that the Corporation of the Mines Royal should set him and his inventions at work to enable Scotland to enjoy the benefit of a cheap and abundant supply of the manufactured article.

entirely the fortunes of the king. He was sworn surveyor
of the Mews or Armoury in 1640, but being unable to pay
for the patent, another was sworn in in his place. Yet his
loyalty did not falter, for in the beginning of 1642, when
Charles set out from London, shortly after the fall of
Strafford and Laud, Dud went with him.* He was present
before Hull when Sir John Hotham shut its gates in the
king's face; at York when the royal commissions of array
were sent out enjoining all loyal subjects to send men,
arms, money, and horses, for defence of the king and
maintenance of the law; at Nottingham, where the royal
standard was raised; at Coventry, where the townspeople
refused the king entrance and fired upon his troops from
the walls; at Edgehill, where the first great but indecisive
battle was fought between the contending parties; in short,
as Dud Dudley states in his petition, he was " in most of
the battailes that year, and also supplyed his late sacred
Majestie's magazines of Stafford, Worcester, Dudley Castle,
and Oxford, with arms, shot, drakes, and cannon; and also,
became major unto Sir Frauncis Worsley's regiment, which
was much decaied."

In 1643, according to the statement contained in his
petition above referred to, Dud Dudley acted as military
engineer in setting out the fortifications of Worcester and
Stafford, and furnishing them with ordnance. After the
taking of Lichfield, in which he had a share, he was made
Colonel of Dragoons, and accompanied the Queen with his
regiment to the royal head-quarters at Oxford. The year
after we find him at the siege of Gloucester, then at the
first battle of Newbury leading the forlorn hope with Sir
George Lisle, afterwards marching with Sir Charles Lucas
into the associate counties, and present at the royalist rout

---

* The Journals of the House of
Commons, of the 13th June, 1642,
contain the resolution " that Cáptain
Wolseley, Ensign Dudley, and John
Lometon be forthwith sent for, as de-
linquents, by the Serjeant-at-Arms
attending on the House, for giving
interruption to the execution of the
ordinance of the militia in the county
of Leicester."

at Newport. That he was esteemed a valiant and skilful officer is apparent from the circumstance, that in 1645 he was appointed general of Prince Maurice's train of artillery, and afterwards held the same rank under Lord Ashley. The iron districts being still for the most part occupied by the royal armies, our military engineer turned his practical experience to account by directing the forging of drakes * of bar-iron, which were found of great use, giving up his own dwelling-house in the city of Worcester for the purpose of carrying on the manufacture of these and other arms. But Worcester and the western towns fell before the Parliamentarian armies in 1646, and all the iron-works belonging to royalists, from which the principal supplies of arms had been drawn by the King's army, were forthwith destroyed.

Dudley fully shared in the dangers and vicissitudes of that trying period, and bore his part throughout like a valiant soldier. For two years nothing was heard of him, until in 1648, when the king's party drew together again, and made head in different parts of the .country, north and south. Goring raised his standard in Essex, but was driven by Fairfax into Colchester, where he defended himself for two months. While the siege was in progress, the royalists determined to make an attempt to raise it. On this Dud Dudley again made his appearance in the field, and, joining sundry other counties, he proceeded to raise 200 men, mostly at his own charge. They were, however, no sooner mustered in Bosco Bello woods near Madeley, than they were attacked by the Parliamentarians, and dispersed or taken prisoners. Dud was among those so taken, and he was first carried to Hartlebury Castle and thence to Worcester, where he was imprisoned. Recounting the sufferings of himself and his followers on this occasion, in the petition presented to Charles II. in

---

* Small pieces of artillery, specimens of which are still to be seen in the museum at Woolwich Arsenal and at the Tower.

1660,* he says, " 200 men were dispersed, killed, and some taken, namely, Major Harcourt, Major Elliotts, Capt. Long, and Cornet Hodgetts, of whom Major Harcourt was miserably burned with matches. The petitioner and the rest were stripped almost naked, and in triumph and scorn carried up to the city of Worcester (which place Dud had fortified for the king), and kept close prisoners, with double guards set upon the prison and the city."

Notwithstanding this close watch and durance, Dudley and Major Elliotts contrived to break out of gaol, making their way over the tops of the houses, afterwards passing the guards at the city gates, and escaping into the open country. Being hotly pursued, they travelled during the night, and took to the trees during the daytime. They succeeded in reaching London, but only to drop again into the lion's mouth; for first Major Elliotts was captured, then Dudley, and both were taken before Sir John Warner, the Lord Mayor, who forthwith sent them before the "cursed committee of insurrection," as Dudley calls them. The prisoners were summarily sentenced to be shot to death, and were meanwhile closely imprisoned in the Gatehouse at Westminster, with other Royalists.

The day before their intended execution, the prisoners formed a plan of escape. It was Sunday morning, the 20th August, 1648, when they seized their opportunity, "at ten of the clocke in sermon time;" and, overpowering the gaolers, Dudley, with Sir Henry Bates, Major Elliotts, Captain South, Captain Paris, and six others, succeeded in getting away, and making again for the open country. Dudley had received a wound in the leg, and could only get along with great difficulty. He records that he proceeded on crutches, through Worcester, Tewkesbury, and Gloucester, to Bristol, having been " fed three weeks in private in an enemy's hay mow." Even the most lynx-eyed Parliamentarian must have failed to recognise the

---

* State Paper Office, Dom. Charles II., vol. xi. 54.

quondam royalist general of artillery in the helpless creature dragging himself along upon crutches; and he reached Bristol in safety.

His military career now over, he found himself absolutely penniless. His estate of about 200*l.* per annum had been sequestrated and sold by the government;* his house in Worcester had been seized and his sickly wife turned out of doors; and his goods, stock, great shop, and ironworks, which he himself valued at 2000*l.*, were destroyed. He had also lost the offices of Serjeant-at-arms, Lieutenant of Ordnance, and Surveyor of the Mews, which he had held under the king; in a word, he found himself reduced to a state of utter destitution.

Dudley was for some time under the necessity of living in great privacy at Bristol; but when the king had been executed, and the royalists were finally crushed at Worcester, Dud gradually emerged from his concealment. He was still the sole possessor of the grand secret of smelting iron with pit-coal, and he resolved upon one more commercial adventure, in the hope of yet turning it to good account. He succeeded in inducing Walter Stevens, linendraper, and John Stone, merchant, both of Bristol, to join him as partners in an ironwork, which they proceeded to erect near that city. The buildings were well advanced, and nearly 700*l.* had been expended, when a quarrel occurred between Dudley and his partners, which ended in the stoppage of the works, and the concern being thrown into Chancery. Dudley alleges that the other partners " cunningly drew him into a bond," and " did unjustly enter staple actions in Bristol of great value against him, because he was of the king's party;" but it would appear as if there had been some twist or infirmity of temper in Dudley himself, which

---

* The Journals of the House of Commons, on the 2nd Nov. 1652, have the following entry: "The House this day resumed the debate upon the additional Bill for sale of several lands and estates forfeited to the Commonwealth for treason, when it was resolved that the name of Dud Dudley of Green Lodge be inserted into this Bill."

prevented him from working harmoniously with such persons as he became associated with in affairs of business.

In the mean time other attempts were made to smelt iron with pit-coal. Dudley says that Cromwell and the then Parliament granted a patent to Captain Buck for the purpose; and that Cromwell himself, Major Wildman, and various others were partners in the patent. They erected furnaces and works in the Forest of Dean;* but, though Cromwell and his officers could fight and win battles, they could not smelt and forge iron with pit-coal. They brought one Dagney, an Italian glass-maker, from Bristol, to erect a new furnace for them, provided with sundry pots of glass-house clay; but no success attended their efforts. The partners knowing of Dudley's possession of the grand secret, invited him to visit their works; but all they could draw from him was that they would never succeed in making iron to profit by the methods they were pursuing. They next proceeded to erect other works at Bristol, but still they failed. Major Wildman † bought Dudley's sequestrated estate, in the hope of being able to extort his secret of making iron with pit-coal; but all their attempts proving abortive, they at length abandoned the enterprise in despair. In 1656, one Captain Copley obtained from Cromwell a further patent with a similar object; and erected works near Bristol, and also in the Forest of Kingswood. The mechanical engineers employed

---

* Mr. Mushet, in his 'Papers on Iron,' says, that "although he had carefully examined every spot and relic in Dean Forest likely to denote the site of Dud Dudley's enterprising but unfortunate experiment of making pig-iron with pit coal," it had been without success; neither could he find any traces of the like operations of Cromwell and his partners.

† Dudley says, "Major Wildman, more barbarous to me than a wild man, although a minister, bought the author's estate, near 200l. per annum, intending to compell from the author his inventions of making iron with pit-cole, but afterwards passed my estate unto two barbarous brokers of London, that pulled down the author's two mantion houses, sold 500 timber trees off his land, and to this day are his houses unrepaired." Wildman himself fell under the grip of Cromwell. Being one of the chiefs of the Republican party, he was seized at Exton, near Marlborough, in 1654, and imprisoned in Chepstow Castle.

by Copley failed in making his bellows blow; on which
he sent for Dudley, who forthwith "made his bellows to
be blown feisibly;" but Copley failed, like his predecessors, in making iron, and at length he too desisted from
further experiments.

Such continued to be the state of things until the Restoration, when we find Dud Dudley a petitioner to the king
for the renewal of his patent. He was also a petitioner
for compensation in respect of the heavy losses he had
sustained during the civil wars. The king was besieged
by crowds of applicants of a similar sort, but Dudley was
no more successful than the others. He failed in obtaining the renewal of his patent. Another applicant for the
like privilege, probably having greater interest at court,
proved more successful. Colonel Proger and three others *
were granted a patent to make iron with coal; but Dudley
knew the secret, which the new patentees did not; and
their patent came to nothing.

Dudley continued to address the king in importunate
petitions, asking to be restored to his former offices of Serjeant-at-arms, Lieutenant of Ordnance, and Surveyor of the
Mews or Armoury. He also petitioned to be appointed
Master of the Charter House in Smithfield, professing himself willing to take anything, or hold any living.† We
find him sending in two petitions to a similar effect in
June, 1660; and a third shortly after. The result was,

---

* June 13, 1661. Petition of Col.
Jas. Proger and three others to the
king for a patent for the sole exercise
of their invention of melting down
iron and other metals with coal instead
of wood, as the great consumption of
coal [charcoal?] therein causes detriment to shipping, &c. With reference
thereon to Attorney-General Palmer,
and his report, June 18, in favour of
the petition.—*State Papers*, Charles
II. (Dom.) vol. xxxvii. 49.

† In his second petition he prays

that a dwelling-house situated in Worcester, and belonging to one Baldwin,
"a known traitor," may be assigned
to him in lieu of Alderman Nash's,
which had reverted to that individual
since his return to loyalty; Dudley
reminding the king that his own
house in that city had been given
up by him for the service of his father
Charles I., and turned into a factory for arms. It does not appear
that this part of his petition was successful.

that he was reappointed to the office of Serjeant-at-Arms; but the Mastership of the Charter-House was not disposed of until 1662, when it fell to the lot of one Thomas Watson.* In 1661, we find a patent granted to Wm. Chamberlaine and —— Dudley, Esq., for the sole use of their new invention of plating steel, &c., and tinning the said plates; but whether Dud Dudley was the person referred to, we are unable precisely to determine. A few years later, he seems to have succeeded in obtaining the means of prosecuting his original invention; for in his *Metallum Martis*, published in 1665, he describes himself as living at Green's Lodge, in Staffordshire; and he says that near it are four forges, Green's Forge, Swin Forge, Heath Forge, and Cradley Forge, where he practises his " perfect invention." These forges, he adds, " have barred all or most part of their iron with pit-coal since the author's first invention in 1618, which hath preserved much wood. In these four, besides many other forges, do the like [*sic*]; yet the author hath had no benefit thereby to this present." From that time forward, Dud becomes lost to sight. He seems eventually to have retired to St. Helen's in Worcestershire, where he died in 1684, in the 85th year of his age. He was buried in the parish church there, and a monument, now destroyed, was erected to his memory, bearing the inscription partly set forth underneath.†

---

* State Papers, vol. xxxi.   Doquet Book, p. 89.

† Pulvis et umbra sumus
    Memento mori.

Dodo Dudley chiliarchi nobilis Edwardi nuper domini de Dudley filius, patri charus et regiæ Majestatis fidissimus subditus et servus in asserendo regem, in vindicando ecclesiam, in propugnando legem ac libertatem Anglicanam, sæpe captus, anno 1648, semel condemnatus et tamen non decollatus, renatum denuo vidit diadæma hic inconcussa semper virtute senex.

Differt non aufert mortem longissima vita
Sed differt multam cras hodiere mori.
Quod nequeas vitare, fugis:
Nec formidanda est.

Plot frequently alludes to Dudley in his *Natural History of Staffordshire*, and when he does so he describes him as the " worshipful Dud Dudley," showing the estimation in which he was held by his contemporaries.

CHAPTER IV.

ANDREW YARRANTON.

" There never have been wanting men to whom England's improvement
by sea and land was one of the dearest thoughts of their lives, and to whom
England's good was the foremost of their worldly considerations. And
such, emphatically, was Andrew Yarranton, a true patriot in the best
sense of the word."—DOVE, *Elements of Political Science.*

THAT industry had a sore time of it during the civil wars
will further appear from the following brief account of
Andrew Yarranton, which may be taken as a companion
memoir to that of Dud Dudley. For Yarranton also was
a Worcester ironmaster and a soldier—though on the
opposite side,—but more even than Dudley was he a
man of public spirit and enterprise, an enlightened political economist (long before political economy had been
recognised as a science), and in many respects a true national benefactor. Bishop Watson said that he ought to
have had a statue erected to his memory because of his
eminent public services; and an able modern writer has
gone so far as to say of him that he was " the founder of
English political economy, the first man in England who
saw and said that peace was better than war, that trade
was better than plunder, that honest industry was better
than martial greatness, and that the best occupation of a
government was to secure prosperity at home, and let other
nations alone."* Yet the name of Andrew Yarranton is
scarcely remembered, or is at most known to only a few
readers of half-forgotten books. The following brief out-

---

* PATRICK EDWARD DOVE, *Elements of Political Science.* Edinburgh, 1854.

line of his history is gathered from his own narrative and from documents in the State Paper Office.

Andrew Yarranton was born at the farmstead of Larford, in the parish of Astley, in Worcestershire, in the year 1616.* In his sixteenth year he was put apprentice to a Worcester linendraper, and remained at that trade for some years; but not liking it, he left it, and was leading a country life when the civil wars broke out. Unlike Dudley, he took the side of the Parliament, and joined their army, in which he served for some time as a soldier. His zeal and abilities commended him to his officers, and he was raised from one position to another, until in the course of a few years we find him holding the rank of captain. "While a soldier," says he, "I had sometimes the honour and misfortune to lodge and dislodge an army;" but this is all the information he gives us of his military career. In the year 1648 he was instrumental in discovering and frustrating a design on the part of the Royalists to seize Doyley House in the county of Hereford, and other strongholds, for which he received the thanks of Parliament "for his ingenuity, discretion, and valour," and a substantial reward of 500l.† He was also recommended to the Committee of Worcester for further employment. But from that time we hear no more of him in connection with the civil wars. When Cromwell assumed the supreme control of affairs, Yarranton retired from the army with most of the Presbyterians, and devoted himself to industrial pursuits.

---

* A copy of the entries in the parish register relating to the various members of the Yarranton family, kindly forwarded to us by the Rev. H. W. Cookes, rector of Astley, shows them to have resided in that parish for many generations. There were the Yarrantons of Yarranton, of Redstone, of Larford, of Brockenton, and of Longmore. With that disregard for orthography in proper names which prevailed some three hundred years since, they are indifferently designated as Yarran, Yarranton, and Yarrington. The name was most probably derived from two farms named Great and Little Yarranton, or Yarran (originally Yarhampton), situated in the parish of Astley. The Yarrantons frequently filled local offices in that parish, and we find several of them officiating at different periods as bailiffs of Bewdley.

† Journals of the House of Commons, 1st July, 1648.

We then find him engaged in carrying on the manufacture of iron at Ashley, near Bewdley, in Worcestershire. "In the year 1652," says he, "I entered upon iron-works, and plied them for several years."* He made it a subject of his diligent study how to provide employment for the poor, then much distressed by the late wars. With the help of his wife, he established a manufacture of linen, which was attended with good results. Observing how the difficulties of communication, by reason of the badness of the roads, hindered the development of the rich natural resources of the western counties,† he applied himself to the improvement of the navigation of the larger rivers, making surveys of them at his own cost, and endeavouring to stimulate local enterprise so as to enable him to carry his plans into effect.

While thus occupied, the restoration of Charles II. took place, and whether through envy or enmity Yarranton's activity excited the suspicion of the authorities. His journeys from place to place seemed to them to point to some Presbyterian plot on foot. On the 13th of November, 1660, Lord Windsor, Lord-Lieutenant of the county, wrote to the Secretary of State—"There is a quaker in prison for speaking treason against his Majesty, and a countryman also, and Captain Yarrington for refusing to obey my authority." ‡ It would appear from subsequent letters that Yarranton must have lain in prison for nearly two years, charged with conspiring against the king's authority, the only evidence against him consisting

---

* YARRANTON'S *England's Improvement by Sea and Land*. Part I. London, 1677.

† There seems a foundation of truth in the old English distich—

The North for Greatness, the East for Health,
The South for Neatness, the West for Wealth.

‡ State Paper Office. Dom. Charles

II. 1660-1. Yarranton afterwards succeeded in making a friend of Lord Windsor, as would appear from his dedication of *England's Improvement* to his Lordship, whom he thanks for the encouragement he had given to him in his survey of several rivers with a view to their being rendered navigable.

of some anonymous letters. At the end of May, 1662, he succeeded in making his escape from the custody of the Provost Marshal. The High Sheriff scoured the country after him at the head of a party of horse, and then he communicated to the Secretary of State, Sir Edward Nicholas, that the suspected conspirator could not be found, and was supposed to have made his way to London. Before the end of a month Yarranton was again in custody, as appears from the communication of certain justices of Surrey to Sir Edward Nicholas.* As no further notice of Yarranton occurs in the State Papers, and as we shortly after find him publicly occupied in carrying out his plans for improving the navigation of the western rivers, it is probable that his innocency of any plot was established after a legal investigation. A few years later he published in London a 4to. tract entitled 'A Full Discovery of the First Presbyterian Sham Plot,' which most probably contained a vindication of his conduct.†

Yarranton was no sooner at liberty than we find him again occupied with his plans of improved inland navigation. His first scheme was to deepen the small river Salwarp, so as to connect Droitwich with the Severn by a water communication, and thus facilitate the transport of the salt so abundantly yielded by the brine springs near that town. In 1665, the burgesses of Droitwich agreed to

---

* The following is a copy of the document from the State Papers:— "John Bramfield, Geo. Moore, and Thos. Lee, Esqrs. and Justices of Surrey, to Sir Edw. Nicholas.—There being this day brought before us one Andrew Yarranton, and he accused to have broken prison, or at least made his escape out of the Marshalsea at Worcester, being there committed by the Deputy-Lieuts. upon suspicion of a plot in November last; we having thereupon examined him, he allegeth that his Majesty hath been sought unto on his behalf, and hath given

order to yourself for his discharge, and a supersedeas against all persons and warrants, and thereupon hath desired to appeal unto you. The which we conceiving to be convenient and reasonable (there being no positive charge against him before us), have accordingly herewith conveyed him unto you by a safe hand, to be further examined or disposed of as you shall find meet."—*S. P. O. Dom. Chas. II.* 23rd June, 1662.

† We have been unable to refer to this tract, there being no copy of it in the British Museum.

give him 750*l.* and eight salt vats in Upwich, valued at
80*l.* per annum, with three-quarters of a vat in Northwich,
for twenty-one years, in payment for the work. But the
times were still unsettled, and Yarranton and his partner
Wall not being rich, the scheme was not then carried
into effect.* In the following year we find him occupied
with a similar scheme to open up the navigation of the
river Stour, passing by Stourport and Kidderminster, and
connect it by an artificial cut with the river Trent. Some
progress was made with this undertaking, so far in advance
of the age, but, like the other, it came to a stand still for
want of money, and more than a hundred years passed
before it was carried out by a kindred genius—James
Brindley, the great canal maker. Mr. Chambers says that
when Yarranton's scheme was first brought forward, it met
with violent opposition and ridicule. The undertaking was
thought wonderfully bold, and, joined to its great extent,
the sandy, spongy nature of the ground, the high banks
necessary to prevent the inundation of the Stour on the
canal, furnished its opponents, if not with sound argument,
at least with very specious topics for opposition and
laughter.† Yarranton's plan was to make the river itself
navigable, and by uniting it with other rivers, open up a
communication with the Trent; while Brindley's was to
cut a canal parallel with the river, and supply it with
water from thence. Yarranton himself thus accounts for
the failure of his scheme in ' England's Improvement by
Sea and Land ':—" It was my projection," he says, " and
I will tell you the reason why it was not finished. The
river Stour and some other rivers were granted by an Act
of Parliament to certain persons of honor, and some progress was made in the work, but within a small while after
the Act passed ‡ it was let fall again; but it being a brat

---

* Nash's *Worcestershire*, i. 306.

† John Chambers, *Biographical
Illustrations of Worcestershire.* London, 1820.

‡ The Act for making the Stour
and Salwarp navigable originated in
the Lords and was passed in the year
1661.

of my own, I was not willing it should be abortive, wherefore I made offers to perfect it, having a third part of the inheritance to me and my heirs for ever, and we came to an agreement, upon which I fell on, and made it completely navigable from Stourbridge to Kidderminster, and carried down many hundred tons of coal, and laid out near 1000*l.*, and there it was obstructed for want of money." *

Another of Yarranton's far-sighted schemes of a similar kind was one to connect the Thames with the Severn by means of an artificial cut, at the very place where, more than a century after his death, it was actually carried out by modern engineers. This canal, it appears, was twice surveyed under his direction by his son. He did, however, succeed in his own time in opening up the navigation of the Avon, and was the first to carry barges upon its waters from Tewkesbury to Stratford.

The improvement of agriculture, too, had a share of Yarranton's attention. He saw the soil exhausted by long tillage and constantly repeated crops of rye, and he urged that the land should have rest or at least rotation of crop. With this object he introduced clover-seed, and supplied it largely to the farmers of the western counties, who found their land doubled in value by the new method of husbandry, and it shortly became adopted throughout the country. Seeing how commerce was retarded by the small accommodation provided for shipping at the then prin-

---

* Nash, in his *Hist. of Worc.*, intimates that Lord Windsor subsequently renewed the attempt to make the Salwarp navigable. He constructed five out of the six locks, and then abandoned the scheme. Gough, in his edition of *Camden's Brit.* ii. 357, Lond. 1789, says, " It is not long since some of the boats made use of in Yarranton's navigation were found. Neither tradition nor our projector's account of the matter perfectly satisfy us why this navigation was neglected. . . . . We must therefore conclude that the numerous works and glass-houses upon the Stour, and in the neighbourhood of Stourbridge, did not then exist, A.D. 1666. . . . . The navigable communication which now connects Trent and Severn, and which runs in the course of Yarranton's project, is already of general use. . . . . The canal since executed under the inspection of Mr. Brindley, running parallel with the river . . . . . cost the proprietors 105,000*l.*"

cipal ports, Yarranton next made surveys and planned docks for the city of London; but though he zealously advocated the subject, he found few supporters, and his plans proved fruitless. In this respect he was nearly a hundred and fifty years before his age, and the London importers continued to conduct their shipping business in the crowded tideway of the Thames down even to the beginning of the present century.

While carrying on his iron works, it occurred to Yarranton that it would be of great national advantage if the manufacture of tin-plate could be introduced into England. Although the richest tin mines then known existed in this country, the mechanical arts were at so low an ebb that we were almost entirely dependent upon foreigners for the supply of the articles manufactured from the metal. The Saxons were the principal consumers of English tin, and we obtained from them in return nearly the whole of our tin-plates. All attempts made to manufacture them in England had hitherto failed; the beating out of the iron by hammers into laminæ sufficiently thin and smooth, and the subsequent distribution and fixing of the film of tin over the surface of the iron, proving difficulties which the English manufacturers were unable to overcome. To master these difficulties the indefatigable Yarranton set himself to work. "Knowing," says he, "the usefulness of tin-plates and the goodness of our metals for that purpose, I did, about sixteen years since (*i. e.* about 1665), endeavour to find out the way for making thereof; whereupon I acquainted a person of much riches, and one that was very understanding in the iron manufacture, who was pleased to say that he had often designed to get the trade into England, but never could find out the way. Upon which it was agreed that a sum of monies should be advanced by several persons,* for the defraying of my charges

* In the dedication of his book, entitled *England's Improvement by Sea and Land,* Part I., Yarranton gives | the names of the "noble patriots" who sent him on his journey of inquiry. They were Sir Walter Kirtham Blount,

of travelling to the place where these plates are made, and from thence to bring away the art of making them. Upon which, an able fire-man, that well understood the nature of iron, was made choice of to accompany me; and being fitted with an ingenious interpreter that well understood the language, and that had dealt much in that commodity, we marched first for Hamburgh, then to Leipsic, and from thence to Dresden, the Duke of Saxony's court, where we had notice of the place where the plates were made ; which was in a large tract of mountainous land, running from a place called Seger-Hutton unto a town called Awe [Au], being in length about twenty miles." *

It is curious to find how much the national industry of England has been influenced by the existence from time to time of religious persecutions abroad, which had the effect of driving skilled Protestant artisans, more particularly from Flanders and France, into England, where they enjoyed the special protection of successive English Governments, and founded various important branches of manufacture. But it appears from the history of the tin manufactures of Saxony, that that country also had profited in like manner by the religious persecutions of Germany, and even of England itself. Thus we are told by Yarranton that it was a Cornish miner, a Protestant, banished out of England for his religion in Queen Mary's time, who discovered the tin mines at Awe, and that a Romish

---

Bart., Sir Samuel Baldwin and Sir Timothy Baldwin, Knights, Thomas Foley and Philip Foley, Esquires, and six other gentlemen. The father of the Foleys was himself supposed to have introduced the art of iron-splitting into England by an expedient similar to that adopted by Yarranton in obtaining a knowledge of the tin-plate manufacture (*Self-Help*, p. 145). The secret of the silk-throwing machinery of Piedmont was in like manner introduced into England by Mr. Lombe of Derby, who shortly succeeded in founding a flourishing branch of manufacture. These were indeed the days of romance and adventure in manufactures.

* The district is known as the Erzgebirge or Ore Mountains, and the Riesengebirge or Giant Mountains. MacCulloch says that upwards of 500 mines are wrought in the former district, and that one-thirtieth of the entire population of Saxony to this day derive their subsistence from mining industry and the manufacture of metallic products.—*Geographical Dict.* ii. 643, edit. 1854.

priest of Bohemia, who had been converted to Lutheranism and fled into Saxony for refuge, " was the chief instrument in the manufacture until it was perfected." These two men were held in great regard by the Duke of Saxony as well as by the people of the country; for their ingenuity and industry proved the source of great prosperity and wealth, " several fine cities," says Yarranton, " having been raised by the riches proceeding from the tin-works "—not less than 80,000 men depending upon the trade for their subsistence; and when Yarranton visited Awe, he found that a statue had been erected to the memory of the Cornish miner who first discovered the tin.

Yarranton was very civilly received by the miners, and, contrary to his expectation, he was allowed freely to inspect the tinworks and examine the methods by which the iron-plates were rolled out, as well as the process of tinning them. He was even permitted to engage a number of skilled workmen, whom he brought over with him to England for the purpose of starting the manufacture in this country. A beginning was made, and the tin-plates manufactured by Yarranton's men were pronounced of better quality even than those made in Saxony. "Many thousand plates," Yarranton says, " were made from iron raised in the Forest of Dean, and were tinned over with Cornish tin; and the plates proved far better than the German ones, by reason of the toughness and flexibleness of our forest iron. One Mr. Dison, a tinman in Worcester, Mr. Lydiate near Fleet Bridge, and Mr. Harrison near the King's Bench, have wrought many, and know their goodness." As Yarranton's account was written and published during the lifetime of the parties, there is no reason to doubt the accuracy of his statement.

Arrangements were made to carry on the manufacture upon a large scale; but the secret having got wind, a patent was taken out, or " trumpt up " as Yarranton calls it, for the manufacture, " the patentee being countenanced by some persons of quality," and Yarranton was precluded from carrying his operations further.   It is not improbable that the patentee in question was William Chamberlaine, Dud Dudley's quondam partner in the iron manufacture.* " What with the patent being in our way," says Yarranton, " and the richest of our partners being afraid to offend great men in power, who had their eye upon us, it caused the thing to cool, and the making of the tin-plates was neither proceeded in by us, nor possibly could be by him that had the patent; because neither he that hath the patent, nor those that have countenanced him, can make one plate fit for use."   Yarranton's labours were thus lost to the English public for a time ; and we continued to import all our tin-plates from Germany until about sixty years later, when a tin-plate manufactory was established by Capel Hanbury at Pontypool in Monmouthshire, where it has since continued to be successfully carried on.

We can only briefly refer to the subsequent history of Andrew Yarranton.   Shortly after his journey into Saxony, he proceeded to Holland to examine the inland navigations of the Dutch, to inspect their linen and other manufactures, and to inquire into the causes of the then extraordinary prosperity of that country compared with England.   Industry was in a very languishing state at home. " People confess they are sick," said Yarranton, " that trade is in a consumption, and the whole nation languishes." He therefore determined to ascertain whether something useful might not be learnt from the example of Holland. The Dutch were then the hardest working and the most thriving people in Europe.   They were manufacturers and carriers for the world.   Their fleets floated on every known sea ; and their herring-busses swarmed along our coasts as far north as the Hebrides.   The Dutch supplied our markets with fish caught within sight of our own shores,

---

* Chamberlaine and Dudley's first licence was granted in 1661 for plating steel and tinning the said plates ; and Chamberlaine's sole patent for " plating and tinning iron, copper, &c.," was granted in 1673, probably the patent in question.

while our coasting population stood idly looking on. Yarranton regarded this state of things as most discreditable, and he urged the establishment of various branches of home industry as the best way of out-doing the Dutch without fighting them.

Wherever he travelled abroad, in Germany or in Holland, he saw industry attended by wealth and comfort, and idleness by poverty and misery. The same pursuits, he held, would prove as beneficial to England as they were abundantly proved to have been to Holland. The healthy life of work was good for all—for individuals as for the whole nation ; and if we would out-do the Dutch, he held that we must out-do them in industry. But all must be done honestly and by fair means. " Common Honesty," said Yarranton, " is as necessary and needful in kingdoms and commonwealths that depend upon Trade, as discipline is in an army ; and where there is want of common Honesty in a kingdom or commonwealth, from thence Trade shall depart. For as the Honesty of all governments is, so shall be their Riches; and as their Honour, Honesty, and Riches are, so will be their Strength; and as their Honour, Honesty, Riches, and Strength are, so will be their Trade. These are five sisters that go hand in hand, and must not be parted." Admirable sentiments, which are as true now as they were two hundred years ago, when Yarranton urged them upon the attention of the English public.

On his return from Holland, he accordingly set on foot various schemes of public utility. He stirred up a movement for the encouragement of the British fisheries. He made several journeys into Ireland for the purpose of planting new manufactures there. He surveyed the River Slade with the object of rendering it navigable, and proposed a plan for improving the harbour of Dublin. He also surveyed the Dee in England with a view to its being connected with the Severn. Chambers says that on the decline of his popularity in 1677, he was taken by Lord

Clarendon to Salisbury to survey the River Avon, and find out how that river might be made navigable, and also whether a safe harbour for ships could be made at Christchurch; and that having found where he thought safe anchorage might be obtained, his Lordship proceeded to act upon Yarranton's recommendations.*

Another of his grand schemes was the establishment of the linen manufacture in the central counties of England, which, he showed, were well adapted for the growth of flax; and he calculated that if success attended his efforts, at least two millions of money then sent out of the country for the purchase of foreign linen would be retained at home, besides increasing the value of the land on which the flax was grown, and giving remunerative employment to our own people, then emigrating for want of work. "Nothing but Sloth or Envy," he said, "can possibly hinder my labours from being crowned with the wished-for success; our habitual fondness for the one hath already brought us to the brink of ruin, and our proneness to the other hath almost discouraged all pious endeavours to promote our future happiness."

In 1677 he published the first part of his *England's Improvement by Sea and Land*—a very remarkable book, full of sagacious insight as respected the future commercial and manufacturing greatness of England. Mr. Dove says of this book that Yarranton "chalks out in it the future course of Britain with as free a hand as if second-sight had revealed to him those expansions of her industrial career which never fail to surprise us, even when we behold them realized." Besides his extensive plans for making harbours and improving internal navigation with the object of creating new channels for domestic industry, his schemes for extending the iron and the woollen trades, establishing the linen manufacture, and cultivating the home fisheries, we find him throwing out various valuable suggestions with reference to the means of facilitating commercial

---

* JOHN CHAMBERS, *Biographical Illustrations of Worcestershire*. London, 1820.

transactions, some of which have only been carried out in our own day. One of his grandest ideas was the establishment of a public bank, the credit of which, based upon the security of freehold land,* should enable its paper " to go in trade equal with ready money." A bank of this sort formed one of the principal means by which the Dutch had been enabled to extend their commercial transactions, and Yarranton accordingly urged its introduction into England. Part of his scheme consisted of a voluntary register of real property, for the purpose of effecting simplicity of title, and obtaining relief from the excessive charges for law,† as well as enabling money to be readily raised for commercial purposes on security of the land registered.

He pointed out very graphically the straits to which a man is put who is possessed of real property enough, but in a time of pressure is unable to turn himself round for want of ready cash. " Then," says he, " all his creditors crowd to him as pigs do through a hole to a bean and pease rick." " Is it not a sad thing," he asks, " that a goldsmith's boy in Lombard Street, who gives notes for the monies handed him by the merchants, should take up more monies upon his notes in one day than two lords, four knights, and eight esquires in twelve months upon all their personal securities? We are, as it were, cutting off our legs and arms to see who will feed the trunk. But we cannot expect this from any of our neighbours abroad, whose interest depends upon our loss."

He therefore proposed his registry of property as a ready means of raising a credit for purposes of trade. Thus, he says, " I can both in England and Wales register my wedding, my burial, and my christening, and a poor parish-clerk is entrusted with the keeping of the book ; and that

---

* Yarranton's Land Bank was actually projected in 1695, and received the sanction of Parliament ; though the Bank of England (founded in the preceding year) petitioned against it, and the scheme was dropped.

† It is interesting to note in passing, that part of Yarranton's scheme has recently been carried into effect by the Act (25 and 26 Vict. c. 53) passed in 1862 for the Registration of Real Estate.

which is registered there is held good by our law.   But I cannot register my lands, to be honest, to pay every man his own, to prevent those sad things that attend families for want thereof, and to have the great benefit and advantage that would come thereby.   A register will quicken trade, and the land registered will be equal as cash in a man's hands, and the credit thereof will go and do in trade what ready money now doth."   His idea was to raise money, when necessary, on the land registered, by giving security thereon after a form which he suggested.   He would, in fact, have made land, as gold now is, the basis of an extended currency; and he rightly held that the value of land as a security must always be unexceptionable, and superior to any metallic basis that could possibly be devised.

This indefatigable man continued to urge his various designs upon the attention of the public until he was far advanced in years.   He professed that he was moved to do so (and we believe him) solely by an ardent love for his country, "whose future flourishing," said he, "is the only reward I ever hope to see of all my labours."   Yarranton, however, received but little thanks for his persistency, while he encountered many rebuffs.   The public for the most part turned a deaf ear to his entreaties; and his writings proved of comparatively small avail, at least during his own lifetime.   He experienced the lot of many patriots, even the purest—the suspicion and detraction of his contemporaries.   His old political enemies do not seem to have forgotten him, of which we have the evidence in certain rare "broadsides" still extant, twitting him with the failure of his schemes, and even trumping up false charges of disloyalty against him.*

---

* One of these is entitled 'A Coffee-house Dialogue, or a Discourse between Captain Y—— and a Young Barrister of the Middle Temple; with some Reflections upon the Bill against the D. of Y.'   In this broadside, of 3½ pages folio, published about 1679, Yarranton is made to favour the Duke of York's exclusion from the throne, not only because he was a papist, but for graver reasons than he dare express.   Another scurrilous pamphlet, entitled 'A Word Without Doors,' was also aimed at him.   Yarranton,

In 1681 he published the second part of 'England's Improvement,'* in which he gave a summary account of its then limited growths and manufactures, pointing out that England and Ireland were the only northern kingdoms remaining unimproved; he re-urged the benefits and necessity of a voluntary register of real property; pointed out a method of improving the Royal Navy, lessening the growing power of France, and establishing home fisheries; proposed the securing and fortifying of Tangier; described a plan for preventing fires in London, and reducing the charge for maintaining the Trained Bands; urged the formation of a harbour at Newhaven in Sussex; and, finally, discoursed at considerable length upon the tin, iron, linen, and woollen trades, setting forth various methods for their improvement. In this last section, after referring to the depression in the domestic tin trade (Cornish tin selling so low as 70s. the cwt.), he suggested a way of reviving it. With the Cornish tin he would combine "the Roman cinders and iron-stone in the Forest

---

or his friends, replied to the first attack in a folio of two pages, entitled 'The Coffee-house Dialogue Examined and Refuted, by some Neighbours in the Country, well-wishers to the Kingdom's interest.' The controversy was followed up by 'A Continuation of the Coffee-house Dialogue,' in which the chief interlocutor hits Yarranton rather hard for the miscarriage of his "improvements." "I know," says he, "when and where you undertook for a small charge to make a river navigable, and it has cost the proprietors about six times as much, and is not yet effective; nor can any man rationally predict when it will be. I know since you left it your son undertook it, and this winter shamefully left his undertaking." Yarranton's friends immediately replied in a four-page folio, entitled 'England's Improvements Justified; and the Author

thereof, Captain Y., vindicated from the Scandals in a paper called a Coffee-house Dialogue; with some Animadversions upon the Popish Designs therein contained.' The writer says he writes without the privity or sanction of Yarranton, but declares the dialogue to be a forgery, and that the alleged conference never took place. "His innocence, when he heard of it, only provoked a smile, with this answer, *Spreta vilescunt*, falsehoods must perish, and are soonest destroyed by contempt; so that he needs no further vindication." The writer then proceeds at some length to vindicate the Captain's famous work and the propositions contained in it.

* This work (especially with the plates) is excessively rare. There is a copy of it in perfect condition in the Grenville Library, British Museum.

The Huntsman Process:
ming crucible steel
heffield in 1955
courtesy of the
ce Museum)

The Puddling Process:
oving the 'ball' from
furnace, Netherton
ks, Dudley, in 1959
courtesy of the
ce Museum)

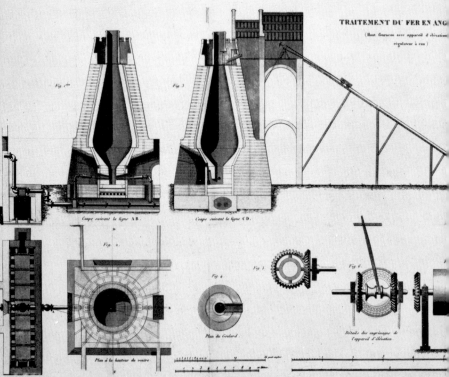

10 Lymington Ironworks on Tyneside, 1835. Engraved by J. Sands after Thomas A

11 Coke blast furnace showing hot-blast stove and charging gear. From *Voyage M urgique en Angleterre*, 1837 (*by courtesy of the Science Museum*)

of Dean, which makes the best iron for most uses in the world, and works up to the best advantage, with delight and pleasure to the workmen." He then described the history of his own efforts to import the manufacture of tin-plates into England some sixteen years before, in which he had been thwarted by Chamberlaine's patent, as above described,—and offered sundry queries as to the utility of patents generally, which, says he, "have the tendency to drive trade out of the kingdom." Appended to the chapter on Tin is an exceedingly amusing dialogue between a tin-miner of Cornwall, an iron-miner of Dean Forest, and a traveller (himself). From this we gather that Yarranton's business continued to be that of an iron-manufacturer at his works at Ashley near Bewdley. Thus the iron-miner says, "About 28 years since Mr. Yarranton found out a vast quantity of Roman cinders, near the walls of the city of Worcester, from whence he and others carried away many thousand tons or loads up the river Severn, unto their iron-furnaces, to be melted down into iron, with a mixture of the Forest of Dean iron-stone; and within 100 yards of the walls of the city of Worcester there was dug up one of the hearths of the Roman foot-blasts, it being then firm and in order, and was 7 foot deep in the earth; and by the side of the work there was found a pot of Roman coin to the quantity of a peck, some of which was presented to Sir [Wm.] Dugdale, and part thereof is now in the King's Closet." *

In the same year (1681) in which the second part of 'England's Improvement' appeared, Yarranton proceeded to Dunkirk for the purpose of making a personal survey of that port, then belonging to England; and on his return he published a map of the town, harbour, and castle on the sea, with accompanying letterpress, in which he recom-

---

* Dr. Nash, in his *History of Worcestershire*, has thrown some doubts upon this story; but Mr. Green, in his *Historical Antiquities* of the city, has made a most able defence of Yarranton's statement (vol. i. 9, in foot-note).

mended, for the safety of British trade, the demolition of
the fortifications of Dunkirk before they were completed,
which he held would only be for the purpose of their being
garrisoned by the French king. His 'Full Discovery
of the First Presbyterian Sham Plot' was published in the
same year; and from that time nothing further is known
of Andrew Yarranton. His name and his writings have
been alike nearly forgotten; and, though Bishop Watson
declared of him that he deserved to have a statue erected
to his memory as a great public benefactor, we do not
know that he was so much as honoured with a tombstone;
for we have been unable, after careful inquiry, to discover
when and where he died.

Yarranton was a man whose views were far in advance
of his age. The generation for whom he laboured and
wrote were not ripe for their reception and realization; and
his voice sounded among the people like that of one crying
in the wilderness. But though his exhortations to industry
and his large plans of national improvement failed to work
themselves into realities in his own time, he broke the
ground, he sowed the seed, and it may be that even at this
day we are in some degree reaping the results of his
labours. At all events, his books still live to show how
wise and sagacious Andrew Yarranton was beyond his contemporaries as to the true methods of establishing upon
solid foundations the industrial prosperity of England.

CHAPTER V.

Coalbrookdale Iron Works — The Darbys and Reynoldses.

———

"The triumph of the industrial arts will advance the cause of civilization more rapidly than its warmest advocates could have hoped, and contribute to the permanent prosperity and strength of the country far more than the most splendid victories of successful war."—C. BABBAGE, *The Exposition of* 1851.

———

DUD DUDLEY'S invention of smelting iron with coke made of pit-coal was, like many others, born before its time. It was neither appreciated by the iron-masters nor by the workmen. All schemes for smelting ore with any other fuel than charcoal made from wood were regarded with incredulity. As for Dudley's *Metallum Martis*, as it contained no specification, it revealed no secret; and when its author died, his secret, whatever it might be, died with him. Other improvements were doubtless necessary before the invention could be turned to useful account. Thus, until a more powerful blowing-furnace had been contrived, the production of pit-coal iron must necessarily have been limited. Dudley himself does not seem to have been able to make more on an average than five tons a-week, and seven tons at the outside. Nor was the iron so good as that made by charcoal; for it is admitted to have been especially liable to deterioration by the sulphureous fumes of the coal in the process of manufacture.

Dr. Plot, in his 'History of Staffordshire,' speaks of an experiment made by one Dr. Blewstone, a High German, as "the last effort" made in that county to smelt iron-ore with pit-coal. He is said to have "built his furnace at

Wednesbury, so ingeniously contrived (that only the flame
of the coal should come to the ore, with several other con-
veniences), that many were of opinion he would succeed
in it.   But experience, that great baffler of speculation,
showed it would not be; the sulphureous vitriolic steams
that issue from the pyrites, which frequently, if not always,
accompanies pit-coal, ascending with the flame, and poi-
soning the ore sufficiently to make it render much worse
iron than that made with charcoal, though not perhaps so
much worse as the body of the coal itself would possibly
do." *   Dr. Plot does not give the year in which this "last
effort" was made; but as we find that one Dr. Frederic de
Blewston obtained a patent from Charles II. on the 25th
October, 1677, for " a new and effectual way of melting
down, forging, extracting, and reducing of iron and all
metals and minerals with pit-coal and sea-coal, as well
and effectually as ever hath yet been done by charcoal,
and with much less charge ;" and as Dr. Plot's History, in
which he makes mention of the experiment and its failure,
was published in 1686, it is obvious that the trial must
have been made between those years.

As the demand for iron steadily increased with the
increasing population of the country, and as the supply of
timber for smelting purposes was diminishing from year
to year, England was compelled to rely more and more
upon foreign countries for its supply of manufactured iron.
The number of English forges rapidly dwindled, and the
amount of the home production became insignificant in
comparison with what was imported from abroad.   Yarranton, writing in 1676, speaks of " the many iron-works
laid down in Kent, Sussex, Surrey, and in the north of
England, because the iron of Sweadland, Flanders, and
Spain, coming in so cheap, it cannot be made to profit
here."   There were many persons, indeed, who held that
it was better we should be supplied with iron from Spain

---

* Dr. PLOT, *Natural History of Staffordshire*, 2nd ed. 1686, p. 128.

than make it at home, in consequence of the great waste
of wood involved by the manufacture; but against this
view Yarranton strongly contended, and held, what is as
true now as it was then, that the manufacture of iron was
the keystone of England's industrial prosperity. He also
apprehended great danger to the country from want of iron
in event of the contingency of a foreign war. " When the
greatest part of the iron-works are asleep," said he, " if
there should be occasion for great quantities of guns and
bullets, and other sorts of iron commodities, for a present
unexpected war, and the Sound happen to be locked up,
and so prevent iron coming to us, truly we should then be
in a fine case! "

Notwithstanding these apprehended national perils arising
from the want of iron, no steps seem to have been taken
to supply the deficiency, either by planting woods on a
large scale, as recommended by Yarranton, or by other
methods; and the produce of English iron continued steadily
to decline.   In 1720-30 there were found only ten furnaces
remaining in blast in the whole Forest of Dean, where the
iron-smelters were satisfied with working up merely the
cinders left by the Romans.   A writer of the time states
that we then bought between two and three hundred thousand pounds' worth of foreign iron yearly, and that England was the best customer in Europe for Swedish and
Russian iron.*   By the middle of the eighteenth century
the home manufacture had so much fallen off, that the total
production of Great Britain is supposed to have amounted
to not more than 18,000 tons a year; four-fifths of the iron
used in the country being imported from Sweden.†

---

* Joshua Gee, *The Trade and Navigation of Great Britain considered*, 1731.

† When a bill was introduced into Parliament in 1750 with the object of encouraging the importation of iron from our American colonies, the Sheffield tanners petitioned against it, on the ground that, if it passed, English iron would be undersold; many forges would consequently be discontinued; in which case the timber used for fuel would remain uncut, and the tanners would thereby be deprived of bark for the purposes of their trade!

The more that the remaining ironmasters became straitened for want of wood, the more they were compelled to resort to cinders and coke made from coal as a substitute. And it was found that under certain circumstances this fuel answered the purpose almost as well as charcoal of wood. The coke was made by burning the coal in heaps in the open air, and it was usually mixed with coal and peat in the process of smelting the ore. Coal by itself was used by the country smiths for forging whenever they could procure it for their smithy fires; and in the midland counties they had it brought to them, sometimes from great distances, slung in bags across horses' backs,—for the state of the roads was then so execrable as not to admit of its being led for any considerable distance in carts. At length we arrive at a period when coal seems to have come into general use, and when necessity led to its regular employment both in smelting the ore and in manufacturing the metal. And this brings us to the establishment of the Coalbrookdale works, where the smelting of iron by means of coke and coal was first adopted on a large scale as the regular method of manufacture.

Abraham Darby, the first of a succession of iron manufacturers who bore the same name, was the son of a farmer residing at Wrensnest, near Dudley. He served an apprenticeship to a maker of malt-kilns near Birmingham, after which he married and removed to Bristol in 1700, to begin business on his own account. Industry is of all politics and religions: thus Dudley was a Royalist and a Churchman, Yarranton was a Parliamentarian and a Presbyterian, and Abraham Darby was a Quaker. At Bristol he was joined by three partners of the same persuasion, who provided the necessary capital to enable him to set up works at Baptist Mills, near that city, where he carried on the business of malt-mill making, to which he afterwards added brass and iron founding.

At that period cast-iron pots were in very general use, forming the principal cooking utensils of the working class.

The art of casting had, however, made such small progress in England that the pots were for the most part imported from abroad. Darby resolved, if possible, to enter upon this lucrative branch of manufacture ; and he proceeded to make a number of experiments in pot-making. Like others who had preceded him, he made his first moulds of clay ; but they cracked and burst, and one trial failed after another. He then determined to find out the true method of manufacturing the pots, by travelling into the country from whence the best were imported, in order to master the grand secret of the trade. With this object he went over to Holland in the year 1706, and after diligent inquiry he ascertained that the only sure method of casting " Hilton ware," as such castings were then called, was in moulds of fine dry sand. This was the whole secret.

Returning to Bristol, accompanied by some skilled Dutch workmen, Darby began the new manufacture, and succeeded to his satisfaction. The work was at first carried on with great secrecy, lest other makers should copy the art; and the precaution was taken of stopping the keyhole of the workshop-door while the casting was in progress. To secure himself against piracy, he proceeded to take out a patent for the process in the year 1708, and it was granted for the term of fourteen years. The recital of the patent is curious, as showing the backward state of English iron-founding at that time. It sets forth that " whereas our trusty and well-beloved Abraham Darby, of our city of Bristol, smith, hath by his petition humbly represented to us, that by his study, industry, and expense, he hath found out and brought to perfection a new way of casting iron bellied pots and other iron bellied ware in sand only, without loam or clay, by which such iron pots and other ware may be cast fine and with more ease and expedition, and may be afforded cheaper than they can be by the way commonly used ; and in regard to their cheapness may be of great advantage to the poor of this our kingdom, who for the most part use such ware, and in all probability will prevent the merchants of England going to foreign markets for such ware, from whence great quantities are imported, and likewise may in time supply other markets with that manufacture of our dominions," &c. . . . . . grants the said Abraham Darby the full power and sole privilege to make and sell such pots and ware for and during the term of fourteen years thence ensuing."

Darby proceeded to make arrangements for carrying on the manufacture upon a large scale at the Baptist Mills; but the other partners hesitated to embark more capital in the concern, and at length refused their concurrence. Determined not to be baulked in his enterprise, Darby abandoned the Bristol firm; and in the year 1709 he removed to Coalbrookdale in Shropshire, with the intention of prosecuting the enterprise on his own account. He took the lease of a little furnace which had existed at the place for more than a century, as the records exist of a "smethe" or "smeth-house" at Coalbrookdale in the time of the Tudors. The woods of oak and hazel which at that time filled the beautiful dingles of the dale, and spread in almost a continuous forest to the base of the Wrekin, furnished abundant fuel for the smithery. As the trade of the Coalbrookdale firm extended, these woods became cleared, until the same scarcity of fuel began to be experienced that had already desolated the forests of Sussex, and brought the manufacture of iron in that quarter to a stand-still.

It appears from the ' Blast Furnace Memorandum Book' of Abraham Darby, which we have examined, that the make of iron at the Coalbrookdale foundry, in 1713, varied from five to ten tons a week. The principal articles cast were pots, kettles, and other "hollow ware," direct from the smelting-furnace; the rest of the metal was run into pigs. In course of time we find that other castings were turned out: a few grates, smoothing-irons, door-frames, weights, baking-plates, cart-bushes, iron pestles and mortars, and occasionally a tailor's goose. The trade gradually increased, until we find as many as 150 pots and kettles cast in a week.

The fuel used in the furnaces appears, from the Darby Memorandum-Book, to have been at first entirely charcoal; but the growing scarcity of wood seems to have gradually led to the use of coke, brays or small coke, and peat.   An abundance of coals existed in the neighbourhood: by rejecting those of inferior quality, and coking the others with great care, a combustible was obtained better fitted even than charcoal itself for the fusion of that particular kind of ore which is found in the coal-measures. Thus we find Darby's most favourite charge for his furnaces to have been five baskets of coke, two of brays, and one of peat; next followed the ore, and then the limestone.   The use of charcoal was gradually given up as the art of smelting with coke and brays improved, most probably aided by the increased power of the furnace-blast, until at length we find it entirely discontinued.

The castings of Coalbrookdale gradually acquired a reputation, and the trade of Abraham Darby continued to increase until the date of his death, which occurred at Madeley Court in 1717.   His sons were too young at the time to carry on the business which he had so successfully started, and several portions of the works were sold at a serious sacrifice.   But when the sons had grown up to manhood, they too entered upon the business of iron-founding; and Abraham Darby's son and grandson, both of the same name, largely extended the operations of the firm, until Coalbrookdale, or, as it was popularly called, " Bedlam," became the principal seat of one of the most important branches of the iron trade.

There seems to be some doubt as to the precise time when pit-coal was first regularly employed at Coalbrookdale in smelting the ore.   Mr. Scrivenor says, " pit-coal was first used by Mr. Abraham Darby, in his furnace at Coalbrookdale, in 1713;" * but we can find no confirmation of this statement in the records of the Company.   It is probable

---

* *History of the Iron Trade*, p. 56.

that Mr. Darby used raw coal, as was done in the Forest of Dean at the same time,* in the process of calcining the ore; but it would appear from his own Memoranda that coke only was used in the process of smelting. We infer from other circumstances that pit-coal was not employed for the latter purpose until a considerably later period. The merit of its introduction, and its successful use in iron-smelting, is due to Mr. Richard Ford, who had married a daughter of Abraham Darby, and managed the Coalbrookdale works in 1747. In a paper by the Rev. Mr. Mason, Woodwardian Professor at Cambridge, given in the 'Philosophical Transactions' for that year,† the first account of its successful employment is stated as follows :—" Several attempts have been made to run iron-ore with pit-coal : he (Mr. Mason) thinks it has not succeeded anywhere, as we have had no account of its being practised; but Mr. Ford, of Coalbrookdale in Shropshire, from iron-ore and coal, both got in the same dale, makes iron brittle or tough as he pleases, there being cannon thus cast so soft as to bear turning like wrought-iron." Most probably, however, it was not until the time of Richard Reynolds, who succeeded Abraham Darby the second in the management of the works in 1757, that pit-coal came into large and regular use in the blasting-furnaces as well as the fineries of Coalbrookdale.

Richard Reynolds was born at Bristol in 1735. His pa-

---

* See Mr. Powle's account of the Iron Works in the Forest of Dean (1677-8), in the *Philosophical Transactions*, vol. ii. p. 418, where he says, " After they have pounded their ore, their first work is to calcine it, which is done in kilns, much after the fashion of ordinary lime-kilns. These they fill up to the top with coal and ore, stratum *super* stratum, until it be full; and so setting fire to the bottom, they let it burn till the coal be wasted, and then renew the kilns with fresh ore and coal, in the same manner as before. This is done without fusion of the metal, and serves to consume the more drossy parts of the ore and to make it friable." The writer then describes the process of smelting the ore mixed with cinder in the furnaces, where, he says, the fuel is "always of charcoal." " Several attempts," he adds, " have been made to introduce the use of sea-coal in these works instead of charcoal, the former being to be had at an easier rate than the latter; but hitherto they have proved ineffectual, the workmen finding by experience that a sea-coal fire, how vehement soever, will not penetrate the most fixed parts of the ore, and so leaves much of the metal unmelted."

† *Phil. Trans.* vol. xliv. 305.

rents, like the Darbys, belonged to the Society of Friends, and he was educated in that persuasion. Being a spirited, lively youth, the " old Adam " occasionally cropped out in him; and he is even said, when a young man, to have been so much fired by the heroism of the soldier's character that he felt a strong desire to embrace a military career; but this feeling soon died out, and he dropped into the sober and steady rut of the Society. After serving an apprenticeship in his native town, he was sent to Coalbrookdale on a mission of business, where he became acquainted with the Darby family, and shortly after married Hannah, the daughter of Abraham the second. He then entered upon the conduct of the iron and coal works at Ketley and Horsehay, where he resided for six years, removing to Coalbrookdale in 1763, to take charge of the works there, on the death of his father-in-law.

By the exertions and enterprise of the Darbys, the Coalbrookdale Works had become greatly enlarged, giving remunerative employment to a large and increasing population. The firm had extended their operations far beyond the boundaries of the Dale : they had established foundries at London, Bristol, and Liverpool, and agencies at Newcastle and Truro for the disposal of steam-engines and other iron machinery used in the deep mines of those districts. Watt had not yet perfected his steam-engine; but there was a considerable demand for pumping-engines of Newcomen's construction, many of which were made at the Coalbrookdale Works. The increasing demand for iron gave an impetus to coal-mining, which in its turn stimulated inventors in their improvement of the power of the steam-engine; for the coal could not be worked quickly and advantageously unless the pits could be kept clear of water. Thus one invention stimulates another; and when the steam-engine had been perfected by Watt, and enabled powerful-blowing apparatus to be worked by its agency, we shall find that the production of iron by means of pit-coal being rendered cheap and expeditious, soon became enormously increased.

We are informed that it was while Richard Reynolds had charge of the Coalbrookdale works that a further important improvement was effected in the manufacture of iron by pit-coal. Up to this time the conversion of crude or cast iron into malleable or bar iron had been effected entirely by means of charcoal. The process was carried on in a fire called a finery, somewhat like that of a smith's forge; the iron being exposed to the blast of powerful bellows, and in constant contact with the fuel. In the first process of fusing the ironstone, coal had been used for some time with increasing success; but the question arose, whether coal might not also be used with effect in the second or refining stage. Two of the foremen, named Cranege, suggested to Mr. Reynolds that this might be performed in what is called a reverberatory furnace,[*] in which the iron should not mix with the coal, but be heated solely by the flame. Mr. Reynolds greatly doubted the feasibility of the operation, but he authorized the Craneges to make an experiment of their process, the result of which will be found described in the following extract of a letter from Mr. Reynolds to Mr. Thomas Goldney of Bristol, dated " Coalbrookdale, 25th April, 1766 ":—

---

[*] Reverberatory, so called because the flame or current of heated gases from the fuel is caused to be reverberated or reflected down upon the substance under operation before passing into the chimney. It is curious that Rovenson, in his *Treatise of Metallica* of 1613, describes a reverberatory furnace in which iron was to be smelted by pit-coal, though it does not appear that he succeeded in perfecting his invention. Dr. Percy, in his excellent work on *Metallurgy*, thus describes a reverberatory furnace:—" It consists essentially of three parts—a fireplace at one end, a stack or chimney at the other, and a bed between both on which the matter is heated. The fireplace is separated from the bed by a low partition wall called the firebridge, and both are covered by an arched roof which rises from the end wall of the fireplace and gradually dips toward the furthest end of the bed connected with the stack. On one or both sides of the bed, or at the end near the stack, may be openings through which the ore spread over the surface of the bed may be stirred about and exposed to the action of the air. The matter is heated in such a furnace by flame, and is kept from contact with the solid fuel. The flame in its course from the fireplace to the stack is reflected downwards or *reverberated* on the matter beneath, whence the name *reverberatory* furnace."

. . . . " I come now to what I think a matter of very great consequence. It is some time since Thos. Cranege, who works at Bridgenorth Forge, and his brother George, of the Dale, spoke to me about a notion they had conceived of making bar iron without wood charcoal. I told them, consistent with the notion I had adopted in common with all others I had conversed with, that I thought it impossible, because the vegetable salts in the charcoal being an alkali acted as an absorbent to the sulphur of the iron, which occasions the red-short quality of the iron, and pit coal abounding with sulphur would increase it. This specious answer, which would probably have appeared conclusive to most, and which indeed was what I really thought, was not so to them. They replied that from the observations they had made, and repeated conversations together, they were both firmly of opinion that the alteration from the quality of pig iron into that of bar iron was effected merely by heat, and if I would give them leave, they would make a trial some day. I consented, but, I confess, without any great expectation of their success; and so the matter rested some weeks, when it happening that some repairs had to be done at Bridgenorth, Thomas came up to the Dale, and, with his brother, made a trial in Thos. Tilly's air-furnace with such success as I thought would justify the erection of a small air-furnace at the Forge for the more perfectly ascertaining the merit of the invention. This was accordingly done, and a trial of it has been made this week, and the success has surpassed the most sanguine expectations. The iron put into the furnace was old Bushes, which thou knowest are always made of hard iron, and the iron drawn out is the toughest I ever saw. A bar 1¼ inch square, when broke, appears to have very little cold short in it. I look upon it as one of the most important discoveries ever made, and take the liberty of recommending thee and earnestly requesting thou wouldst take out a patent for it immediately. . . . The specification of the invention will be comprised in a few words, as it will only set forth that a reverberatory furnace being built of a proper construction, the pig or cast iron is put into it, and without the addition of anything else than common raw pit coal, is converted into good malleable iron, and, being taken red-hot from the reverberatory furnace to the forge hammer, is drawn out into bars of various shapes and sizes, according to the will of the workmen."

Mr. Reynolds's advice was implicitly followed. A patent was secured in the name of the brothers Cranege, dated the 17th June, 1766; and the identical words in the above letter were adopted in the specification as descriptive of the process. By this method of puddling, as it is termed, the manufacturer was thenceforward enabled to produce iron in increased quantity at a large reduction in price; and though the invention of the Craneges was greatly improved upon by Onions, and subsequently by Cort, there can be no doubt as to the originality and the importance of their invention. Mr. Tylor states that he was informed by the son of Richard Reynolds that the wrought iron made at Coalbrookdale by the Cranege process " was very good, quite tough, and broke with a long, bright, fibrous fracture: that made by Cort afterwards was quite different."* Though Mr. Reynolds's generosity to the Craneges is apparent in the course which he adopted in securing for them a patent for the invention in their own names, it does not appear to have proved of much advantage to them; and they failed to rise above the rank which they occupied when their valuable discovery was patented. This, however, was no fault of Richard Reynolds, but was mainly attributable to the circumstance of other inventions in a great

---

* Mr. TYLOR *on Metal Work—Reports on the Paris Exhibition of* 1855. Part II. 182. We are informed by Mr. Reynolds of Coed-du, a grandson of Richard Reynolds, that " on further trials many difficulties arose. The bottoms of the furnaces were destroyed by the heat, and the quality of the iron varied. Still, by a letter dated May, 1767, it appears there had been sold of iron made in the new way to the value of 247*l.* 14*s.* 6*d.*"

measure superseding their process, and depriving them of the benefits of their ingenuity.

Among the important improvements introduced by Mr. Reynolds while managing the Coalbrookdale Works, was the adoption by him for the first time of iron instead of wooden rails in the tram-roads along which coal and iron were conveyed from one part of the works to another, as well as to the loading-places along the river Severn. He observed that the wooden rails soon became decayed, besides being liable to be broken by the heavy loads passing over them, occasioning much loss of time, interruption to business, and heavy expenses in repairs. It occurred to him that these inconveniences would be obviated by the use of rails of cast-iron; and, having tried an experiment with them, it answered so well, that in 1767 the whole of the wooden rails were taken up and replaced by rails of iron. Thus was the era of iron railroads fairly initiated at Coalbrookdale, and the example of Mr. Reynolds was shortly after followed on all the tramroads throughout the country.

It is also worthy of note that the first iron bridge ever erected was cast and made at the Coalbrookdale Works—its projection as well as its erection being mainly due to the skill and enterprise of Abraham Darby the third. When but a young man, he showed indications of that sagacity and energy in business which seemed to be hereditary in his family. One of the first things he did on arriving at man's estate was to set on foot a scheme for throwing a bridge across the Severn at Coalbrookdale, at a point where the banks were steep and slippery, to accommodate the large population which had sprung up along both banks of the river. There were now thriving iron, brick, and pottery works established in the parishes of Madeley and Broseley; and the old ferry on the Severn was found altogether inadequate for ready communication between one bank and the other. The want of a bridge had long been felt, and a plan of one had been prepared during the lifetime of Abraham Darby the second; but the project was suspended at his death. When his son came of age, he resolved to take up his father's dropped scheme, and prosecute it to completion, which he did. Young Mr. Darby became lord of the manor of Madeley in 1776, and was the owner of one-half of the ferry in right of his lordship. He was so fortunate as to find the owner of the other or Broseley half of the ferry equally anxious with himself to connect the two banks of the river by means of a bridge. The necessary powers were accordingly obtained from Parliament, and a bridge was authorized to be built "of cast-iron, stone, brick, or timber." A company was formed for the purpose of carrying out the project, and the shares were taken by the adjoining owners, Abraham Darby being the principal subscriber.[*]

The construction of a bridge of iron was an entirely new idea. An attempt had indeed been made at Lyons, in France, to construct such a bridge more than twenty years before; but it had entirely failed, and a bridge of timber was erected instead. It is not known whether the Coalbrookdale masters had heard of that attempt; but, even if they had, it could have been of no practical use to them.

---

[*] Among the other subscribers were the Rev. Mr. Harris, Mr. Jennings, and Mr. John Wilkinson, an active promoter of the scheme, who gave the company the benefit of his skill and experience when it was determined to construct the bridge of iron. For an account of John Wilkinson see *Lives of the Engineers*, vol. ii. 337, 356. In the description of the first iron bridge given in that work we have, it appears, attributed rather more credit to Mr. Wilkinson than he is entitled to. Mr. Darby was the most active promoter of the scheme, and had the principal share in the design. Wilkinson nevertheless was a man of great energy and originality. Besides being the builder of the first iron ship, he was the first to invent, for James Watt, a machine that would bore a tolerably true cylinder. He afterwards established iron works in France, and Arthur Young says, that " until that well-known English manufacturer arrived, the French knew nothing of the art of casting cannon solid and then boring them" (*Travels in France*, 4to. ed. London, 1792, p. 90). Yet England had borrowed her first cannon-maker from France in the person of Peter Baude, as described in chap. iii. Wilkinson is also said to have invented a kind of hot-blast, in respect of which various witnesses gave evidence on the trial of Neilson's patent in 1839; but the invention does not appear to have been perfected by him.

ater-powered tilt hammer still working at Sheffield in 1933 (*by courtesy of the ence Museum*)

rly iron rolling mills from Wortley Forge, Penistone, Yorkshire (*by courtesy of the ence Museum*)

15 Spring-winding machine, one of the three surviving examples

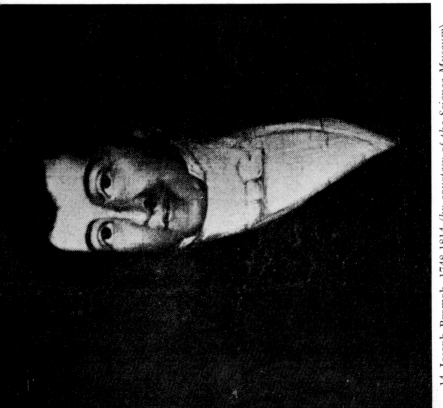

14 Joseph Bramah, 1748-1814 (*by courtesy of the Science Museum*)

Mr. Pritchard, an architect of Shrewsbury, was first employed to prepare a design of the intended structure, which is still preserved.   Although Mr. Pritchard proposed to introduce cast-iron in the arch of the bridge, which was to be of 120 feet span, it was only as a sort of key, occupying but a few feet at the crown of the arch.   This sparing use of cast iron indicates the timidity of the architect in dealing with the new material—his plan exhibiting a desire to effect a compromise between the tried and the untried in bridge-construction.   But the use of iron to so limited an extent, and in such a part of the structure, was of more than questionable utility; and if Mr. Pritchard's plan had been adopted, the problem of the iron bridge would still have remained unsolved.

The plan, however, after having been duly considered, was eventually set aside, and another, with the entire arch of cast-iron, was prepared under the superintendence of Abraham Darby, by Mr. Thomas Gregory, his foreman of pattern-makers.   This plan was adopted, and arrangements were forthwith made for carrying it into effect.   The abutments of the bridge were built in 1777-8, during which the castings were made at the foundry, and the ironwork was successfully erected in the course of three months. The bridge was opened for traffic in 1779, and proved a most serviceable structure.   In 1788 the Society of Arts recognised Mr. Darby's merit as its designer and erector by presenting him with their gold medal; and the model of the bridge is still to be seen in the collection of the Society.   Mr. Robert Stephenson has said of the structure : " If we consider that the manipulation of cast-iron was then completely in its infancy, a bridge of such dimensions was doubtless a bold as well as an original undertaking, and the efficiency of the details is worthy of the boldness of the conception." *   Mr. Stephenson adds that from a defect in the construction the abutments were thrust inwards at the

---

* *Encyclopædia Britannica*, 8th ed.   Art. " Iron Bridges."

approaches and the ribs partially fractured. We are, however, informed that this is a mistake, though it does appear that the apprehension at one time existed that such an accident might possibly occur.

To remedy the supposed defect, two small land arches were, in the year 1800, substituted for the stone approach on the Broseley side of the bridge. While the work was in progress, Mr. Telford, the well-known engineer, carefully examined the bridge, and thus spoke of its condition at the time:—"The great improvement of erecting upon a navigable river a bridge of cast-iron of one arch only was first put in practice near Coalbrookdale. The bridge was executed in 1777 by Mr. Abraham Darby, and the ironwork is now quite as perfect as when it was first put up. Drawings of this bridge have long been before the public, and have been much and justly admired."* A Coalbrookdale correspondent, writing in May, 1862, informs us that "at the present time the bridge is undergoing repair; and, special examination having been made, there is no appearance either that the abutments have moved, or that the ribs have been broken in the centre or are out of their proper right line. There has, it is true, been a strain on the land arches, and on the roadway plates, which, however, the main arch has been able effectually to resist."

The bridge has now been in profitable daily use for upwards of eighty years, and has during that time proved of the greatest convenience to the population of the district. So judicious was the selection of its site, and so great its utility, that a thriving town of the name of Ironbridge has grown up around it upon what, at the time of its erection, was a nameless part of "the waste of the manor of Madeley." And it is probable that the bridge will last for centuries to come. Thus, also, was the use of iron as an important material in bridge-building fairly initiated at Coalbrookdale by Abraham Darby, as the use

---

* PLYMLEY, *General View of the Agriculture of Shropshire.*

of iron rails was by Richard Reynolds. We need scarcely add that since the invention and extensive adoption of railway locomotion, the employment of iron in various forms in railway and bridge structures has rapidly increased, until iron has come to be regarded as the very sheet-anchor of the railway engineer.

In the mean time the works at Coalbrookdale had become largely extended. In 1784, when the government of the day proposed to levy a tax on pit-coal, Richard Reynolds strongly urged upon Mr. Pitt, then Chancellor of the Exchequer, as well as on Lord Gower, afterwards Marquis of Stafford, the impolicy of such a tax. To the latter he represented that large capitals had been invested in the iron trade, which was with difficulty carried on in the face of the competition with Swedish and Russian iron. At Coalbrookdale, sixteen " fire engines," as steam engines were first called, were then at work, eight blast-furnaces and nine forges, besides the air furnaces and mills at the foundry, which, with the levels, roads, and more than twenty miles of iron railways, gave employment to a very large number of people. " The advancement of the iron trade within these few years," said he, " has been prodigious. It was thought, and justly, that the making of pig-iron with pit coal was a great acquisition to the country by saving the wood and supplying a material to manufactures, the production of which, by the consumption of all the wood the country produced, was formerly unequal to the demand, and the nail trade, perhaps the most considerable of any one article of manufactured iron, would have been lost to this country had it not been found practicable to make nails of iron made with pit coal. We have now another process to attempt, and that is to make *bar iron* with pit coal; and it is for that purpose we have made, or rather are making, alterations at Donnington Wood, Ketley, and elsewhere, which we expect to complete in the present year, but not at a less expense than twenty thousand pounds, which will be lost to us, and gained by nobody, if this tax

is laid upon our coals." He would not, however, have it
understood that he sought for any *protection* for the home-
made iron, notwithstanding the lower prices of the foreign
article. " From its most imperfect state as pig-iron," he
observed to Lord Sheffield, " to its highest finish in the
regulating springs of a watch, we have nothing to fear if
the importation into each country should be permitted
without duty." We need scarcely add that the subsequent
history of the iron trade abundantly justified these sagacious anticipations of Richard Reynolds.

He was now far advanced in years. His business had
prospered, his means were ample, and he sought retirement. He did not desire to possess great wealth, which in
his opinion entailed such serious responsibilities upon its
possessor; and he held that the accumulation of large property was more to be deprecated than desired. He therefore determined to give up his shares in the ironworks at
Ketley to his sons William and Joseph, who continued to
carry them on. William was a man of eminent ability,
well versed in science, and an excellent mechanic. He introduced great improvements in the working of the coal
and iron mines, employing new machinery for the purpose,
and availing himself with much ingenuity of the discoveries
then being made in the science of chemistry. He was also
an inventor, having been the first to employ (in 1788)
inclined planes, consisting of parallel railways, to connect
and work canals of different levels,—an invention errone-
ously attributed to Fulton, but which the latter himself
acknowledged to belong to William Reynolds. In the first
chapter of his 'Treatise on Canal Navigation,' published
in 1796, Fulton says :—" As local prejudices opposed the
Duke of Bridgewater's canal in the first instance, prejudices
equally strong as firmly adhered to the principle on which
it was constructed; and it was thought impossible to lead
one through a country, or to work it to any advantage,
unless by locks and boats of at least twenty-five tons, till
the genius of Mr. William Reynolds, of Ketley, in Shrop-

shire, stepped from the accustomed path, constructed the
first inclined plane, and introduced boats of five tons. This,
like the Duke's canal, was deemed a visionary project, and
particularly by his Grace, who was partial to locks; yet
this is also introduced into practice, and will in many
instances supersede lock canals." Telford, the engineer,
also gracefully acknowledged the valuable assistance he
received from William Reynolds in planning the iron
aqueduct by means of which the Ellesmere Canal was
carried over the Pont Cysylltau, and in executing the necessary castings for the purpose at the Ketley foundry.

The future management of his extensive ironworks being
thus placed in able hands, Richard Reynolds finally left
Coalbrookdale in 1804, for Bristol, his native town, where
he spent the remainder of his life in works of charity and
mercy. Here we might leave the subject, but cannot
refrain from adding a few concluding words as to the moral
characteristics of this truly good man. Though habitually
religious, he was neither demure nor morose, but cheerful,
gay, and humorous. He took great interest in the pleasures of the young people about him, and exerted himself
in all ways to promote their happiness. He was fond of
books, pictures, poetry, and music, though the indulgence
of artistic tastes is not thought becoming in the Society
to which he belonged. His love for the beauties of nature
amounted almost to a passion, and when living at The
Bank, near Ketley, it was his great delight in the summer
evenings to retire with his pipe to a rural seat commanding a full view of the Wrekin, the Ercall Woods, with
Cader Idris and the Montgomeryshire hills in the distance,
and watch the sun go down in the west in his glory. Once
in every year he assembled a large party to spend a day
with him on the Wrekin, and amongst those invited were
the principal clerks in the company's employment, together
with their families. At Madeley, near Coalbrookdale, where
he bought a property, he laid out, for the express use of
the workmen, extensive walks through the woods on Lin-

coln Hill, commanding beautiful views. They were called "The Workmen's Walks," and were a source of great enjoyment to them and their families, especially on Sunday afternoons.

When Mr. Reynolds went to London on business, he was accustomed to make a round of visits, on his way home, to places remarkable for their picturesque beauty, such as Stowe, Hagley Park, and the Leasowes. After a visit to the latter place in 1767, he thus, in a letter to his friend John Maccappen, vindicated his love for the beautiful in nature :—" I think it not only lawful but expedient to cultivate a disposition to be pleased with the beauties of nature, by frequent indulgences for that purpose. The mind, by being continually applied to the consideration of ways and means to gain money, contracts an indifferency if not an insensibility to the profusion of beauties which the benevolent Creator has impressed upon every part of the material creation. A sordid love of gold, the possession of what gold can purchase, and the reputation of being rich, have so depraved the finer feelings of some men, that they pass through the most delightful grove, filled with the melody of nature, or listen to the murmurings of the brook in the valley, with as little pleasure and with no more of the vernal delight which Milton describes, than they feel in passing through some obscure alley in a town."

When in the prime of life, Mr. Reynolds was an excellent rider, performing all his journeys on horseback. He used to give a ludicrous account of a race he once ran with another youth, each having a lady seated on a pillion behind him ; Mr. Reynolds reached the goal first, but when he looked round he found that he had lost his fair companion, who had fallen off in the race ! On another occasion he had a hard run with Lord Thurlow during a visit paid by the latter to the Ketley Iron-Works. Lord Thurlow pulled up his horse first, and observed, laughing, " I think, Mr. Reynolds, this is probably the first time that ever a Lord Chancellor rode a race with a

Quaker!" But a stranger rencontre was one which befel
Mr. Reynolds on Blackheath. Though he declined Government orders for cannon, he seems to have had a secret
hankering after the "pomp and circumstance" of military
life. At all events he was present on Blackheath one day
when George III. was reviewing some troops. Mr. Reynolds's horse, an old trooper, no sooner heard the sound of
the trumpet than he started off at full speed, and made
directly for the group of officers before whom the troops
were defiling. Great was the surprise of the King when
he saw the Quaker draw up alongside of him, but still
greater, perhaps, was the confusion of the Quaker at finding
himself in such company.

During the later years of his life, while living at
Bristol, his hand was in every good work; and it was
often felt where it was not seen. For he carefully avoided
ostentation, and preferred doing his good in secret. He
strongly disapproved of making charitable bequests by
will, which he observed in many cases to have been the
foundation of enormous abuses, but held it to be the duty
of each man to do all the possible good that he could
during his lifetime. Many were the instances of his
princely, though at the time unknown, munificence. Unwilling to be recognised as the giver of large sums, he
employed agents to dispense his anonymous benefactions.
He thus sent 20,000*l.* to London to be distributed during
the distress of 1795. He had four almoners constantly
employed in Bristol, finding out cases of distress, relieving
them, and presenting their accounts to him weekly, with
details of the cases relieved. He searched the debtors'
prisons, and where, as often happened, deserving but unfortunate men were found confined for debt, he paid the
claims against them and procured their release. Such a
man could not fail to be followed with blessings and gratitude; but these he sought to direct to the Giver of all
Good. "My talent," said he to a friend, "is the meanest
of all talents—a little sordid dust; but as the man in the

parable who had but one talent was held accountable, I also am accountable for the talent that I possess, humble as it is, to the great Lord of all." On one occasion the case of a poor orphan boy was submitted to him, whose parents, both dying young, had left him destitute, on which Mr. Reynolds generously offered to place a sum in the names of trustees for his education and maintenance until he could be apprenticed to a business. The lady who represented the case was so overpowered by the munificence of the act that she burst into tears, and, struggling to express her gratitude, concluded with—" and when the dear child is old enough, I will teach him to thank his benefactor." "Thou must teach him to look higher," interrupted Reynolds: "Do we thank the clouds for rain? When the child grows up, teach him to thank Him who sendeth both the clouds and the rain." Reynolds himself deplored his infirmity of temper, which was by nature hasty; and, as his benevolence was known, and appeals were made to him at all times, seasonable and unseasonable, he sometimes met them with a sharp word, which, however, he had scarcely uttered before he repented of it; and he is known to have followed a poor woman to her home and ask forgiveness for having spoken hastily in answer to her application for help.

This " great good man " died on the 10th of September, 1816, in the 81st year of his age. At his funeral the poor of Bristol were the chief mourners. The children of the benevolent societies which he had munificently supported during his lifetime, and some of which he had founded, followed his body to the grave. The procession was joined by the clergy and ministers of all denominations, and by men of all classes and persuasions. And thus was Richard Reynolds laid to his rest, leaving behind him a name full of good odour, which will long be held in grateful remembrance by the inhabitants of Bristol.

CHAPTER VI.

INVENTION OF CAST STEEL — BENJAMIN HUNTSMAN.

" It may be averred that as certainly as the age of iron superseded that of bronze, so will the age of steel reign triumphant over iron."—HENRY BESSEMER.

" Aujourd'hui la révolution que devait amener en Grande-Bretagne la mémorable découverte de Benjamin Huntsman est tout à fait accomplie, et chaque jour les conséquences s'en feront plus vivement sentir sur le continent."—LE PLAY, *Sur la Fabrication de l'Acier en Yorkshire.*

IRON, besides being used in various forms as bar and cast iron, is also used in various forms as bar and cast steel ; and it is principally because of its many admirable qualities in these latter forms that iron maintains its supremacy over all the other metals.

The process of converting iron into steel had long been known among the Eastern nations before it was introduced into Europe. The Hindoos were especially skilled in the art of making steel, as indeed they are to this day ; and it is supposed that the tools with which the Egyptians covered their obelisks and temples of porphyry and syenite with hieroglyphics were made of Indian steel, as probably no other metal was capable of executing such work. The art seems to have been well known in Germany in the Middle Ages, and the process is on the whole very faithfully described by Agricola in his great work on Metallurgy.* England then produced very little steel, and was mainly dependent for its supply of the article upon the continental makers.

---

* AGRICOLA, *De Re Metallica.* Basle, 1621.

From an early period Sheffield became distinguished for its manufacture of iron and steel into various useful articles. We find it mentioned in the thirteenth century as a place where the best arrowheads were made,—the Earl of Richmond owing his success at the battle of Bosworth partly to their superior length, sharpness, and finish. The manufactures of the town became of a more pacific character in the following centuries, during which knives, tools, and implements of husbandry became the leading articles.

Chaucer's reference to the 'Sheffield thwytel' (or case-knife) in his Canterbury Tales, written about the end of the fourteenth century, shows that the place had then become known for its manufacture of knives. In 1575 we find the Earl of Shrewsbury presenting to his friend Lord Burleigh "a case of Hallamshire whittells, being such fruites as his pore cuntrey affordeth with fame throughout the realme." Fuller afterwards speaks of the Sheffield knives as "for common use of the country people," and he cites an instance of a knave who cozened him out of fourpence for one when it was only worth a penny.

In 1600 Sheffield became celebrated for its tobacco-boxes and Jew's-harps. The town was as yet of small size and population; for when a survey of it was made in 1615 it was found to contain not more than 2207 householders, of whom one-third, or 725, were "not able to live without the charity of their neighbours: these are all begging poor."* It must, however, have continued its manufacture of knives; for we find that the knife with which Felton stabbed the Duke of Buckingham at Portsmouth in 1628 was traced to Sheffield. The knife was left sticking in the duke's body, and when examined was found to bear the Sheffield corporation mark. It was ultimately ascertained to have been made by one Wild, a cutler, who had sold the knife for tenpence to Felton when recruiting in the town.

At a still later period, the manufacture of clasp or spring

---

* The Rev. Joseph Hunter, *History of Hallamshire.*

knives was introduced into Sheffield by Flemish workmen.
Harrison says this trade was begun in 1650. The clasp-
knife was commonly known in the North as a *jocteleg*.
Hence Burns, describing the famous article treasured by
Captain Grose the antiquarian, says that—

> " It was a faulding *jocteleg*,
>   Or lang-kail gully ;"

the word being merely a corruption of *Jacques de Liege*, a
famous foreign cutler, whose knives were as well known
throughout Europe as those of Rogers or Mappin are now.
Scythes and sickles formed other branches of manufacture
introduced by the Flemish artisans, the makers of the
former principally living in the parish of Norton, those of
the latter in Eckington.

Many improvements were introduced from time to time in
the material of which these articles were made. Instead of
importing the German steel, as it was called, the Sheffield
manufacturers began to make it themselves, principally
from Dannemora iron imported from Sweden. The first
English manufacturer of the article was one Crowley, a
Newcastle man ; and the Sheffield makers shortly followed
his example. We may here briefly state that the ordinary
method of preparing this valuable material of manufactures
is by exposing iron bars, placed in contact with roughly-
granulated charcoal, to an intense heat,—the process lasting
for about a week, more or less, according to the degree of
carbonization required. By this means, what is called
blistered steel is produced, and it furnishes the material out
of which razors, files, knives, swords, and various articles
of hardware are manufactured. A further process is the
manufacture of the metal thus treated into *shear steel*, by
exposing a fasciculus of the blistered steel rods, with sand
scattered over them for the purposes of a flux, to the heat
of a wind-furnace until the whole mass becomes of a
welding heat, when it is taken from the fire and drawn
out under a forge-hammer,—the process of welding being

repeated, after which the steel is reduced to the required sizes. The article called *faggot* steel is made after a somewhat similar process.

But the most valuable form in which steel is now used in the manufactures of Sheffield is that of cast-steel, in which iron is presented in perhaps its very highest state of perfection. Cast-steel consists of iron united to carbon in an elastic state together with a small portion of oxygen; whereas crude or pig iron consists of iron combined with carbon in a material state.* The chief merits of cast-steel consist in its possessing great cohesion and closeness of grain, with an astonishing degree of tenacity and flexibility,—qualities which render it of the highest value in all kinds of tools and instruments where durability, polish, and fineness of edge are essential requisites. It is to this material that we are mainly indebted for the exquisite cutting instrument of the surgeon, the chisel of the sculptor, he steel plate on which the engraver practises his art, the cutting tools employed in the various processes of skilled handicraft, down to the common saw or the axe used by the backwoodsman in levelling the primeval forest.

The invention of cast-steel is due to Benjamin Huntsman, of Attercliffe, near Sheffield. M. Le Play, Professor of Metallurgy in the Royal School of Mines of France, after making careful inquiry and weighing all the evidence on the subject, arrived at the conclusion that the invention fairly belongs to Huntsman. The French professor speaks of it as a "memorable discovery," made and applied with admirable perseverance; and he claims for its inventor the distinguished merit of advancing the steel manufactures of Yorkshire to the first rank, and powerfully contributing to the establishment on a firm foundation of the industrial and commercial supremacy of Great Britain. It is remarkable that a French writer should have been among the

---

* Mushet, *Papers on Iron and Steel.*

first to direct public attention to the merits of this inventor, and to have first published the few facts known as to his history in a French Government Report,—showing the neglect which men of this class have heretofore received at home, and the much greater esteem in which they are held by scientific foreigners.* Le Play, in his enthusiastic admiration of the discoverer of so potent a metal as cast-steel, paid a visit to Huntsman's grave in Attercliffe Churchyard, near Sheffield, and from the inscription on his tombstone recites the facts of his birth, his death, and his brief history. With the assistance of his descendants, we are now enabled to add the following record of the life and labours of this remarkable but almost forgotten man.

Benjamin Huntsman was born in Lincolnshire in the year 1704. His parents were of German extraction, and had settled in this country only a few years previous to his birth. The boy being of an ingenious turn, was bred to a mechanical calling; and becoming celebrated for his expertness in repairing clocks, he eventually set up in business as a clock maker and mender in the town of Doncaster. He also undertook various other kinds of metal work, such as the making and repairing of locks, smoke-jacks, roasting-jacks, and other articles requiring mechanical skill. He was remarkably shrewd, observant, thoughtful, and practical; so much so that he came to be regarded as the " wise man " of his neighbourhood, and was not only consulted as to the repairs of machinery, but also of the human frame. He practised surgery with dexterity, though after an empirical fashion, and was held in especial esteem as an oculist. His success was such that his advice was sought in many surgical diseases, and he was always ready to give it, but declined receiving any payment in return.

---

* M. Le Play's two elaborate and admirable reports on the manufacture of steel, published in the *Annales des Mines*, vols. iii. and ix., 4th series, are unique of their kind, and have as yet no counterpart in English literature. They are respectively entitled ' Mémoire sur la Fabrication de l'Acier en Yorkshire,' and ' Mémoire sur le Fabrication et le Commerce des Fers à Acier dans le Nord de l'Europe.'

In the exercise of his mechanical calling, he introduced several improved tools, but was much hindered by the inferior quality of the metal supplied to him, which was common German steel. He also experienced considerable difficulty in finding a material suitable for the springs and pendulums of his clocks. These circumstances induced him to turn his attention to the making of a better kind of steel than was then procurable, for the purposes of his trade. His first experiments were conducted at Doncaster; * but as fuel was difficult to be had at that place, he determined, for greater convenience, to remove to the neighbourhood of Sheffield, which he did in 1740. He first settled at Handsworth, a few miles to the south of that town, and there pursued his investigations in secret. Unfortunately, no records have been preserved of the methods which he adopted in overcoming the difficulties he had necessarily to encounter. That they must have been great is certain, for the process of manufacturing cast-steel of a first-rate quality even at this day is of a most elaborate and delicate character, requiring to be carefully watched in its various stages. He had not only to discover the fuel and flux suitable for his purpose, but to build such a furnace and make such a crucible as should sustain a heat more intense than any then known in metallurgy. Ingot-moulds had not yet been cast, nor were there hoops and wedges made that would hold them together, nor, in short, were any of those materials at his disposal which are now so familiar at every melting-furnace.

Huntsman's experiments extended over many years before the desired result was achieved. Long after his death, the memorials of the numerous failures through which he

* There are several clocks still in existence in the neighbourhood of Doncaster made by Benjamin Huntsman; and there is one in the possession of his grandson, with a pendulum made of cast-steel. The manufacture of a pendulum of such a material at that early date is certainly curious; its still perfect spring and elasticity showing the scrupulous care with which it had been made.

toilsomely worked his way to success, were brought to light in the shape of many hundredweights of steel, found buried in the earth in different places about his manufactory. From the number of these wrecks of early experiments, it is clear that he had worked continuously upon his grand idea of purifying the raw steel then in use, by melting it with fluxes at an intense heat in closed earthen crucibles. The buried masses were found in various stages of failure, arising from imperfect melting, breaking of crucibles, and bad fluxes; and had been hid away as so much spoiled steel of which nothing could be made.   At last his perseverance was rewarded, and his invention perfected; and though a hundred years have passed since Huntsman's discovery, the description of fuel (coke) which he first applied for the purpose of melting the steel, and the crucibles and furnaces which he used, are for the most part similar to those in use at the present day. Although the making of cast-steel is conducted with greater economy and dexterity, owing to increased experience, it is questionable whether any maker has since been able to surpass the quality of Huntsman's manufacture.

The process of making cast-steel, as invented by Benjamin Huntsman, may be thus summarily described. The melting is conducted in clay pots or crucibles manufactured for the purpose, capable of holding about 34 lbs. each. Ten or twelve of such crucibles are placed in a melting-furnace similar to that used by brass founders; and when the furnace and pots are at a white heat, to which they are raised by a coke fire, they are charged with bar steel reduced to a certain degree of hardness, and broken into pieces of about a pound each.   When the pots are all thus charged with steel, lids are placed over them, the furnace is filled with coke, and the cover put down. Under the intense heat to which the metal is exposed, it undergoes an apparent ebullition.   When the furnace requires feeding, the workmen take the opportunity of lifting the lid of each crucible and judging how far the process has advanced. After about three hours' exposure to the heat, the metal is ready for " teeming." The completion of the melting process is known by the subsidence of all ebullition, and by the clear surface of the melted metal, which is of a dazzling brilliancy like the sun when looked at with the naked eye on a clear day. The pots are then lifted out of their place, and the liquid steel is poured into ingots of the shape and size required. The pots are replaced, filled again, and the process is repeated; the red-hot pots thus serving for three successive charges, after which they are rejected as useless.

When Huntsman had perfected his invention, it would naturally occur to him that the new metal might be employed for other purposes besides clock-springs and pendulums. The business of clock-making was then of a very limited character, and it could scarcely have been worth his while to pursue so extensive and costly a series of experiments merely to supply the requirements of that trade. It is more probable that at an early stage of his investigations he shrewdly foresaw the extensive uses to which cast-steel might be applied in the manufacture of tools and cutlery of a superior kind; and we accordingly find him early endeavouring to persuade the manufacturers of Sheffield to employ it in the manufacture of knives and razors. But the cutlers obstinately refused to work a material so much harder than that which they had been accustomed to use; and for a time he gave up all hopes of creating a demand in that quarter. Foiled in his endeavours to sell his steel at home, Huntsman turned his attention to foreign markets; and he soon found he could readily sell abroad all that he could make. The merit of employing cast-steel for general purposes belongs to the French, always so quick to appreciate the advantages of any new discovery, and for a time the whole of the cast-steel that Huntsman could manufacture was exported to France.

When he had fairly established his business with that country, the Sheffield cutlers became alarmed at the reputation which cast-steel was acquiring abroad ; and when they heard of the preference displayed by English as well as French consumers for the cutlery manufactured of that metal, they readily apprehended the serious consequences that must necessarily result to their own trade if cast-steel came into general use.   They then appointed a deputation to wait upon Sir George Savile, one of the members for the county of York, and requested him to use his influence with the government to obtain an order to prohibit the exportation of cast-steel.   But on learning from the deputation that the Sheffield manufacturers themselves would not make use of the new steel, he positively declined to comply with their request.   It was indeed fortunate for the interests of the town that the object of the deputation was defeated, for at that time Mr. Huntsman had very pressing and favourable offers from some spirited manufacturers in Birmingham to remove his furnaces to that place ; and it is extremely probable that had the business of cast-steel making become established there, one of the most important and lucrative branches of its trade would have been lost to the town of Sheffield.

The Sheffield makers were therefore under the necessity of using the cast-steel, if they would retain their trade in cutlery against France ; and Huntsman's home trade rapidly increased.   And then began the efforts of the Sheffield men to wrest his secret from him.   For Huntsman had not taken out any patent for his invention, his only protection being in preserving his process as much a mystery as possible.   All the workmen employed by him were pledged to inviolable secrecy; strangers were carefully excluded from the works ; and the whole of the steel made was melted during the night.   There were many speculations abroad as to Huntsman's process.   It was generally believed that his secret consisted in the flux which he employed to make the metal melt more readily; and it leaked out amongst the workmen that he used broken bottles for the purpose.   Some of the manufacturers, who by prying and

bribing got an inkling of the process, followed Huntsman
implicitly in this respect ; and they would not allow their
own workmen to flux the pots lest they also should obtain
possession of the secret.   But it turned out eventually that
no such flux was necessary, and the practice has long since
been discontinued.   A Frenchman named Jars, frequently
quoted by Le Play in his account of the manufacture of
steel in Yorkshire,* paid a visit to Sheffield towards the
end of last century, and described the process so far as he
was permitted to examine it.   According to his statement
all kinds of fragments of broken steel were used ; but this
is corrected by Le Play, who states that only the best bar
steel manufactured of Dannemora iron was employed.
Jars adds that "the steel is put into the crucible with *a
flux*, the composition of which is kept secret;" and he
states that the time then occupied in the conversion was
five hours.

It is said that the person who first succeeded in copying
Huntsman's process was an ironfounder named Walker,
who carried on his business at Greenside near Sheffield,
and it was certainly there that the making of cast-steel
was next begun.   Walker adopted the "ruse" of disguising
himself as a tramp, and, feigning great distress and abject
poverty, he appeared shivering at the door of Huntsman's
foundry late one night when the workmen were about to
begin their labours at steel-casting, and asked for admission
to warm himself by the furnace fire.   The workmen's
hearts were moved, and they permitted him to enter.   We
have the above facts from the descendants of the Huntsman
family; but we add the traditional story preserved in the
neighbourhood, as given in a well-known book on metallurgy :—

"One cold winter's night, while the snow was falling
in heavy flakes, and the manufactory threw its red glare of
light over the neighbourhood, a person of the most abject

---

* *Annales des Mines,* vols. iii. and ix., 4th Series.

appearance presented himself at the entrance, praying for permission to share the warmth and shelter which it afforded. The humane workmen found the appeal irresistible, and the apparent beggar was permitted to take up his quarters in a warm corner of the building. A careful scrutiny would have discovered little real sleep in the drowsiness which seemed to overtake the stranger; for he eagerly watched every movement of the workmen while they went through the operations of the newly discovered process. He observed, first of all, that bars of blistered steel were broken into small pieces, two or three inches in length, and placed in crucibles of fire clay. When nearly full, a little green glass broken into small fragments was spread over the top, and the whole covered over with a closely-fitting cover. The crucibles were then placed in a furnace previously prepared for them, and after a lapse of from three to four hours, during which the crucibles were examined from time to time to see that the metal was thoroughly melted and incorporated, the workmen proceeded to lift the crucible from its place on the furnace by means of tongs, and its molten contents, blazing, sparkling, and spurting, were poured into a mould of cast-iron previously prepared: here it was suffered to cool, while the crucibles were again filled, and the process repeated. When cool, the mould was unscrewed, and a bar of cast-steel presented itself, which only required the aid of the hammerman to form a finished bar of cast-steel. How the unauthorized spectator of these operations effected his escape without detection tradition does not say; but it tells us that, before many months had passed, the Huntsman manufactory was not the only one where cast-steel was produced." [*]

However the facts may be, the discovery of the elder Huntsman proved of the greatest advantage to Sheffield;

---

[*] *The Useful Metals and their Alloys* (p. 348), an excellent little work, in which the process of cast- steel making will be found fully described.

for there is scarcely a civilized country where Sheffield steel is not largely used, either in its most highly finished forms of cutlery, or as the raw material for some home manufacture.   In the mean time the demand for Huntsman's steel steadily increased, and in 1770, for the purpose of obtaining greater scope for his operations, he removed to a large new manufactory which he erected at Attercliffe, a little to the north of Sheffield, more conveniently situated for business purposes.   There he continued to flourish for six years more, making steel and practising benevolence ; for, like the Darbys and Reynoldses of Coalbrookdale, he was a worthy and highly respected member of the Society of Friends.   He was well versed in the science of his day, and skilled in chemistry, which doubtless proved of great advantage to him in pursuing his experiments in metallurgy.*   That he was possessed of great perseverance will be obvious from the difficulties he encountered and overcame in perfecting his valuable invention.   He was, however, like many persons of strong original character, eccentric in his habits and reserved in his manner.   The Royal Society wished to enrol him as a member in acknowledgment of the high merit of his discovery of cast-steel, as well as because of his skill in practical chemistry ; but as this would have drawn him in some measure from his seclusion, and was also, as he imagined, opposed to the principles of the Society to which he belonged, he declined the honour.   Mr. Huntsman died in 1776, in his seventy-second year, and was buried in the churchyard at Attercliffe, where a gravestone with an inscription marks his resting-place.

His son continued to carry on the business, and largely extended its operations.   The Huntsman mark became known throughout the civilised world.   Le Play, the French Professor of Metallurgy, in his *Mémoire* of 1846,

---

* We are informed that a mirror is still preserved at Attercliffe, made by Huntsman in the days of his early experiments.

still speaks of the cast-steel bearing the mark of " Hunts-man and Marshall" as the best that is made, and he adds, "the buyer of this article, who pays a higher price for it than for other sorts, is not acting merely in the blind spirit of routine, but pays a logical and well-deserved homage to all the material and moral qualities of which the true Huntsman mark has been the guarantee for a cen-tury." *

Many other large firms now compete for their share of the trade; and the extent to which it has grown, the num-ber of furnaces constantly at work, and the quantity of steel cast into ingots, to be tilted or rolled for the various purposes to which it is applied, have rendered Sheffield the greatest laboratory in the world of this valuable material. Of the total quantity of cast-steel manufactured in Eng-land, not less than five-sixths are produced there; and the facilities for experiment and adaptation on the spot have enabled the Sheffield steel-makers to keep the lead in the manufacture, and surpass all others in the perfection to which they have carried this important branch of our national industry. It is indeed a remarkable fact that this very town, which was formerly indebted to Styria for the steel used in its manufactures, now exports a material of its own conversion to the Austrian forges and other places on the Continent from which it was before accustomed to draw its own supplies.

Among the improved processes invented of late years for the manufacture of steel are those of Heath, Mushet, and Bessemer. The last promises to effect before long an entire revolution in the iron and steel trade. By it the crude metal is converted by one simple process, directly as it comes from the blast-furnace. This is effected by driving through it, while still in a molten state, several streams of atmospheric air, on which the carbon of the crude iron unites with the oxygen of the atmosphere, the

---

* *Annales des Mines*, vol. ix., 4th Series, 266.

temperature is greatly raised, and a violent ebullition takes place, during which, if the process be continued, that part of the carbon which appears to be mechanically mixed and diffused through the crude iron is entirely consumed. The metal becomes thoroughly cleansed, the slag is ejected and removed, while the sulphur and other volatile matters are driven off; the result being an ingot of malleable iron of the quality of charcoal iron. An important feature in the process is, that by stopping it at a particular stage, immediately following the boil, before the whole of the carbon has been abstracted by the oxygen, the crude iron will be found to have passed into the condition of cast-steel of ordinary quality. By continuing the process, the metal losing its carbon, it passes from hard to soft steel, thence to steely iron, and last of all to very soft iron; so that by interrupting the process at any stage, or continuing it to the end, almost any quality of iron and steel may be obtained. One of the most valuable forms of the metal is described by Mr. Bessemer as "semi-steel," being in hardness about midway between ordinary cast-steel and soft malleable iron. The Bessemer processes are now in full operation in England as well as abroad, both for converting crude into malleable iron, and for producing steel; and the results are expected to prove of the greatest practical utility in all cases where iron and steel are extensively employed.

Yet, like every other invention, this of Mr. Bessemer had long been dreamt of, if not really made. We are informed in Warner's Tour through the Northern Counties of England, published at Bath in 1801, that a Mr. Reed of Whitehaven had succeeded at that early period in making steel direct from the ore; and Mr. Mushet clearly alludes to the process in his " Papers on Iron and Steel." Nevertheless, Mr. Bessemer is entitled to the merit of working out the idea, and bringing the process to perfection, by his great skill and indomitable perseverance.

In the Heath process, carburet of manganese is employed to aid the conversion of iron into steel, while it also confers on the metal the property of welding and working more soundly under the hammer—a fact discovered by Mr. Heath while residing in India.   Mr. Mushet's process is of a similar character.   Another inventor, Major Uchatius, an Austrian engineer, granulates crude iron while in a molten state by pouring it into water, and then subjecting it to the process of conversion.   Some of the manufacturers still affect secrecy in their operations; but as one of the Sanderson firm—famous for the excellence of their steel— remarked to a visitor when showing him over their works, "the great secret is to have the courage to be honest—a spirit to purchase the best material, and the means and disposition to do justice to it in the manufacture."

It remains to be added, that much of the success of the Sheffield manufactures is attributable to the practical skill of the workmen, who have profited by the accumulated experience treasured up by their class through many generations.   The results of the innumerable experiments conducted before their eyes have issued in a most valuable though unwritten code of practice, the details of which are known only to themselves.   They are also a most laborious class; and Le Play says of them, when alluding to the fact of a single workman superintending the operations of three steel-casting furnaces—"I have found nowhere in Europe, except in England, workmen able for an entire day, without any interval of rest, to undergo such toilsome and exhausting labour as that performed by these Sheffield workmen."

CHAPTER VII.

THE INVENTIONS OF HENRY CORT.

"I have always found it in mine own experience an easier matter to devise manie and profitable inventions, than to dispose of one of them to the good of the author himself."—Sir Hugh Platt, 1589.

HENRY CORT was born in 1740 at Lancaster, where his father carried on the trade of a builder and brickmaker. Nothing is known as to Henry's early history; but he seems to have raised himself by his own efforts to a respectable position. In 1765 we find him established in Surrey Street, Strand, carrying on the business of a navy agent, in which he is said to have realized considerable profits. It was while conducting this business that he became aware of the inferiority of British iron compared with that obtained from foreign countries. The English wrought iron was considered so bad that it was prohibited from all government supplies, while the cast iron was considered of too brittle a nature to be suited for general use. * Indeed the Russian government became so persuaded that the English nation could not carry on their manufactures without Russian iron, that in 1770 they ordered the price to be raised from 70 and 80 copecs per pood to 200 and 220 copecs per pood.†

Such being the case, Cort's attention became directed to the subject in connection with the supply of iron to the Navy, and he entered on a series of experiments with the object of improving the manufacture of English iron. What the particular experiments were, and by what steps he arrived at results of so much importance to the British iron

---

* *Life of Brunel*, p. 60.   † SCRIVENOR, *History of the Iron Trade*, 169.

trade, no one can now tell. All that is known is, that about the year 1775 he relinquished his business as a navy agent, and took a lease of certain premises at Fontley, near Fareham, at the north-western corner of Portsmouth Harbour, where he erected a forge and an iron mill. He was afterwards joined in partnership by Samuel Jellicoe (son of Adam Jellicoe, then Deputy-Paymaster of Seamen's Wages), which turned out, as will shortly appear, a most unfortunate connection for Cort.

As in the case of other inventions, Cort took up the manufacture of iron at the point to which his predecessors had brought it, carrying it still further, and improving upon their processes. We may here briefly recite the steps by which the manufacture of bar-iron by means of pit-coal had up to this time been advanced. In 1747, Mr. Ford succeeded at Coalbrookdale in smelting iron ore with pit-coal, after which it was refined in the usual way by means of coke and charcoal. In 1762, Dr. Roebuck (hereafter to be referred to) took out a patent for melting the cast or pig iron in a hearth heated with pit-coal by the blast of bellows, and then working the iron until it was reduced to nature, or metallized, as it was termed ; after which it was exposed to the action of a hollow pit-coal fire urged by a blast, until it was reduced to a loop and drawn out into bar-iron under a common forge-hammer. Then the brothers Cranege, in 1766, adopted the reverberatory or air furnace, in which they placed the pig or cast iron, and without blast or the addition of anything more than common raw pit-coal, converted the same into good malleable iron, which being taken red hot from the reverberatory furnace to the forge hammer, was drawn into bars according to the will of the workman. Peter Onions of Merthyr Tydvil, in 1783, carried the manufacture a stage further, as described by him in his patent of that year. Having charged his furnace (" bound with iron work and well annealed ") with pig or fused cast iron from the smelting furnace, it was closed up and the

doors were luted with sand. The fire was urged by a
blast admitted underneath, apparently for the purpose of
keeping up the combustion of the fuel on the grate. Thus
Onions' furnace was of the nature of a puddling furnace, the
fire of which was urged by a blast. The fire was to be kept
up until the metal became less fluid, and "thickened into
a kind of froth, which the workman, by opening the door,
must turn and stir with a bar or other iron instrument,
and then close the aperture again, applying the blast and
fire until there was a ferment in the metal." The patent
further describes that "as the workman stirs the metal,"
the scoriæ will separate, "and the particles of iron will adhere, which particles the workman must collect or gather
into a mass or lump." This mass or lump was then to be
raised to a white heat, and forged into malleable iron at
the forge-hammer.

Such was the stage of advance reached in the manufacture of bar-iron, when Henry Cort published his patents
in 1783 and 1784. In dispensing with a blast, he had
been anticipated by the Craneges, and in the process of
puddling by Onions; but he introduced so many improvements of an original character, with which he combined the inventions of his predecessors, as to establish
quite a new era in the history of the iron manufacture, and,
in the course of a few years, to raise it to the highest state
of prosperity. As early as 1786, Lord Sheffield recognised
the great national importance of Cort's improvements in
the following words:—" If Mr. Cort's very ingenious and
meritorious improvements in the art of making and working iron, the steam-engine of Boulton and Watt, and Lord
Dundonald's discovery of making coke at half the present
price, should all succeed, it is not asserting too much to
say that the result will be more advantageous to Great
Britain than the possession of the thirteen colonies (of
America); for it will give the complete command of the
iron trade to this country, with its vast advantages to navigation." It is scarcely necessary here to point out how

completely the anticipations of Lord Sheffield have been fulfilled, sanguine though they might appear to be when uttered some seventy-six years ago.*

We will endeavour as briefly as possible to point out the important character of Mr. Cort's improvements, as embodied in his two patents of 1783 and 1784. In the first he states that, after "great study, labour, and expense, in trying a variety of experiments, and making many discoveries, he had invented and brought to perfection a peculiar method and process of preparing, welding, and working various sorts of iron, and of reducing the same into uses by machinery: a furnace, and other apparatus, adapted and applied to the said process." He first describes his method of making iron for "large uses," such as shanks, arms, rings, and palms of anchors, by the method of piling and faggoting, since become generally practised,— by laying bars of iron of suitable lengths, forged on purpose, and tapering so as to be thinner at one end than the other, laid over one another in the manner of bricks in buildings, so that the ends should everywhere overlay each other. The faggots so prepared, to the amount of half a ton more or less, were then to be put into a common air or balling furnace, and brought to a welding heat, which was accomplished by his method in a much shorter time than in any hollow fire; and when the heat was perfect, the faggots were then brought under a forge-hammer of great

---

* Although the iron manufacture had gradually been increasing since the middle of the century, it was as yet comparatively insignificant in amount. Thus we find, from a statement by W. Wilkinson, dated Dec. 25, 1791, contained in the memorandum-book of Wm. Reynolds of Coalbrookdale, that the produce in England and Scotland was then estimated to be—

	Coke Furnaces.			Charcoal Furnaces.	
In England	73 producing	67,548 tons	20 producing	8500 tons.	
In Scotland	12 ,,	12,480 ,,	2 ,,	1000 ,,	
	85 ,,	80,028 ,,	22 ,,	9500 ,,	

At the same time the annual import of Oregrounds iron from Sweden amounted to about 20,000 tons, and of bars and slabs from Russia about 50,000 tons, at an average cost of 35l. a ton!

size and weight, and welded into a solid mass. Mr. Cort alleges in the specification that iron for " larger uses " thus finished, is in all respects possessed of the highest degree of perfection; and that the fire in the balling furnace is better suited, from its regularity and penetrating quality, to give the iron a perfect welding heat throughout its whole mass, without fusing in any part, than any fire blown by a blast. Another process employed by Mr. Cort for the purpose of cleansing the iron and producing a metal of purer grain, was that of working the faggots by passing them through rollers. " By this simple process," said he, " all the earthy particles are pressed out and the iron becomes at once free from dross, and what is usually called cinder, and is compressed into a fibrous and tough state." The objection has indeed been taken to the process of passing the iron through rollers, that the cinder is not so effectually got rid of as by passing it under a tilt hammer, and that much of it is squeezed into the bar and remains there, interrupting its fibre and impairing its strength.

It does not appear that there was any novelty in the use of rollers by Cort; for in his first specification he speaks of them as already well known.* His great merit consisted in apprehending the value of certain processes, as tested by his own and others' experience, and combining and applying them in a more effective practical form than had ever been done before. This power of apprehending the best methods, and embodying the details in one complete whole, marks the practical, clear-sighted man, and in certain cases amounts almost to a genius. The merit of combining the

---

* " It is material to observe," says Mr. Webster, " that Cort, in this specification, speaks of the rollers, furnaces, and separate processes, as well known. There is no claim to any of them separately; the claim is to the reducing of the faggots of piled iron into bars, and the welding of such bars by rollers instead of by forge-hammers."—Memoir of Henry Cort, in *Mechanic's Magazine*, 15 July, 1859, by Thomas Webster, M.A., F.R.S.

inventions of others in such forms as that they shall work to advantage, is as great in its way as that of the man who strikes out the inventions themselves, but who, for want of tact and experience, cannot carry them into practical effect.

It was the same with Cort's second patent, in which he described his method of manufacturing bar-iron from the ore or from cast-iron. All the several processes therein described had been practised before his time; his merit chiefly consisting in the skilful manner in which he combined and applied them. Thus, like the Craneges, he employed the reverberatory or air furnace, without blast, and, like Onions, he worked the fused metal with iron bars until it was brought into lumps, when it was removed and forged into malleable iron. Cort, however, carried the process further, and made it more effectual in all respects. His method may be thus briefly described: the bottom of the reverberatory furnace was hollow, so as to contain the fluid metal, introduced into it by ladles; the heat being kept up by pit-coal or other fuel. When the furnace was charged, the doors were closed until the metal was sufficiently fused, when the workman opened an aperture and worked or stirred about the metal with iron bars, when an ebullition took place, during the continuance of which a bluish flame was emitted, the carbon of the cast-iron was burned off, the metal separated from the slag, and the iron, becoming reduced to nature, was then collected into lumps or loops of sizes suited to their intended uses, when they were drawn out of the doors of the furnace. They were then stamped into plates, and piled or worked in an air furnace, heated to a white or welding heat, shingled under a forge hammer, and passed through the grooved rollers after the method described in the first patent.

The processes described by Cort in his two patents have been followed by iron manufacturers, with various modifications, the results of enlarged experience, down to the present time. After the lapse of seventy-eight years, the language employed by Cort continues on the whole a faithful description of the processes still practised: the same methods of manufacturing bar from cast-iron, and of puddling, piling, welding, and working the bar-iron through grooved rollers—all are nearly identical with the methods of manufacture perfected by Henry Cort in 1784. It may be mentioned that the development of the powers of the steam-engine by Watt had an extraordinary effect upon the production of iron. It created a largely increased demand for the article for the purposes of the shafting and machinery which it was employed to drive; while at the same time it cleared pits of water which before were unworkable, and by being extensively applied to the blowing of iron-furnaces and the working of the rolling-mills, it thus gave a still further impetus to the manufacture of the metal. It would be beside our purpose to enter into any statistical detail on the subject; but it will be sufficient to state that the production of iron, which in the early part of last century amounted to little more than 12,000 tons, about the middle of the century to about 18,000 tons, and at the time of Cort's inventions to about 90,000 tons, was found, in 1820, to have increased to 400,000 tons; and now the total quantity produced is upwards of four millions of tons of pig-iron every year, or more than the entire production of all other European countries. There is little reason to doubt that this extraordinary development of the iron manufacture has been in a great measure due to the inventions of Henry Cort. It is said that at the present time there are not fewer than 8200 of Cort's furnaces in operation in Great Britain alone.*

Practical men have regarded Cort's improvement of the process of rolling the iron as the most valuable of his inventions. A competent authority has spoken of Cort's grooved rollers as of "high philosophical interest, being scarcely less than the discovery of a new mechanical

---

* Letter by Mr. Truran in *Mechanic's Magazine*.

power, in reversing the action of the wedge, by the application of force to four surfaces, so as to elongate a mass,
instead of applying force to a mass to divide the four surfaces."   One of the best authorities in the iron trade of
last century, Mr. Alexander Raby of Llanelly, like many
others, was at first entirely sceptical as to the value of
Cort's invention; but he had no sooner witnessed the process than with manly candour he avowed his entire conversion to his views.

We now return to the history of the chief author of this
great branch of national industry. As might naturally be
expected, the principal ironmasters, when they heard of
Cort's success, and the rapidity and economy with which
he manufactured and forged bar-iron, visited his foundry
for the purpose of examining his process, and, if found expedient, of employing it at their own works.   Among the
first to try it were Richard Crawshay of Cyfartha, Samuel
Homfray of Penydarran (both in South Wales), and William
Reynolds of Coalbrookdale.   Richard Crawshay was then
(in 1787) forging only ten tons of bar-iron weekly under
the hammer; and when he saw the superior processes invented by Cort he readily entered into a contract with him
to work under his patents at ten shillings a ton royalty.
In 1812 a letter from Mr. Crawshay to the Secretary of
Lord Sheffield was read to the House of Commons, descriptive of his method of working iron, in which he said, " I
took it from a Mr. Cort, who had a little mill at Fontley in
Hampshire: I have thus acquainted you with my method,
by which I am now making more than ten thousand tons of
bar-iron per annum."   Samuel Homfray was equally prompt
in adopting the new process.   He not only obtained from
Cort plans of the puddling-furnaces and patterns of the
rolls, but borrowed Cort's workmen to instruct his own in
the necessary operations; and he soon found the method so
superior to that invented by Onions that he entirely confined himself to manufacturing after Cort's patent.   We
also find Mr. Reynolds inviting Cort to conduct a trial of

his process at Ketley, though it does not appear that it was adopted by the firm at that time.*

The quality of the iron manufactured by the new process was found satisfactory; and the Admiralty having, by the persons appointed by them to test it in 1787, pronounced it to be superior to the best Oregrounds iron, the use of the latter was thenceforward discontinued, and Cort's iron only was directed to be used for the anchors and other ironwork in the ships of the Royal Navy. The merits of the invention seem to have been generally conceded, and numerous contracts for licences were entered into with Cort and his partner by the manufacturers of bar-iron throughout the country.† Cort himself made arrangements for carrying on the manufacture on a large scale, and with that object entered upon the possession of a wharf at Gosport, belonging to Adam Jellicoe, his partner's father, where he succeeded in obtaining considerable Government orders for iron made after his patents. To all ordinary eyes the inventor now appeared to be on the high road to fortune; but there was a fatal canker at the root of this seeming prosperity, and in a few years the fabric which he had so laboriously raised crumbled into ruins.

On the death of Adam Jellicoe, the father of Cort's part-

---

* In the memorandum-book of Wm. Reynolds appears the following entry on the subject :—

" *Copy of a paper given to H. Cort,
Esq.*

" W. Reynolds saw H. C. in a trial which he made at Ketley, Dec. 17, 1784, produce from the same pig both cold short and tough iron by a variation of the process used in reducing them from the state of cast-iron to that of malleable or bar-iron; and in point of yield his processes were quite equal to those at Pitchford, which did not exceed the proportion of 31 cwt. to the ton of bars. The experiment was made by stamping and potting the blooms or loops made in his furnace, which then produced a cold short iron; but when they were immediately shingled and drawn, the iron was of a black tough."

The Coalbrookdale ironmasters are said to have been deterred from adopting the process because of what was considered an excessive waste of the metal —about 25 per cent.—though, with greater experience, this waste was very much diminished.

† Mr. Webster, in the ' Case of Henry Cort,' published in the *Mechanic's Magazine* (2 Dec. 1859), states that " licences were taken at royalties estimated to yield 27,500*l.* to the owners of the patents."

16 Henry Maudslay, 1781-1831 (by courtesy of the Science Museum)

17 Marc Isambard Brunel. 1769-1849 (by courtesy of the Science Museum)

ner, in August, 1789,* defalcations were discovered in his
public accounts to the extent of 39,676*l.*, and his books and
papers were immediately taken possession of by the Government.   On examination it was found that the debts due to
Jellicoe amounted to 89,657*l.*, included in which was a
sum of not less than 54,853*l.* owing to him by the Cort partnership.   In the public investigation which afterwards took
place, it appeared that the capital possessed by Cort being
insufficient to enable him to pursue his experiments,
which were of a very expensive character, Adam Jellicoe
had advanced money from time to time for the purpose,
securing himself by a deed of agreement entitling him to
one-half the stock and profits of all his contracts; and in
further consideration of the capital advanced by Jellicoe
beyond his equal share, Cort subsequently assigned to him
all his patent rights as collateral security.   As Jellicoe
had the reputation of being a rich man, Cort had not the
slightest suspicion of the source from which he obtained
the advances made by him to the firm, nor has any con-
nivance whatever on the part of Cort been suggested.   At
the same time it must be admitted that the connexion was not
free from suspicion, and, to say the least, it was a singularly
unfortunate one.   It was found that among the moneys
advanced by Jellicoe to Cort there was a sum of 27,500*l.*
entrusted to him for the payment of seamen's and officers'
wages.   How his embarrassments had tempted him to make
use of the public funds for the purpose of carrying on his
speculations, appears from his own admissions.   In a memorandum dated the 11th November, 1782, found in his strong
box after his death, he set forth that he had always had
much more than his proper balance in hand, until his en-

---

* In the ' Case of Henry Cort,' by
Mr. Webster, above referred to (*Mechanic's Magazine*, 2 Dec. 1859), it is
stated that Adam Jellicoe " committed
suicide under the pressure of dread of
exposure," but this does not appear to
be confirmed by the accounts in the
newspapers of the day.   He died at his
private dwelling-house, No. 14, High-
bury Place, Islington, on the 30th
August, 1789, after a fortnight's ill-
ness.

gagement, about two years before, with Mr. Cort, "which by degrees has so reduced me, and employed so much more of my money than I expected, that I have been obliged to turn most of my Navy bills into cash, and at the same time, to my great concern, am very deficient in my balance. This gives me great uneasiness, nor shall I live or die in peace till the whole is restored." He had, however, made the first false step, after which the downhill career of dishonesty is rapid. His desperate attempts to set himself right only involved him the deeper; his conscious breach of trust caused him a degree of daily torment which he could not bear; and the discovery of his defalcations, which was made only a few days before his death, doubtless hastened his end.

The Government acted with promptitude, as they were bound to do in such a case. The body of Jellicoe was worth nothing to them, but they could secure the property in which he had fraudulently invested the public moneys intrusted to him. With this object the then Paymaster of the Navy proceeded to make an affidavit in the Exchequer that Henry Cort was indebted to His Majesty in the sum of 27,500l. and upwards, in respect of moneys belonging to the public treasury, which "Adam Jellicoe had at different times lent and advanced to the said Henry Cort, from whom the same now remains justly due and owing; and the deponent saith he verily believes that the said Henry Cort is much decayed in his credit and in very embarrassed circumstances; and therefore the deponent verily believes that the aforesaid debt so due and owing to His Majesty is in great danger of being lost if some more speedy means be not taken for the recovery than by the ordinary process of the Court." Extraordinary measures were therefore adopted. The assignments of Cort's patents, which had been made to Jellicoe in consideration of his advances, were taken possession of; but Samuel Jellicoe, the son of the defaulter, singular to say, was put in possession of the properties at Fontley and Gosport, and continued to enjoy them, to Cort's exclusion, for a period of fourteen years. It does not however appear that any patent right was ever levied by the assignees, and the result of the proceeding was that the whole benefit of Cort's inventions was thus made over to the ironmasters and to the public. Had the estate been properly handled, and the patent rights due under the contracts made by the ironmasters with Cort been duly levied, there is little reason to doubt that the whole of the debt owing to the Government would have been paid in the course of a few years. " When we consider," says Mr. Webster, " how very simple was the process of demanding of the contracting ironmasters the patent dues (which for the year 1789 amounted to 15,000*l.*, in 1790 to 15,000*l.*, and in 1791 to 25,000*l.*), and which demand might have been enforced by the same legal process used to ruin the inventor, it is not difficult to surmise the motive for abstaining." The case, however, was not so simple as Mr. Webster puts it ; for there was such a contingency as that of the ironmasters combining to dispute the patent right, and there is every reason to believe that they were prepared to adopt that course.*

---

* This is confirmed by the report of a House of Commons Committee on the subject (Mr. Davies Gilbert chairman), in which they say, " Your committee have not been able to satisfy themselves that either of the two inventions, one for subjecting cast-iron to an operation termed puddling during its conversion to malleable iron, and the other for passing it through fluted or grooved rollers, were so novel in their principle or their application as fairly to entitle the petitioners [Mr. Cort's survivors] to a parliamentary reward." It is, however, stated by Mr. Mushet that the evidence was not fairly taken by the committee—that they were overborne by the audacity of Mr. Samuel Homfray, one of the great Welsh ironmasters, whose statements were altogether at variance with known facts—and that it was under his influence that Mr. Gilbert drew up the fallacious report of the committee. The illustrious James Watt, writing to Dr. Black in 1784, as to the iron produced by Cort's process, said, " Though I cannot perfectly agree with you as to its goodness, yet there is much ingenuity in the idea of forming the bars in that manner, which is the only part of his process which has any pretensions to novelty. . . . Mr. Cort has, as you observe, been most illiberally treated by the trade : they are ignorant brutes ; but he exposed himself to it by showing them the process before it was perfect, and seeing his ignorance of the common operations of making iron, laughed at and despised him ; yet they

Although the Cort patents expired in 1796 and 1798 respectively, they continued the subject of public discussion for some time after, more particularly in connection with the defalcations of the deceased Adam Jellicoe. It does not appear that more than 2654*l.* was realised by the Government from the Cort estate towards the loss sustained by the public, as a balance of 24,846*l.* was still found standing to the debit of Jellicoe in 1800, when the deficiencies in the naval accounts became matter of public inquiry. A few years later, in 1805, the subject was again revived in a remarkable manner. In that year, the Whigs, perceiving the bodily decay of Mr. Pitt, and being too eager to wait for his removal by death, began their famous series of attacks upon his administration. Fearing to tackle the popular statesman himself, they inverted the ordinary tactics of an opposition, and fell foul of Dundas, Lord Melville, then Treasurer of the Navy, who had successfully carried the country through the great naval war with revolutionary France. They scrupled not to tax him with gross peculation, and exhibited articles of impeachment against him, which became the subject of elaborate investigation, the result of which is matter of history. In those articles, no reference whatever was made to Lord Melville's supposed complicity with Jellicoe; nor, on the trial that followed, was any reference made to the defalcations of that official. But when Mr. Whitbread, on the 8th of April, 1805, spoke to the "Resolutions" in the Commons for impeaching the Treasurer of the Navy, he thought proper to intimate that he "had a strong suspicion that Jellicoe was in the same partnership with Mark Sprott, Alexander Trotter, and Lord Melville. He had been suffered to remain a public debtor for a whole year after

---

will contrive by some dirty evasion to use his process, or such parts as they like, without acknowledging him in it. I shall be glad to be able to be of any use to him." Watt's fellow-feel-ing was naturally excited in favour of the plundered inventor, he himself having all his life been exposed to the attacks of like piratical assailants.

he was known to be in arrears upwards of 24,000*l.*   During
next year 11,000*l.* more had accrued.   It would not have
been fair to have turned too short on an old companion.
It would perhaps, too, have been dangerous, since un-
pleasant discoveries might have met the public eye.   It
looked very much as if, mutually conscious of criminality,
they had agreed to be silent, and keep their own secrets."

In making these offensive observations Whitbread was
manifestly actuated by political enmity.   They were
utterly unwarrantable.   In the first place, Melville had
been formally acquitted of Jellicoe's deficiency by a writ
of Privy Seal, dated 31st May, 1800; and secondly, the
committee appointed in that very year (1805) to reinvesti-
gate the naval accounts, had again exonerated him, but
intimated that they were of opinion there was remissness
on his part in allowing Jellicoe to remain in his office after
the discovery of his defalcations.

In the report made by the commissioners to the Houses
of Parliament in 1805,* the value of Cort's patents was
estimated at only 100*l.*   Referring to the schedule of
Jellicoe's alleged assets, they say "Many of the debts are
marked as bad; and we apprehend that the debt from Mr.
Henry Cort, not so marked, of 54,000*l.* and upwards, is of
that description."   As for poor bankrupt Henry Cort, these
discussions availed nothing.   On the death of Jellicoe, he
left his iron works, feeling himself a ruined man.   He
made many appeals to the Government of the day for restoral of his patents, and offered to find security for payment of the debt due by his firm to the Crown, but in vain.
In 1794, an appeal was made to Mr. Pitt by a number of
influential members of Parliament, on behalf of the inventor
and his destitute family of twelve children, when a pension
of 200*l.* a-year was granted him.   This Mr. Cort enjoyed
until the year 1800, when he died, broken in health and

---

* *Tenth Report of the Commis-* *Report of Select Committee on the*
sioners of Naval Inquiry.   See also *10th Naval Report.*   May, 1805.

spirit, in his sixtieth year. He was buried in Hampstead Churchyard, where a stone marking the date of his death is still to be seen. A few years since it was illegible, but it has recently been restored by his surviving son.

Though Cort thus died in comparative poverty, he laid the foundations of many gigantic fortunes. He may be said to have been in a great measure the author of our modern iron aristocracy, who still manufacture after the processes which he invented or perfected, but for which they never paid him a shilling of royalty. These men of gigantic fortunes have owed much—we might almost say everything—to the ruined projector of " the little mill at Fontley." Their wealth has enriched many families of the older aristocracy, and has been the foundation of several modern peerages. Yet Henry Cort, the rock from which they were hewn, is already all but forgotten; and his surviving children, now aged and infirm, are dependent for their support upon the slender pittance wrung by repeated entreaty and expostulation from the state.

The career of Richard Crawshay, the first of the great ironmasters who had the sense to appreciate and adopt the methods of manufacturing iron invented by Henry Cort, is a not unfitting commentary on the sad history we have thus briefly described. It shows how, as respects mere money-making, shrewdness is more potent than invention, and business faculty than manufacturing skill. Richard Crawshay was born at Normanton near Leeds, the son of a small Yorkshire farmer. When a youth, he worked on his father's farm, and looked forward to occupying the same condition in life; but a difference with his father unsettled his mind, and at the age of fifteen he determined to leave his home, and seek his fortune elsewhere. Like most unsettled and enterprising lads, he first made for London, riding to town on a pony of his own, which, with the clothes on his back, formed his entire fortune. It took him a fortnight to make the journey, in consequence of the badness of the roads. Arrived in London, he sold his pony for fifteen pounds, and the money kept him until he succeeded in finding employment. He was so fortunate as to be taken upon trial by a Mr. Bicklewith, who kept an ironmonger's shop in York Yard, Upper Thames Street; and his first duty there was to clean out the office, put the stools and desks in order for the other clerks, run errands, and act as porter when occasion required. Young Crawshay was very attentive, industrious, and shrewd; and became known in the office as " The Yorkshire Boy." Chiefly because of his " cuteness," his master appointed him to the department of selling flat irons. The London washerwomen of that day were very sharp and not very honest, and it used to be said of them that where they bought one flat iron they generally contrived to steal two. Mr. Bicklewith thought he could not do better than set the Yorkshireman to watch the washerwomen, and, by way of inducement to him to be vigilant, he gave young Crawshay an interest in that branch of the business, which was soon found to prosper under his charge. After a few more years, Mr. Bicklewith retired, and left to Crawshay the cast-iron business in York Yard. This he still further increased. There was not at that time much enterprise in the iron trade, but Crawshay endeavoured to connect himself with what there was of it. The price of iron was then very high, and the best sorts were still imported from abroad; a good deal of the foreign iron and steel being still landed at the Steelyard on the Thames, in the immediate neighbourhood of Crawshay's ironmongery store.

It seems to have occurred to some London capitalists that money was then to be made in the iron trade, and that South Wales was a good field for an experiment. The soil there was known to be full of coal and ironstone, and several small iron works had for some time been carried on, which were supposed to be doing well. Merthyr Tydvil was one of the places at which operations had been begun, but the place being situated in a hill district, of difficult access, and the manufacture being still in a very imperfect state, the progress made was for some time very slow.   Land containing coal and iron was deemed of very little value, as may be inferred from the fact that in the year 1765, Mr. Anthony Bacon, a man of much foresight, took a lease from Lord Talbot, for 99 years, of the minerals under forty square miles of country surrounding the then insignificant hamlet of Merthyr Tydvil, at the trifling rental of 200l. a-year.   There he erected iron works, and supplied the Government with considerable quantities of cannon and iron for different purposes; and having earned a competency, he retired from business in 1782, subletting his mineral tract in four divisions—the Dowlais, the Peny-darran, the Cyfartha, and the Plymouth Works, north, east, west, and south, of Merthyr Tydvil.

Mr. Richard Crawshay became the lessee of what Mr. Mushet has called " the Cyfartha flitch of the great Bacon domain."   There he proceeded to carry on the works established by Mr. Bacon with increased spirit; his son William, whom he left in charge of the ironmongery store in London, supplying him with capital to put into the iron works as fast as he could earn it by the retail trade. In 1787, we find Richard Crawshay manufacturing with difficulty ten tons of bar-iron weekly, and it was of a very inferior character,*—the means not having yet been devised at Cyfartha for malleableizing the pit-coal cast-iron with economy or good effect.   Yet Crawshay found a ready market for all the iron he could make, and he is said to have counted the gains of the forge-hammer close by his house at the rate of a penny a stroke.   In course of time he found it necessary to erect new furnaces, and, having adopted the processes invented by Henry Cort, he was

---

* Mr. Mushet says of the early manufacture of iron at Merthyr Tydvil that " A modification of the charcoal refinery, a hollow fire, was worked with coke as a substitute for charcoal, but the bar-iron hammered from the produce was very inferior."   The pit-coal cast-iron was nevertheless found of a superior quality for castings, being more fusible and more homogeneous than charcoal-iron.   Hence it was well adapted for cannon, which was for some time the principal article of manu-facture at the Welsh works.

thereby enabled greatly to increase the production of his forges, until in 1812 we find him stating to a committee of the House of Commons that he was making ten thousand tons of bar-iron yearly, or an average produce of two hundred tons a week. But this quantity, great though it was, has since been largely increased, the total produce of the Crawshay furnaces of Cyfartha, Ynysfach, and Kirwan, being upwards of 50,000 tons of bar-iron yearly.

The distance of Merthyr from Cardiff, the nearest port, being considerable, and the cost of carriage being very great by reason of the badness of the roads, Mr. Crawshay set himself to overcome this great impediment to the prosperity of the Merthyr Tydvil district; and, in conjunction with Mr. Homfray of the Penydarran Works, he planned and constructed the canal* to Cardiff, the opening of which, in 1795, gave an immense impetus to the iron trade of the neighbourhood. Numerous other extensive iron works became established there, until Merthyr Tydvil attained the reputation of being at once the richest and the dirtiest district in all Britain. Mr. Crawshay became known in the west of England as the "Iron King," and was quoted as the highest authority in all questions relating to the trade. Mr. George Crawshay, recently describing the founder of the family at a social meeting at Newcastle, said,—"In these days a name like ours is lost in the infinity of great manufacturing firms which exist throughout the land; but in those early times the man who opened out the iron district of Wales stood upon an eminence seen by all the world. It is preserved in the traditions of the family that when the 'Iron King' used to drive from home in his coach-and-four into Wales, all the country turned out to see him, and quite a commotion

---

* It may be worthy of note that the first locomotive run upon a railroad was that constructed by Trevithick for Mr. Homfray in 1803, which was employed to bring down metal from the furnaces to the Old Forge. The engine was taken off the road because the tram-plates were found too weak to bear its weight without breaking.

took place when he passed through Bristol on his way to
the works. My great grandfather was succeeded by his
son, and by his grandson; the Crawshays have followed
one another for four generations in the iron trade in Wales,
and there they still stand at the head of the trade." The occasion on which these words were uttered was at a Christmas
party, given to the men, about 1300 in number, employed
at the iron works of Messrs. Hawks, Crawshay, and Co., at
Newcastle-upon-Tyne. These works were founded in 1754
by William Hawks, a blacksmith, whose principal trade
consisted in making claw-hammers for joiners. He became
a thriving man, and eventually a large manufacturer of
bar-iron. Partners joined him, and in the course of the
changes wrought by time, one of the Crawshays, in 1842,
became a principal partner in the firm.

Illustrations of a like kind might be multiplied to any
extent, showing the growth in our own time of an iron
aristocracy of great wealth and influence, the result mainly
of the successful working of the inventions of the unfortunate and unrequited Henry Cort. He has been the
very Tubal Cain of England—one of the principal founders
of our iron age. To him we mainly owe the abundance of
wrought-iron for machinery, for steam-engines, and for
railways, at one-third the price we were before accustomed
to pay to the foreigner. We have by his inventions, not
only ceased to be dependent upon other nations for our
supply of iron for tools, implements, and arms, but we
have become the greatest exporters of iron, producing
more than all other European countries combined. In the
opinion of Mr. Fairbairn of Manchester, the inventions of
Henry Cort have already added six hundred millions
sterling to the wealth of the kingdom, while they have
given employment to some six hundred thousand working
people during three generations. And while the great
ironmasters, by freely availing themselves of his inventions,
have been adding estate to estate, the only estate secured
by Henry Cort was the little domain of six feet by two in
which he lies interred in Hampstead Churchyard.

CHAPTER VIII.

THE SCOTCH IRON MANUFACTURE — DR. ROEBUCK — DAVID MUSHET.

"Were public benefactors to be allowed to pass away, like hewers of wood and drawers of water, without commemoration, genius and enterprise would be deprived of their most coveted distinction."—*Sir Henry Englefield.*

THE account given of Dr. Roebuck in a Cyclopedia of Biography, recently published in Glasgow, runs as follows:— "Roebuck, John, a physician and experimental chemist, born at Sheffield, 1718; died, after ruining himself by his projects, 1794." Such is the short shrift which the man receives who fails. Had Dr. Roebuck wholly succeeded in his projects, he would probably have been esteemed as among the greatest of Scotland's benefactors. Yet his life was not altogether a failure, as we think will sufficiently appear from the following brief account of his labours:—

At the beginning of last century, John Roebuck's father carried on the manufacture of cutlery at Sheffield,* in the course of which he realized a competency. He intended his son to follow his own business, but the youth was irresistibly attracted to scientific pursuits, in which his father liberally encouraged him; and he was placed first under the care of Dr. Doddridge, at Northampton, and afterwards at the University of Edinburgh, where he applied himself to the study of medicine, and especially of chemistry, which was then attracting considerable attention at the principal seats

---

* Dr. Roebuck's grandson, John Arthur Roebuck, by a singular coincidence, at present represents Sheffield in the British Parliament.

of learning in Scotland.   While residing at Edinburgh
young Roebuck contracted many intimate friendships with
men who afterwards became eminent in literature, such as
Hume and Robertson the historians, and the circumstance
is supposed to have contributed not a little to his partiality
in favour of Scotland, and his afterwards selecting it as the
field for his industrial operations.

After graduating as a physician at Leyden, Roebuck returned to England, and settled at Birmingham in the year
1745 for the purpose of practising his profession.   Birmingham was then a principal seat of the metal manufacture, and its mechanics were reputed to be among the most
skilled in Britain.   Dr. Roebuck's attention was early
drawn to the scarcity and dearness of the material in which
the mechanics worked, and he sought by experiment to
devise some method of smelting iron otherwise than by
means of charcoal.   He had a laboratory fitted up in his
house for the purpose of prosecuting his inquiries, and
there he spent every minute that he could spare from his
professional labours.   It was thus that he invented the
process of smelting iron by means of pit-coal which he
afterwards embodied in the patent hereafter to be referred
to.   At the same time he invented new methods of refining
gold and silver, and of employing them in the arts, which
proved of great practical value to the Birmingham tradesmen, who made extensive use of them in their various
processes of manufacture.

Dr. Roebuck's inquiries had an almost exclusively
practical direction, and in pursuing them his main
object was to render them subservient to the improvement of the industrial arts.   Thus he sought to devise
more economical methods of producing the various che-
micals used in the Birmingham trade, such as ammonia,
sublimate, and several of the acids; and his success was
such as to induce him to erect a large laboratory for their
manufacture, which was conducted with complete success
by his friend Mr. Garbett.   Among his inventions of this

character, was the modern process of manufacturing vitriolic acid in leaden vessels in large quantities, instead of in glass vessels in small quantities as formerly practised. His success led him to consider the project of establishing a manufactory for the purpose of producing oil of vitriol on a large scale; and, having given up his practice as a physician, he resolved, with his partner Mr. Garbett, to establish the proposed works in the neighbourhood of Edinburgh. He removed to Scotland with that object, and began the manufacture of vitriol at Prestonpans in the year 1749. The enterprise proved eminently lucrative, and, encouraged by his success, Roebuck proceeded to strike out new branches of manufacture. He started a pottery for making white and brown ware, which eventually became established, and the manufacture exists in the same neighbourhood to this day.

The next enterprise in which he became engaged was one of still greater importance, though it proved eminently unfortunate in its results as concerned himself. While living at Prestonpans, he made the friendship of Mr. William Cadell, of Cockenzie, a gentleman who had for some time been earnestly intent on developing the industry of Scotland, then in a very backward condition. Mr. Cadell had tried, without success, to establish a manufactory of iron; and, though he had heretofore failed, he hoped that with the aid of Dr. Roebuck he might yet succeed. The Doctor listened to his suggestions with interest, and embraced the proposed enterprise with zeal. He immediately proceeded to organize a company, in which he was joined by a number of his friends and relatives. His next step was to select a site for the intended works, and make the necessary arrangements for beginning the manufacture of iron. After carefully examining the country on both sides of the Forth, he at length made choice of a site on the banks of the river Carron, in Stirlingshire, where there was an abundant supply of water, and an inexhaustible supply of iron, coal, and limestone in the immediate neighbourhood, and there Dr. Roebuck planted the first ironworks in Scotland.

In order to carry them on with the best chances of success, he brought a large number of skilled workmen from England, who formed a nucleus of industry at Carron, where their example and improved methods of working served to train the native labourers in their art. At a subsequent period, Mr. Cadell, of Carronpark, also brought a number of skilled English nail-makers into Scotland, and settled them in the village of Camelon, where, by teaching others, the business has become handed down to the present day.

The first furnace was blown at Carron on the first day of January, 1760; and in the course of the same year the Carron Iron Works turned out 1500 tons of iron, then the whole annual produce of Scotland. Other furnaces were shortly after erected on improved plans, and the production steadily increased. Dr. Roebuck was indefatigable in his endeavours to improve the manufacture, and he was one of the first, as we have said, to revive the use of pit-coal in refining the ore, as appears from his patent of 1762. He there describes his new process as follows:—"I melt pig or any kind of cast-iron in a hearth heated with pit-coal by the blast of bellows, and work the metal until it is reduced to nature, which I take out of the fire and separate to pieces; then I take the metal thus reduced to nature and expose it to the action of a hollow pit-coal fire, heated by the blast of bellows, until it is reduced to a loop, which I draw out under a common forge hammer into bar-iron." This method of manufacture was followed with success, though for some time, as indeed to this day, the principal production of the Carron Works was castings, for which the peculiar quality of the Scotch iron admirably adapts it. The well-known Carronades,* or "Smashers," as they were

---

* The carronade was invented by General Robert Melville [Mr. Nasmyth says it was by Miller of Dalswinton], who proposed it for discharging 68 lb. shot with low charges of powder, in order to produce the increased splinter-

named, were cast in large numbers at the Carron Works.
To increase the power of his blowing apparatus, Dr. Roebuck called to his aid the celebrated Mr. Smeaton, the
engineer, who contrived and erected for him at Carron the
most perfect apparatus of the kind then in existence. It
may also be added, that out of the Carron enterprise, in a
great measure, sprang the Forth and Clyde Canal, the first
artificial navigation in Scotland. The Carron Company,
with a view to securing an improved communication with
Glasgow, themselves surveyed a line, which was only given
up in consequence of the determined opposition of the
landowners ; but the project was again revived through
their means, and was eventually carried out after the designs of Smeaton and Brindley.

While the Carron foundry was pursuing a career of safe
prosperity, Dr. Roebuck's enterprise led him to embark in
coal-mining, with the object of securing an improved
supply of fuel for the iron works. He became the lessee of
the Duke of Hamilton's extensive coal-mines at Boroughstoness, as well as of the salt-pans which were connected with
them. The mansion of Kinneil went with the lease, and there
Dr. Roebuck and his family took up their abode. Kinneil
House was formerly a country seat of the Dukes of Hamilton,
and is to this day a stately old mansion, reminding one of a
French château. Its situation is of remarkable beauty,
its windows overlooking the broad expanse of the Firth of
Forth, and commanding an extensive view of the country
along its northern shores. The place has become in a
measure classical, Kinneil House having been inhabited,
since Dr. Roebuck's time, by Dugald Stewart, who there
wrote his Philosophical Essays.*

---

ing or *smashing* effects which were
known to result from such practice.
The first piece of the kind was cast at
the Carron Foundry, in 1779, and
General Melville's family have now in
their possession a small model of this
gun, with the inscription :—" Gift of

the Carron Company to Lieutenant-
General Melville, inventor of the
smashers and lesser carronades, for
solid, ship, shell, and carcass shot, &c.
First used against French ships in
1779."

* Wilkie the painter once paid him

When Dr. Roebuck began to sink for coal at the new mines, he found it necessary to erect pumping-machinery of the most powerful kind that could be contrived, in order to keep the mines clear of water. For this purpose the Newcomen engine, in its then state, was found insufficient; and when Dr. Roebuck's friend, Professor Black, of Edinburgh, informed him of a young man of his acquaintance, a mathematical instrument maker at Glasgow, having invented a steam-engine calculated to work with increased power, speed, and economy, compared with Newcomen's, Dr. Roebuck was much interested, and shortly after entered into a correspondence with James Watt, the mathematical instrument maker aforesaid, on the subject. The Doctor urged that Watt, who, up to that time, had confined himself to models, should come over to Kinneil House, and proceed to erect a working engine in one of the outbuildings. The English workmen whom he had brought to the Carron works would, he justly thought, give Watt a better chance of success with his engine than if made by the clumsy whitesmiths and blacksmiths of Glasgow, quite unaccustomed as they were to first-class work; and he proposed himself to cast the cylinders at Carron previous to Watt's intended visit to him at Kinneil.

Watt paid his promised visit in May, 1768, and Roebuck was by this time so much interested in the invention, that the subject of his becoming a partner with Watt, with the

---

a visit there while in Scotland studying the subject of his " Penny Wedding;" and Dugald Stewart found for him the old farm-house with the cradle-chimney, which he introduced in that picture. But Kinneil House has had its imaginary inhabitants as well as its real ones, the ghost of a Lady Lilburn, once an occupant of the place, still "haunting" some of the unoccupied chambers. Dugald Stewart told Wilkie one night, as he was going to bed, of the unearthly wailings which he himself had heard proceeding from the ancient apartments; but to him at least they had been explained by the door opening out upon the roof being blown in on gusty nights, when a jarring and creaking noise was heard all over the house. One advantage derived from the house being "haunted" was, that the garden was never broken into, and the winter apples and stores were at all times kept safe from depredation in the apartments of the Lady Lilburn.

20 Richard Roberts, 1789-1864 (by courtesy of the Science Museum)

21 Joseph Whitworth, 1803-1887 (by courtesy of the Science Museum)

22 Back-geared lathe by Richard Roberts, 1817 (*by courtesy of the Science Mus*

23 Screw-cutting lathe by Joseph Clement, c 1820 (*by courtesy of the Science Mus*

24 Lathe with automatic cross-feed by Joseph Whitworth, 1843 (*by courtesy of Science Museum*)

object of introducing the engine into general use, was seriously discussed. Watt had been labouring at his invention for several years, contending with many difficulties, but especially with the main difficulty of limited means. He had borrowed considerable sums of money from Dr. Black to enable him to prosecute his experiments, and he felt the debt to hang like a millstone round his neck. Watt was a sickly, fragile man, and a constant sufferer from violent headaches; besides he was by nature timid, desponding, painfully anxious, and easily cast down by failure. Indeed, he was more than once on the point of abandoning his invention in despair. On the other hand, Dr. Roebuck was accustomed to great enterprises, a bold and undaunted man, and disregardful of expense where he saw before him a reasonable prospect of success. His reputation as a practical chemist and philosopher, and his success as the founder of the Prestonpans Chemical Works and of the Carron Iron Works, justified the friends of Watt in thinking that he was of all men the best calculated to help him at this juncture, and hence they sought to bring about a more intimate connection between the two. The result was that Dr. Roebuck eventually became a partner to the extent of two-thirds of the invention, took upon him the debt owing by Watt to Dr. Black amounting to about 1200*l.*, and undertook to find the requisite money to protect the invention by means of a patent. The necessary steps were taken accordingly, and the patent right was secured by the beginning of 1769, though the perfecting of his model cost Watt much further anxiety and study.

It was necessary for Watt occasionally to reside with Dr. Roebuck at Kinneil House while erecting his first engine there. It had been originally intended to erect it in the neighbouring town of Boroughstoness, but as there might be prying eyes there, and Watt wished to do his work in privacy, determined " not to puff," he at length fixed upon an outhouse still standing, close behind the mansion, by the burnside in the glen, where there was abundance of water and secure privacy. Watt's extreme diffidence was often the subject of remark at Dr. Roebuck's fireside. To the Doctor his anxiety seemed quite painful, and he was very much disposed to despond under apparently trivial difficulties. Roebuck's hopeful nature was his mainstay throughout. Watt himself was ready enough to admit this; for, writing to his friend Dr. Small, he once said, " I have met with many disappointments; and I must have sunk under the burthen of them if I had not been supported by the friendship of Dr. Roebuck."

But more serious troubles were rapidly accumulating upon Dr. Roebuck himself; and it was he, and not Watt, that sank under the burthen. The progress of Watt's engine was but slow, and long before it could be applied to the pumping of Roebuck's mines, the difficulties of the undertaking on which he had entered overwhelmed him. The opening out of the principal coal involved a very heavy outlay, extending over many years, during which he sank not only his own but his wife's fortune, and— what distressed him most of all—large sums borrowed from his relatives and friends, which he was unable to repay. The consequence was, that he was eventually under the necessity of withdrawing his capital from the refining works at Birmingham, and the vitriol works at Prestonpans. At the same time, he transferred to Mr. Boulton of Soho his entire interest in Watt's steam-engine, the value of which, by the way, was thought so small that it was not even included among the assets ; Roebuck's creditors not estimating it as worth one farthing. Watt sincerely deplored his partner's misfortunes, but could not help him. " He has been a most sincére and generous friend," said Watt, " and is a truly worthy man." And again, " My heart bleeds for him, but I can do nothing to help him : I have stuck by him till I have much hurt myself; I can do so no longer; my family calls for my care to provide for them." The later years of Dr.

Roebuck's life were spent in comparative obscurity; and he died in 1794, in his 76th year.

He lived to witness the success of the steam-engine, the opening up of the Boroughstoness coal,* and the rapid extension of the Scotch iron trade, though he shared in the prosperity of neither of those branches of industry. He had been working ahead of his age, and he suffered for it. He fell in the breach at the critical moment, and more fortunate men marched over his body into the fortress which his enterprise and valour had mainly contributed to win. Before his great undertaking of the Carron Works, Scotland was entirely dependent upon other countries for its supply of iron. In 1760, the first year of its operations, the whole produce was 1500 tons. In course of time other iron works were erected, at Clyde Cleugh, Muirkirk, and Devon—the managers and overseers of which, as well as the workmen, had mostly received their training and experience at Carron—until at length the iron trade of Scotland has assumed such a magnitude that its manufacturers are enabled to export to England and other countries upwards of 500,000 tons a-year. How different this state of things from the time when raids were made across the Border for the purpose of obtaining a store of iron plunder to be carried back into Scotland!

The extraordinary expansion of the Scotch iron trade of late years has been mainly due to the discovery by David Mushet of the Black Band ironstone in 1801, and the invention of the Hot Blast by James Beaumont Neilson in 1828. David Mushet was born at Dalkeith, near Edin-

---

* Dr. Roebuck had been on the brink of great good fortune, but he did not know it. Mr. Ralph Moore, in his " *Papers on the Blackband Ironstones* " (Glasgow, 1861), observes :—" Strange to say, he was leaving behind him, almost as the roof of one of the seams of coal which he worked, a valuable blackband ironstone, upon which Kinneil Iron Works are now founded. The coal-field continued to be worked until the accidental discovery of the blackband about 1845. The old coal-pits are now used for working the ironstone."

burgh, in 1772.* Like other members of his family he was brought up to metal-founding. At the age of nineteen he joined the staff of the Clyde Iron Works, near Glasgow, at a time when the Company had only two blast-furnaces at work. The office of accountant, which he held, precluded him from taking any part in the manufacturing operations of the concern. But being of a speculative and ingenious turn of mind, the remarkable conversions which iron underwent in the process of manufacture very shortly began to occupy his attention. The subject was much discussed by the young men about the works, and they frequently had occasion to refer to Fourcroy's well-known book for the purpose of determining various questions of difference which arose among them in the course of their inquiries. The book was, however, in many respects indecisive and unsatisfactory; and, in 1793, when a reduction took place in the Company's staff, and David Mushet was left nearly the sole occupant of the office, he determined to study the subject for himself experimentally, and in the first place to acquire a thorough knowledge of assaying, as the true key to the whole art of iron-making.

He first set up his crucible upon the bridge of the reverberatory furnace used for melting pig-iron, and filled it with a mixture carefully compounded according to the formula of the books; but, notwithstanding the shelter of a brick, placed before it to break the action of the flame, the crucible generally split in two, and not unfrequently melted and disappeared altogether. To obtain better results if possible, he next had recourse to the ordinary smith's fire, carrying on his experiments in the evenings after office-hours. He set his crucible upon the fire on a piece of fire-

---

* The Mushets are an old Kincardine family; but they were almost extinguished by the plague in the reign of Charles the Second. Their numbers were then reduced to two; one of whom remained at Kincardine, and the other, a clergyman, the Rev. George Mushet, accompanied Montrose as chaplain. He is buried in Kincardine churchyard.

brick, opposite the nozzle of the bellows; covering the whole with coke, and then exciting the flame by blowing. This mode of operating produced somewhat better results, but still neither the iron nor the cinder obtained resembled the pig or scoria of the blast-furnace, which it was his ambition to imitate. From the irregularity of the results, and the frequent failure of the crucibles, he came to the conclusion that either his furnace, or his mode of fluxing, was in fault, and he looked about him for a more convenient means of pursuing his experiments. A small square furnace had been erected in the works for the purpose of heating the rivets used for the repair of steam-engine boilers; the furnace had for its chimney a cast-iron pipe six or seven inches in diameter and nine feet long. After a few trials with it, he raised the heat to such an extent that the lower end of the pipe was melted off, without producing any very satisfactory results on the experimental crucible, and his operations were again brought to a standstill. A chimney of brick having been substituted for the cast-iron pipe, he was, however, enabled to proceed with his trials.

He continued to pursue his experiments in assaying for about two years, during which he had been working entirely after the methods described in books; but, feeling the results still unsatisfactory, he determined to borrow no more from the books, but to work out a system of his own, which should ensure results similar to those produced at the blast-furnace. This he eventually succeeded in effecting by numerous experiments performed in the night; as his time was fully occupied by his office-duties during the day. At length these patient experiments bore their due fruits. David Mushet became the most skilled assayer at the works; and when a difficulty occurred in smelting a quantity of new ironstone which had been contracted for, the manager himself resorted to the bookkeeper for advice and information; and the skill and experience which he had gathered during his nightly labours, enabled him readily and satisfactorily to solve the difficulty and suggest a suitable remedy. His reward for this achievement was the permission, which was immediately granted him by the manager, to make use of his own assay-furnace, in which he thenceforward continued his investigations, at the same time that he instructed the manager's son in the art of assaying. This additional experience proved of great benefit to him ; and he continued to prosecute his inquiries with much zeal, sometimes devoting entire nights to experiments in assaying, roasting and cementing iron-ores and ironstone, decarbonating cast-iron for steel and bar-iron, and various like operations. His general practice, however, at that time was, to retire between two and three o'clock in the morning, leaving directions with the engine-man to call him at half-past five, so as to be present in the office at six. But these praiseworthy experiments were brought to a sudden end, as thus described by himself :—

"In the midst of my career of investigation," says he,* "and without a cause being assigned, I was stopped short. My furnaces, at the order of the manager, were pulled in pieces, and an edict was passed that they should never be erected again. Thus terminated my researches at the Clyde Iron Works. It happened at a time when I was interested—and I had been two years previously occupied —in an attempt to convert cast-iron into steel, without fusion, by a process of cementation, which had for its object the dispersion or absorption of the superfluous carbon contained in the cast-iron,—an object which at that time appeared to me of so great importance, that, with the consent of a friend, I erected an assay and cementing furnace at the distance of about two miles from the Clyde Works. Thither I repaired at night, and sometimes at the breakfast and dinner hours during the day. This plan of operation was persevered in for the whole of one

---

* *Papers on Iron and Steel.* By David Mushet. London, 1840.

summer, but was found too uncertain and laborious to be continued. At the latter end of the year 1798 I left my chambers, and removed from the Clyde Works to the distance of about a mile, where I constructed several furnaces for assaying and cementing, capable of exciting a greater temperature than any to which I before had access ; and thus for nearly two years I continued to carry on my investigations connected with iron and the alloys of the metals.

"Though operating in a retired manner, and holding little communication with others, my views and opinions upon the *rationale* of iron-making spread over the establishment. I was considered forward in affecting to see and explain matters in a different way from others who were much my seniors, and who were content to be satisfied with old methods of explanation, or with no explanation at all. . . . . Notwithstanding these early reproaches, I have lived to see the nomenclature of my youth furnish a vocabulary of terms in the art of iron-making, which is used by many of the ironmasters of the present day with freedom and effect, in communicating with each other on the subject of their respective manufactures. Prejudices seldom outlive the generation to which they belong, when opposed by a more rational system of explanation. In this respect, Time (as my Lord Bacon says) is the greatest of all innovators.

"In a similar manner, Time operated in my favour in respect to the Black Band Ironstone.* The discovery of

---

* This valuable description of iron ore was discovered by Mr. Mushet, as he afterwards informs us (*Papers on Iron and Steel,* 121), in the year 1801, when crossing the river Calder, in the parish of Old Monkland. Having subjected a specimen which he found in the river-bed to the test of his crucible, he satisfied himself as to its properties, and proceeded to ascertain its geological position and relations. He shortly found that it belonged to the upper part of the coal-formation, and hence he designated it carboniferous ironstone. He prosecuted his researches, and found various rich beds of the mineral distributed throughout the western counties of Scotland. On analysis, it was found to contain a little over 50 per cent. of protoxide of iron. The coaly matter it contained was not its least valuable

this was made in 1801, when I was engaged in erecting for myself and partners the Calder Iron Works. Great prejudice was excited against me by the ironmasters and others of that day in presuming to class the *wild coals* of the country (as Black Band was called) with ironstone fit and proper for the blast furnace. Yet that discovery has elevated Scotland to a considerable rank among the iron-making nations of Europe, with resources still in store that may be considered inexhaustible. But such are the consolatory effects of Time, that the discoverer of 1801 is no longer considered the intrusive visionary of the laboratory, but the acknowledged benefactor of his country at large, and particularly of an extensive class of coal and mine proprietors and iron masters, who have derived, and are still deriving, great wealth from this important discovery; and who, in the spirit of grateful acknowledgment, have pronounced it worthy of a crown of gold, or a monumental record on the spot where the discovery was first made.

" At an advanced period of life, such considerations are soothing and satisfactory. Many under similar circumstances have not, in their own lifetime, had that measure of justice awarded to them by their country to which they were equally entitled. I accept it, however, as a boon justly due to me, and as an equivalent in some degree for that laborious course of investigation which I had prescribed for myself, and which, in early life, was carried on under circumstances of personal exposure and inconvenience, which nothing but a frame of iron could have supported. They atone also, in part, for that disappointment sustained in early life by the speculative habits of one partner, and the constitutional nervousness of another, which eventually occasioned my separation from the Calder Iron Works, and lost me the possession of extensive tracts

---

ingredient; for by the aid of the hot blast it was afterwards found practicable to smelt it almost without any addition of coal. Seams of black band have since been discovered and successfully worked in Edinburghshire, Staffordshire, and North Wales.

of Black Band iron-stone, which I had secured while the
value of the discovery was known only to myself."

Mr. Mushet published the results of his laborious investigations in a series of papers in the Philosophical Magazine,
—afterwards reprinted in a collected form in 1840 under
the title of " Papers on Iron and Steel."   These papers are
among the most valuable original contributions to the
literature of the iron-manufacture that have yet been given
to the world.   They contain the germs of many inventions
and discoveries in iron and steel, some of which were perfected by Mr. Mushet himself, while others were adopted
and worked out by different experimenters. In 1798 some of
the leading French chemists were endeavouring to prove
by experiment that steel could be made by contact of the
diamond with bar-iron in the crucible, the carbon of the
diamond being liberated and entering into combination with
the iron, forming steel.   In the animated controversy which
occurred on the subject, Mr. Mushet's name was brought
into considerable notice; one of the subjects of his published experiments having been the conversion of bar-iron
into steel in the crucible by contact with regulated proportions of charcoal.   The experiments which he made in
connection with this controversy, though in themselves
unproductive of results, led to the important discovery by
Mr. Mushet of the certain fusibility of malleable iron at a
suitable temperature.

Among the other important results of Mr. Mushet's life-
long labours, the following may be summarily mentioned :
The preparation of steel from bar-iron by a direct process,
combining the iron with carbon ; the discovery of the
beneficial effects of oxide of manganese on iron and steel ;
the use of oxides of iron in the puddling-furnace in various
modes of appliance ; the production of pig-iron from the
blast-furnace, suitable for puddling, without the interven-
tion of the refinery ; and the application of the hot blast
to anthracite coal in iron-smelting.   For the process of
combining iron with carbon for the production of steel,

Mr. Mushet took out a patent in November, 1800; and many years after, when he had discovered the beneficial effects of oxide of manganese on steel, Mr. Josiah Heath founded upon it his celebrated patent for the making of cast-steel, which had the effect of raising the annual production of that metal in Sheffield from 3000 to 100,000 tons. His application of the hot blast to anthracite coal, after a process invented by him and adopted by the Messrs. Hill of the Plymouth Iron Works, South Wales, had the effect of producing savings equal to about 20,000*l.* a year at those works ; and yet, strange to say, Mr. Mushet himself never received any consideration for his invention.

The discovery of Titanium by Mr. Mushet in the hearth of a blast-furnace in 1794 would now be regarded as a mere isolated fact, inasmuch as Titanium was not placed in the list of recognised metals until Dr. Wollaston, many years later, ascertained its qualities. But in connection with the fact, it may be mentioned that Mr. Mushet's youngest son, Robert, reasoning on the peculiar circumstances of the discovery in question, of which ample record is left, has founded upon it his Titanium process, which is expected by him eventually to supersede all other methods of manufacturing steel, and to reduce very materially the cost of its production.

While he lived, Mr. Mushet was a leading authority on all matters connected with Iron and Steel, and he contributed largely to the scientific works of his time. Besides his papers in the Philosophical Journal, he wrote the article "Iron" for Napier's Supplement to the Encyclopædia Britannica ; and the articles "Blast Furnace" and "Blowing Machine" for Rees's Cyclopædia. The two latter articles had a considerable influence on the opposition to the intended tax upon iron in 1807, and were frequently referred to in the discussions on the subject in Parliament. Mr. Mushet died in 1847.

CHAPTER IX.

INVENTION OF THE HOT BLAST — JAMES BEAUMONT NEILSON.

"Whilst the exploits of the conqueror and the intrigues of the demagogue are faithfully preserved through a succession of ages, the persevering and unobtrusive efforts of genius, developing the best blessings of the Deity to man, are often consigned to oblivion."—David Mushet.

THE extraordinary value of the Black Band ironstone was not at first duly recognised, perhaps not even by Mr. Mushet himself. For several years after its discovery by him, its use was confined to the Calder Iron Works, where it was employed in mixture with other ironstones of the argillaceous class. It was afterwards partially used at the Clyde Iron Works, but nowhere else, a strong feeling of prejudice being entertained against it on the part of the iron trade generally. It was not until the year 1825 that the Monkland Company used it alone, without any other mixture than the necessary quantity of limestone for a flux. "The success of this Company," says Mr. Mushet, "soon gave rise to the Gartsherrie and Dundyvan furnaces, in the midst of which progress came the use of raw pit-coal and the Hot Blast—the latter one of the greatest discoveries in metallurgy of the present age, and, above every other process, admirably adapted for smelting the Blackband ironstone." From the introduction of this process the extraordinary development of the iron-manufacture of Scotland may be said to date; and we accordingly propose to devote the present chapter to an account of its meritorious inventor.

James Beaumont Neilson was born at Shettleston, a

roadside village about three miles eastward of Glasgow, on the 22nd of June, 1792.   His parents belonged to the working class. His father's earnings during many laborious years of his life did not exceed sixteen shillings a week. He had been bred to the trade of a mill-wright, and was for some time in the employment of Dr. Roebuck as an engine-wright at his colliery near Boroughstoness.   He was next employed in a like capacity by Mr. Beaumont, the mineral-manager of the collieries of Mrs. Cunningham of Lain-shaw, near Irvine in Ayrshire; after which he was ap-pointed engine-wright at Ayr, and subsequently at the Govan Coal Works near Glasgow, where he remained until his death. It was while working at the Irvine Works that he first became acquainted with his future wife, Marion Smith, the daughter of a Renfrewshire bleacher, a woman remarkable through life for her clever, managing, and industrious habits. She had the charge of Mrs. Cunning-ham's children for some time after the marriage of that lady to Mr. Beaumont, and it was in compliment to her former mistress and her husband that she named her youngest son James Beaumont after the latter.

The boy's education was confined to the common ele-ments of reading, writing, and arithmetic, which he partly acquired at the parish school of Strathbungo near Glasgow, and partly at the Chapel School, as it was called, in the Gorbals at Glasgow. He had finally left school before he was fourteen. Some time before he left, he had been partially set to work, and earned four shillings a week by employing a part of each day in driving a small con-densing engine which his father had put up in a neigh-bouring quarry. After leaving school, he was employed for two years as a gig boy on one of the winding engines at the Govan colliery. His parents now considered him of fit age to be apprenticed to some special trade, and as Beau-mont had much of his father's tastes for mechanical pursuits, it was determined to put him apprentice to a working engineer. His elder brother John was then acting as engineman at Oakbank near Glasgow, and Beaumont was apprenticed under him to learn the trade. John was a person of a studious and serious turn of mind, and had been strongly attracted to follow the example of the brothers Haldane, who were then exciting great interest by their preaching throughout the North; but his father set his face against his son's "preaching at the back o' dikes," as he called it; and so John quietly settled down to his work. The engine which the two brothers managed was a very small one, and the master and apprentice served for engine-man and fireman. Here the youth worked for three years, employing his leisure hours in the evenings in remedying the defects of his early education, and endeavouring to acquire a knowledge of English grammar, drawing, and mathematics.

On the expiry of his apprenticeship, Beaumont continued for a time to work under his brother as journeyman at a guinea a week; after which, in 1814, he entered the employment of William Taylor, coal-master at Irvine, and he was appointed engine-wright of the colliery at a salary of from 70*l.* to 80*l.* a year. One of the improvements which he introduced in the working of the colliery, while he held that office, was the laying down of an edge railway of cast-iron, in lengths of three feet, from the pit to the harbour of Irvine, a distance of three miles. At the age of 23 he married his first wife, Barbara Montgomerie, an Irvine lass, with a "tocher" of 250*l.* This little provision was all the more serviceable to him, as his master, Taylor, becoming unfortunate in business, he was suddenly thrown out of employment, and the little fortune enabled the newly-married pair to hold their heads above water till better days came round. They took a humble tenement, consisting of a room and a kitchen, in the Cowcaddens, Glasgow, where their first child was born.

About this time a gas-work, the first in Glasgow, was projected, and the company having been formed, the directors advertised for a superintendent and foreman, to

whom they offered a "liberal salary." Though Beaumont
had never seen gaslight before, except at the illumination
of his father's colliery office after the Peace of Amiens,—
which was accomplished in a very simple and original
manner, without either condenser, purifier, or gas-holder,—
and though he knew nothing of the art of gas-making, he
had the courage to apply for the situation. He was one of
twenty candidates, and the fortunate one; and in August,
1817, we find him appointed foreman of the Glasgow Gas-
works, for five years, at the salary of 90*l.* a year. Before
the expiry of his term he was reappointed for six years
more, at the advanced salary of 200*l.*, with the status of
manager and engineer of the works. His salary was gradually increased to 400*l.* a year, with a free dwelling-
house, until 1847, when, after a faithful service of thirty
years, during which he had largely extended the central
works, and erected branch works in Tradeston and Partick,
he finally resigned the management.

The situation of manager of the Glasgow Gas-works was
in many respects well suited for the development of Mr.
Neilson's peculiar abilities. In the first place it afforded
him facilities for obtaining theoretical as well as practical
knowledge in Chemical Science, of which he was a diligent
student at the Andersonian University, as well as of Natural Philosophy and Mathematics in their higher branches.
In the next place it gave free scope for his ingenuity in
introducing improvements in the manufacture of gas, then
in its infancy. He was the first to employ clay retorts;
and he introduced sulphate of iron as a self-acting purifier,
passing the gas through beds of charcoal to remove its oily
and tarry elements. The swallow-tail or union jet was
also his invention, and it has since come into general use.

While managing the Gas-works, one of Mr. Neilson's
labours of love was the establishment and direction by him
of a Workmen's Institution for mutual improvement.
Having been a workman himself, and experienced the disadvantages of an imperfect education in early life, as well

as the benefits arising from improved culture in later years, he desired to impart some of these advantages to the workmen in his employment, who consisted chiefly of persons from remote parts of the Highlands or from Ireland.   Most of them could not even read, and his principal difficulty consisted in persuading them that it was of any use to learn.   For some time they resisted his persuasions to form a Workmen's Institution, with a view to the establishment of a library, classes, and lectures, urging as a sufficient plea for not joining it, that they could not read, and that books would be of no use to them.   At last Mr. Neilson succeeded, though with considerable difficulty, in inducing fourteen of the workmen to adopt his plan.   Each member was to contribute a small sum monthly, to be laid out in books, the Gas Company providing the members with a comfortable room in which they might meet to read and converse in the evenings instead of going to the alehouse. The members were afterwards allowed to take the books home to read, and the room was used for the purpose of conversation on the subjects of the books read by them, and occasionally for lectures delivered by the members themselves on geography, arithmetic, chemistry, and mechanics.   Their numbers increased so that the room in which they met became insufficient for their accommodation, when the Gas Company provided them with a new and larger place of meeting, together with a laboratory and workshop.   In the former they studied practical chemistry, and in the latter they studied practical mechanics, making for themselves an air pump and an electrifying machine, as well as preparing the various models used in the course of the lectures.   The effects on the workmen were eminently beneficial, and the institution came to be cited as among the most valuable of its kind in the kingdom.*   Mr. Neilson throughout watched carefully over its working, and exerted

---

* Article by Dugald Bannatyne in *Glasgow Mechanic's Magazine*, No. 53, Dec. 1824.

himself in all ways to promote its usefulness, in which he had the zealous co-operation of the leading workmen themselves, and the gratitude of all. On the opening of the new and enlarged rooms in 1825, we find him delivering an admirable address, which was thought worthy of republication, together with the reply of George Sutherland, one of the workmen, in which Mr. Neilson's exertions as its founder and chief supporter were gratefully and forcibly expressed.*

It was during the period of his connection with the Glasgow Gas-works that Mr. Neilson directed his attention to the smelting of iron. His views in regard to the subject were at first somewhat crude, as appears from a paper read by him before the Glasgow Philosophical Society early in 1825. It appears that in the course of the preceding year his attention had been called to the subject by an ironmaker, who asked him if he thought it possible to purify the air blown into the blast furnaces, in like manner as carburetted hydrogen gas was purified. The ironmaster supposed that it was the presence of sulphur in the air that caused blast-furnaces to work irregularly, and to make bad iron in the summer months. Mr. Neilson was of opinion that this was not the true cause, and he was rather disposed to think it attributable to the want of a due proportion of oxygen in summer, when the air was more rarefied, besides containing more aqueous vapour than in winter. He therefore thought the true remedy was in some way or other to throw in a greater proportion of oxygen; and he suggested that, in order to dry the air, it should be passed, on its way to the furnace, through two long tunnels containing calcined lime. But further inquiry served to correct his views, and eventually led him to the true theory of blasting.

Shortly after, his attention was directed by Mr. James Ewing to a defect in one of the Muirkirk blast-furnaces,

---

* *Glasgow Mechanic's Magazine,* vol. iii. p. 159.

situated about half a mile distant from the blowing-engine, which was found not to work so well as others which were situated close to it. The circumstances of the case led Mr. Neilson to form the opinion that, as air increases in volume according to temperature, if he were to heat it by passing it through a red-hot vessel, its volume would be increased, according to the well-known law, and the blast might thus be enabled to do more duty in the distant furnace. He proceeded to make a series of experiments at the Gas-works, trying the effect of heated air on the illuminating power of gas, by bringing up a stream of it in a tube so as to surround the gas-burner. He found that by this means the combustion of the gas was rendered more intense, and its illuminating power greatly increased. He proceeded to try a similar experiment on a common smith's fire, by blowing the fire with heated air, and the effect was the same; the fire was much more brilliant, and accompanied by an unusually intense degree of heat.

Having obtained such marked results by these small experiments, it naturally occurred to him that a similar increase in intensity of combustion and temperature would attend the application of the process to the blast-furnace on a large scale; but being only a gas-maker, he had the greatest difficulty in persuading any ironmaster to permit him to make the necessary experiments with blast-furnaces actually at work. Besides, his theory was altogether at variance with the established practice, which was to supply air as cold as possible, the prevailing idea being that the coldness of the air in winter was the cause of the best iron being then produced. Acting on these views, the efforts of the ironmasters had always been directed to the cooling of the blast, and various expedients were devised for the purpose. Thus the regulator was painted white, as being the coolest colour; the air was passed over cold water, and in some cases the air pipes were even surrounded by ice, all with the object of keeping the blast cold. When, therefore, Mr. Neilson proposed entirely to reverse the process,

and to employ hot instead of cold blast, the incredulity of
the ironmasters may well be imagined.   What ! Neilson,
a mere maker of gas, undertake to instruct practical men
in the manufacture of iron !   And to suppose that *heated*
air can be used for the purpose !   It was presumption in
the extreme, or at best the mere visionary idea of a person
altogether unacquainted with the subject !

At length, however, Mr. Neilson succeeded in inducing
Mr. Charles Macintosh of Crossbasket, and Mr. Colin
Dunlop of the Clyde Iron Works, to allow him to make a
trial of the hot air process.   In the first imperfect attempts
the air was heated to little more than 80° Fahrenheit, yet
the results were satisfactory, and the scoriæ from the furnace evidently contained less iron.   He was therefore desirous of trying his plan upon a more extensive scale, with
the object, if possible, of thoroughly establishing the soundness of his principle.   In this he was a good deal hampered
even by those ironmasters who were his friends, and had
promised him the requisite opportunities for making a fair
trial of the new process.   They strongly objected to his
making the necessary alterations in the furnaces, and he
seemed to be as far from a satisfactory experiment as ever.
In one instance, where he had so far succeeded as to be
allowed to heat the blast-main, he asked permission to
introduce deflecting plates in the main or to put a bend
in the pipe, so as to bring the blast more closely against
the heated sides of the pipe, and also increase the area of
heating surface, in order to raise the temperature to a
higher point; but this was refused, and it was said that
if even a bend were put in the pipe the furnace would stop
working.   These prejudices proved a serious difficulty in
the way of our inventor, and several more years passed
before he was allowed to put a bend in the blast-main.
After many years of perseverance, he was, however, at
length enabled to work out his plan into a definite shape
at the Clyde Iron Works, and its practical value was
at once admitted.   At the meeting of the Mechanical

Engineers' Society held in May, 1859, Mr. Neilson explained that his invention consisted solely in the principle of heating the blast between the engine and the furnace, and was not associated with any particular construction of the intermediate heating apparatus. This, he said, was the cause of its success; and in some respects it resembled the invention of his countryman, James Watt, who, in connection with the steam-engine, invented the plan of condensing the steam in a separate vessel, and was successful in maintaining his invention by not limiting it to any particular construction of the condenser. On the same occasion he took the opportunity of acknowledging the firmness with which the English ironmasters had stood by him when attempts were made to deprive him of the benefits of his invention; and to them he acknowledged he was mainly indebted for the successful issue of the severe contests he had to undergo. For there were, of course, certain of the ironmasters, both English and Scotch, supporters of the cause of free trade in others' inventions, who sought to resist the patent, after it had come into general use, and had been recognised as one of the most valuable improvements of modern times.*

The patent was secured in 1828 for a term of fourteen years; but, as Mr. Neilson did not himself possess the requisite capital to enable him to perfect the invention, or to defend it if attacked, he found it necessary to invite other gentlemen, able to support him in these respects, to share its profits; retaining for himself only three-tenths of the whole. His partners were Mr. Charles Macintosh, Mr. Colin

---

* Mr. Mushet described it as "a wonderful discovery," and one of the "most novel and beautiful improvements in his time." Professor Gregory of Aberdeen characterized it as "the greatest improvement with which he was acquainted." Mr. Jessop, an extensive English iron manufacturer, declared it to be "of as great advantage in the iron trade as Arkwright's machinery was in the cotton-spinning trade;" and Mr. Fairbairn, in his contribution on "Iron" in the *Encyclopædia Britannica*, says that it "has effected an entire revolution in the iron industry of Great Britain, and forms the last era in the history of this material."

Dunlop, and Mr. John Wilson of Dundyvan. The charge made by them was only a shilling a ton for all iron produced by the new process; this low rate being fixed in order to ensure the introduction of the patent into general use, as well as to reduce to a minimum the temptations of the ironmasters to infringe it.

The first trials of the process were made at the blast-furnaces of Clyde and Calder; from whence the use of the hot blast gradually extended to the other iron-mining districts. In the course of a few years every furnace in Scotland, with one exception (that at Carron), had adopted the improvement; while it was also employed in half the furnaces of England and Wales, and in many of the furnaces on the Continent and in America. In course of time, and with increasing experience, various improvements were introduced in the process, more particularly in the shape of the air-heating vessels; the last form adopted being that of a congeries of tubes, similar to the tubular arrangement in the boiler of the locomotive, by which the greatest extent of heating surface was provided for the thorough heating of the air. By these modifications the temperature of the air introduced into the furnace has been raised from 240° to 600°, or the temperature of melting lead. To protect the nozzle of the air-pipe as it entered the furnace against the action of the intense heat to which it was subjected, a spiral pipe for a stream of cold water constantly to play in has been introduced within the sides of the iron tuyere through which the nozzle passes; by which means the tuyere is kept comparatively cool, while the nozzle of the air-pipe is effectually protected.*

This valuable invention did not escape the usual fate of successful patents, and it was on several occasions the subject of protracted litigation. The first action occurred in 1832; but the objectors shortly gave in, and renewed

---

* The invention of the tubular air-vessels and the water-tuyere belongs, we believe, to Mr. John Condie, sometime manager of the Blair Iron Works.

their licence.   In 1839, when the process had become generally adopted throughout Scotland, and, indeed, was found absolutely essential for smelting the peculiar ores of that country—more especially Mushet's Black Band—a powerful combination was formed amongst the ironmasters to resist the patent.   The litigation which ensued extended over five years, during which period some twenty actions were proceeding in Scotland, and several in England. Three juries sat upon the subject at different times, and on three occasions appeals were carried to the House of Lords.   One jury trial occupied ten days, during which a hundred and two witnesses were examined; the law costs on both sides amounting, it is supposed, to at least 40,000*l.* The result was, that the novelty and merit of Mr. Neilson's invention were finally established, and he was secured in the enjoyment of the patent right.

We are gratified to add, that, though Mr. Neilson had to part with two-thirds of the profits of the invention to secure the capital and influence necessary to bring it into general use, he realized sufficient to enable him to enjoy the evening of his life in peace and comfort.   He retired from active business to an estate which he purchased in 1851 in the Stewartry of Kirkcudbright, where he is found ready to lend a hand in every good work—whether in agricultural improvement, railway extension, or the moral and social good of those about him.   Mindful of the success of his Workmen's Institution at the Glasgow Gas-Works, he has, almost at his own door, erected a similar Institution for the use of the parish in which his property is situated, the beneficial effects of which have been very marked in the district.   We may add that Mr. Neilson's merits have been recognised by many eminent bodies—by the Institution of Civil Engineers, the Chemical Society, and others—the last honour conferred on him being his election as a Member of the Royal Society in 1846.

The invention of the hot blast, in conjunction with the discovery of the Black Band ironstone, has had an extra-

ordinary effect upon the development of the iron-manufacture of Scotland. The coals of that country are generally
unfit for coking, and lose as much as 55 per cent. in the
process. But by using the hot blast, the coal could be sent
to the blast-furnace in its raw state, by which a large
saving of fuel was effected.* Even coals of an inferior
quality were by its means made available for the manufacture of iron. But one of the peculiar qualities of the
Black Band ironstone is that in many cases it contains
sufficient coaly matter for purposes of calcination, without
any admixture of coal whatever. Before its discovery, all
the iron manufactured in Scotland was made from clay-
band; but the use of the latter has in a great measure
been discontinued wherever a sufficient supply of Black
Band can be obtained. And it is found to exist very extensively in most of the midland Scotch counties,—the
coal and iron measures stretching in a broad belt from
the Firth of Forth to the Irish Channel at the Firth of
Clyde. At the time when the hot blast was invented, the
fortunes of many of the older works were at a low ebb,
and several of them had been discontinued; but they were
speedily brought to life again wherever Black Band could
be found. In 1829, the year after Neilson's patent was
taken out, the total make of Scotland was 29,000 tons. As
fresh discoveries of the mineral were made, in Ayrshire and
Lanarkshire, new works were erected, until, in 1845, we
find the production of Scotch pig-iron had increased to

---

* Mr. Mushet says, " The greatest
produce in iron per furnace with the
Black Band and cold blast never exceeded 60 tons a-week. The produce
per furnace now averages 90 tons a-
week. Ten tons of this I attribute to
the use of raw pit-coal, and the other
twenty tons to the use of hot blast."
[*Papers on Iron and Steel*, 127.]
The produce per furnace is now 200
tons a-week and upwards.
The hot blast process was afterwards
applied to the making of iron with the
anthracite or stone coal of Wales; for
which a patent was taken out by
George Crane in 1836. Before the
hot blast was introduced, anthracite
coal would not act as fuel in the blast-
furnace. When put in, it merely had
the effect of putting the fire out.
With the aid of the hot blast, however, it now proves to be a most
valuable fuel in smelting.

475,000 tons.   It has since increased to upwards of a million of tons, nineteen-twentieths of which are made from Black Band ironstone.*

Employment has thus been given to vast numbers of our industrial population, and the wealth and resources of the Scotch iron districts have been increased to an extraordinary extent.   During the last year there were 125 furnaces in blast throughout Scotland, each employing about 400 men in making an average of 200 tons a week; and the money distributed amongst the workmen may readily be computed from the fact that, under the most favourable circumstances, the cost of making iron in wages alone amounts to 36s. a-ton.†

An immense additional value was given to all land in which the Black Band was found.   Mr. Mushet mentions that in 1839 the proprietor of the Airdrie estate derived a royalty of 16,500l. from the mineral, which had not before its discovery yielded him one farthing.   At the same time, many fortunes have been made by pushing and energetic men who have of late years entered upon this new branch of industry.   Amongst these may be mentioned the Bairds of Gartsherrie, who vie with the Guests and Crawshays of South Wales, and have advanced themselves in the course of a very few years from the station of small farmers to that of great capitalists owning estates in many counties, holding the highest character as commercial men, and ranking among the largest employers of labour in the kingdom.

---

* It is stated in the *North British Review* for Nov. 1845, that "As in Scotland every furnace—with the exception of one at Carron—now uses the hot blast, the saving on our present produce of 400,000 tons of pig-iron is 2,000,000 tons of coals, 200,000 tons of limestone, and £650,000 sterling per annum."   But as the Scotch produce is now above a million tons of pig-iron a year, the above figures will have to be multiplied by 2½ to give the present annual savings.

† Papers read by Mr. Ralph Moore, Mining Engineer, Glasgow, before the Royal Scottish Society of Arts, Edin. 1861, pp. 13, 14.

CHAPTER X.

Mechanical Inventions and Inventors.

"L'invention n'est-elle pas la poésie de la science? . . . Toutes les grandes découvertes portent avec elles la trace ineffaçable d'une pensée poétique. Il faut être poëte pour créer. Aussi, sommes-nous convaincus que si les puissantes machines, véritable source de la production et de l'industrie de nos jours, doivent recevoir des modifications radicales, ce sera à des hommes d'imagination, et non point à des hommes purement spéciaux, que l'on devra cette transformation."—E. M. Bataille, *Traité des Machines à Vapeur.*

Tools have played a highly important part in the history of civilization. Without tools and the ability to use them, man were indeed but a "poor, bare, forked animal,"— worse clothed than the birds, worse housed than the beaver, worse fed than the jackal. "Weak in himself," says Carlyle, "and of small stature, he stands on a basis, at most for the flattest-soled, of some half square foot, insecurely enough; has to straddle out his legs, lest the very wind supplant him. Feeblest of bipeds! Three quintals are a crushing load for him; the steer of the meadow tosses him aloft like a waste rag. Nevertheless he can use tools, can devise tools: with these the granite mountain melts into light dust before him; he kneads glowing iron as if it were soft paste; seas are his smooth highway, winds and fire his unvarying steeds. Nowhere do you find him without tools: without tools he is nothing; with tools he is all." His very first contrivances to support life were tools of the simplest and rudest construction; and his latest achievements in the substitution of machinery for the relief of the human hand and intellect are founded on the use of tools of a still higher order. Hence it is not without good reason that man has by some philosophers been defined as *a tool-making animal.*

Tools, like everything else, had small beginnings. With the primitive stone-hammer and chisel very little could be done. The felling of a tree would occupy a workman a month, unless helped by the destructive action of fire. Dwellings could not be built, the soil could not be tilled, clothes could not be fashioned and made, and the hewing out of a boat was so tedious a process that the wood must have been far gone in decay before it could be launched. It was a great step in advance to discover the art of working in metals, more especially in steel, one of the few metals capable of taking a sharp edge and keeping it. From the date of this discovery, working in wood and stone would be found comparatively easy; and the results must speedily have been felt not only in the improvement of man's daily food, but in his domestic and social condition. Clothing could then be made, the primitive forest could be cleared and tillage carried on; abundant fuel could be obtained, dwellings erected, ships built, temples reared; every improvement in tools marking a new step in the development of the human intellect, and a further stage in the progress of human civilization.

The earliest tools were of the simplest possible character, consisting principally of modifications of the wedge; such as the knife, the shears (formed of two knives working on a joint), the chisel, and the axe. These, with the primitive hammer, formed the principal stock-in-trade of the early mechanics, who were handicraftsmen in the literal sense of the word. But the work which the early craftsmen in wood, stone, brass, and iron, contrived to execute, sufficed to show how much expertness in the handling of tools will serve to compensate for their mechanical imperfections. Workmen then sought rather to aid muscular strength than to supersede it, and mainly to facilitate the efforts of manual skill. Another tool became added to those mentioned above, which proved an additional source of power to the workman. We mean the Saw, which was considered of so much importance that its inventor was honoured with a place among the gods in the mythology of the Greeks. This invention is said to have been suggested by the arrangement of the teeth in the jaw of a serpent, used by Talus the nephew of Dædalus in dividing a piece of wood. From the representations of ancient tools found in the paintings at Herculaneum it appears that the frame-saw used by the ancients very nearly resembled that still in use; and we are informed that the tools employed in the carpenters' shops at Nazareth at this day are in most respects the same as those represented in the buried Roman city. Another very ancient tool referred to in the Bible and in Homer was the File, which was used to sharpen weapons and implements. Thus the Hebrews " had a file for the mattocks, and for the coulters, and for the forks, and for the axes, and to sharpen the goads."* When to these we add the adze, plane-irons, the auger, and the chisel, we sum up the tools principally relied on by the early mechanics for working in wood and iron.

Such continued to be the chief tools in use down almost to our own day. The smith was at first the principal tool-maker; but special branches of trade were gradually established, devoted to tool-making. So long, however, as the workman relied mainly on his dexterity of hand, the amount of production was comparatively limited; for the number of skilled workmen was but small. The articles turned out by them, being the product of tedious manual labour, were too dear to come into common use, and were made almost exclusively for the richer classes of the community. It was not until machinery had been invented and become generally adopted that many of the ordinary articles of necessity and of comfort were produced in sufficient abundance and at such prices as enabled them

---

* 1 Samuel, ch. xiii. v. 21.

to enter into the consumption of the great body of the people.

But every improver of tools had a long and difficult battle to fight; for any improvement in their effective power was sure to touch the interests of some established craft. Especially was this the case with machines, which are but tools of a more complete though complicated kind than those above described.

Take, for instance, the case of the Saw. The tedious drudgery of dividing timber by the oldfashioned hand-saw is well known. To avoid it, some ingenious person suggested that a number of saws should be fixed to a frame in a mill, so contrived as to work with a reciprocating motion, upwards and downwards, or backwards and forwards, and that this frame so mounted should be yoked to the mill wheel, and the saws driven by the power of wind or water. The plan was tried, and, as may readily be imagined, the amount of effective work done by this machine-saw was immense, compared with the tedious process of sawing by hand.

It will be observed, however, that the new method must have seriously interfered with the labour of the hand-sawyers; and it was but natural that they should regard the establishment of the saw-mills with suspicion and hostility. Hence a long period elapsed before the hand-sawyers would permit the new machinery to be set up and worked. The first saw-mill in England was erected by a Dutchman, near London, in 1663, but was shortly abandoned in consequence of the determined hostility of the workmen. More than a century passed before a second saw-mill was set up; when, in 1767, Mr. John Houghton, a London timber-merchant, by the desire and with the approbation of the Society of Arts, erected one at Lime-house, to be driven by wind. The work was directed by one James Stansfield, who had gone over to Holland for the purpose of learning the art of constructing and managing the sawing machinery. But the mill was no sooner erected than a mob assembled and razed it to the ground. The principal rioters having been punished, and the loss to the proprietor having been made good by the nation, a new mill was shortly after built, and it was suffered to work without further molestation.

Improved methods of manufacture have usually had to encounter the same kind of opposition. Thus, when the Flemish weavers came over to England in the seventeenth century, bringing with them their skill and their industry, they excited great jealousy and hostility amongst the native workmen. Their competition as workmen was resented as an injury, but their improved machinery was regarded as a far greater source of mischief. In a memorial presented to the king in 1621 we find the London weavers complaining of the foreigners' competition, but especially that " they have made so bould of late as to devise engines for working of tape, lace, ribbin, and such like, wherein one man doth more among them than 7 Englishe men can doe ; so as their cheap sale of commodities beggereth all our Englishe artificers of that trade, and enricheth them."*

At a much more recent period new inventions have had to encounter serious rioting and machine-breaking fury. Kay of the fly-shuttle, Hargreaves of the spinning-jenny, and Arkwright of the spinning-frame, all had to fly from Lancashire, glad to escape with their lives. Indeed, says Mr. Bazley, " so jealous were the people, and also the legislature, of everything calculated to supersede men's labour, that when the Sankey Canal, six miles long, near Warrington, was authorized about the middle of last century, it was on the express condition that the boats plying on it should be drawn by men only ! "† Even improved agricultural tools and machines have had the same oppo-

---

* *State Papers*, Dom. 1621, Vol. 88, No. 112.
† *Lectures on the Results of the*

Great Exhibition of 1851, 2nd Series, 117.

sition to encounter; and in our own time bands of rural labourers have gone from farm to farm breaking drill-ploughs, winnowing, threshing, and other machines, down even to the common drills,—not perceiving that if their policy had proved successful, and tools could have been effectually destroyed, the human race would at once have been reduced to their teeth and nails, and civilization summarily abolished.*

It is, no doubt, natural that the ordinary class of work-men should regard with prejudice, if not with hostility, the introduction of machines calculated to place them at a disadvantage and to interfere with their usual employ-ments; for to poor and not very far-seeing men the loss of daily bread is an appalling prospect. But invention does not stand still on that account. Human brains *will* work. Old tools are improved and new ones invented, super-seding existing methods of production, though the weak and unskilled may occasionally be pushed aside or even trodden under foot. The consolation which remains is, that while the few suffer, society as a whole is vastly bene-fited by the improved methods of production which are suggested, invented, and perfected by the experience of successive generations.

The living race is the inheritor of the industry and skill of all past times; and the civilization we enjoy is but the sum of the useful effects of labour during the past cen-

---

* Dr. Kirwan, late President of the Royal Irish Academy, who had travelled much on the continent of Europe, used to relate, when speaking of the difficulty of introducing im-provements in the arts and manufac-tures, and of the prejudices entertained for old practices, that, in Normandy, the farmers had been so long accus-tomed to the use of ploughs whose shares were made entirely of *wood* that they could not be prevailed on to make trial of those with *iron;* that they considered them to be an idle and use-less innovation on the long-established practices of their ancestors; and that they carried these prejudices so far as to force the government to issue an edict on the subject. And even to the last they were so obstinate in their attachment to ploughshares of wood that a tumultuous opposition was made to the enforcement of the edict, which for a short time threatened a rebellion in the province.—PARKES, *Chemical Essays,* 4th Ed. 473.

turies. *Nihil per saltum.* By slow and often painful steps
Nature's secrets have been mastered. Not an effort has
been made but has had its influence. For no human labour
is altogether lost; some remnant of useful effect surviving
for the benefit of the race, if not of the individual. Even
attempts apparently useless have not really been so, but
have served in some way to advance man to higher knowledge, skill, or discipline. " The loss of a position gained,"
says Professor Thomson, " is an event unknown in the
history of man's struggle with the forces of inanimate
nature." A single step won gives a firmer foothold for
further effort. The man may die, but the race survives
and continues the work,—to use the poet's simile, mounting
on stepping-stones of dead selves to higher selves.

Philarète Chasles, indeed, holds that it is the Human
Race that is your true inventor: " As if to unite all generations," he says, " and to show that man can only act
efficiently by association with others, it has been ordained
that each inventor shall only interpret the first word of
the problem he sets himself to solve, and that every great
idea shall be the *résumé* of the past at the same time that
it is the germ of the future." And rarely does it happen
that any discovery or invention of importance is made by
one man alone. The threads of inquiry are taken up and
traced, one labourer succeeding another, each tracing it a
little further, often without apparent result. This goes
on sometimes for centuries, until at length some man,
greater perhaps than his fellows, seeking to fulfil the
needs of his time, gathers the various threads together,
treasures up the gain of past successes and failures, and
uses them as the means for some solid achievement. Thus
Newton discovered the law of gravitation, and thus James
Watt invented the steam-engine. So also of the Locomotive, of which Robert Stephenson said, " It has not been
the invention of any one man, but of a race of mechanical
engineers." Or, as Joseph Bramah observed, in the pre-
amble to his second Lock patent, " Among the number

of patents granted there are comparatively few which can be called original, so that it is difficult to say where the boundary of one ends and where that of another begins."

The arts are indeed reared but slowly; and it was a wise observation of Lord Bacon that we are too apt to pass those ladders by which they have been reared, and reflect the whole merit on the last new performer. Thus, what is hailed as an original invention is often found to be but the result of a long succession of trials and experiments gradually following each other, which ought rather to be considered as a continuous series of achievements of the human mind than as the conquest of any single individual. It has sometimes taken centuries of experience to ascertain the value of a single fact in its various bearings. Like man himself, experience is feeble and apparently purposeless in its infancy, but acquires maturity and strength with age. Experience, however, is not limited to a lifetime, but is the stored-up wealth and power of our race. Even amidst the death of successive generations it is constantly advancing and accumulating, exhibiting at the same time the weakness and the power, the littleness and the greatness of our common humanity. And not only do we who live succeed to the actual results of our predecessors' labours,—to their works of learning and of art, their inventions and discoveries, their tools and machines, their roads, bridges, canals, and railways,—but to the inborn aptitudes of blood and brain which they bequeath to us,— to that "educability," so to speak, which has been won for us by the labours of many generations, and forms our richest natural heritage.

The beginning of most inventions is very remote. The first idea, born within some unknown brain, passes thence into others, and at last comes forth complete, after a parturition, it may be, of centuries. One starts the idea, another developes it, and so on progressively until at last it is elaborated and worked out in practice; but the first not less than the last is entitled to his share in the merit of the invention, were it only possible to measure and apportion it duly. Sometimes a great original mind strikes upon some new vein of hidden power, and gives a powerful impulse to the inventive faculties of man, which lasts through generations. More frequently, however, inventions are not entirely new, but modifications of contrivances previously known, though to a few, and not yet brought into practical use. Glancing back over the history of mechanism, we occasionally see an invention seemingly full born, when suddenly it drops out of sight, and we hear no more of it for centuries. It is taken up *de novo* by some inventor, stimulated by the needs of his time, and falling again upon the track, he recovers the old footmarks, follows them up, and completes the work.

There is also such a thing as inventions being born before their time—the advanced mind of one generation projecting that which cannot be executed for want of the requisite means; but in due process of time, when mechanism has got abreast of the original idea, it is at length carried out; and thus it is that modern inventors are enabled to effect many objects which their predecessors had tried in vain to accomplish. As Louis Napoleon has said, " Inventions born before their time must remain useless until the level of common intellects rises to comprehend them." For this reason, misfortune is often the lot of the inventor before his time, though glory and profit may belong to his successors. Hence the gift of inventing not unfrequently involves a yoke of sorrow. Many of the greatest inventors have lived neglected and died unrequited, before their merits could be recognised and estimated. Even if they succeed, they often raise up hosts of enemies in the persons whose methods they propose to supersede. Envy, malice, and detraction meet them in all their forms; they are assailed by combinations of rich and unscrupulous persons to wrest from them the profits of their ingenuity; and last and worst of all, the successful inventor often finds his claims to originality decried, and himself branded as a copyist and a pirate.

Among the inventions born out of time, and before the world could make adequate use of them, we can only find space to allude to a few, though they are so many that one is almost disposed to accept the words of Chaucer as true, that " There is nothing new but what has once been old;" or, as another writer puts it, " There is nothing new but what has before been known and forgotten;" or, in the words of Solomon, " The thing that hath been is that which shall be, and there is no new thing under the sun." One of the most important of these is the use of Steam, which was well known to the ancients; but though it was used to grind drugs, to turn a spit, and to excite the wonder and fear of the credulous, a long time elapsed before it became employed as a useful motive-power. The inquiries and experiments on the subject extended through many ages. Friar Bacon, who flourished in the thirteenth century, seems fully to have anticipated, in the following remarkable passage, nearly all that steam could accomplish, as well as the hydraulic engine and the diving-bell, though the flying machine yet remains to be invented :—

" I will now," says the Friar, " mention some of the wonderful works of art and nature in which there is nothing of magic, and which magic could not perform. Instruments may be made by which the largest ships, with only one man guiding them, will be carried with greater velocity than if they were full of sailors. Chariots may be constructed that will move with incredible rapidity, without the help of animals. Instruments of flying may be formed, in which a man, sitting at his ease and meditating on any subject, may beat the air with his artificial wings, after the manner of birds. A small instrument may be made to raise or depress the greatest weights. An instrument may be fabricated by which one man may draw a thousand men to him by force and against their will; as also machines which will enable men to walk at the bottom of seas or rivers without danger."

It is possible that Friar Bacon derived his knowledge

of the powers which he thus described from the traditions handed down of former inventions which had been neglected and allowed to fall into oblivion; for before the invention of printing, which enabled the results of investigation and experience to be treasured up in books, there was great risk of the inventions of one age being lost to the succeeding generations. Yet Disraeli the elder is of opinion that the Romans had invented printing without being aware of it; or perhaps the senate dreaded the inconveniences attending its use, and did not care to deprive a large body of scribes of their employment. They even used stereotypes, or immovable printing-types, to stamp impressions on their pottery, specimens of which still exist. In China the art of printing is of great antiquity. Lithography was well known in Germany, by the very name which it still bears, nearly three hundred years before Senefelder reinvented it; and specimens of the ancient art are yet to be seen in the Royal Museum at Munich.*

Steam-locomotion, by sea and land, had long been dreamt of and attempted. Blasco de Garay made his experiment in the harbour of Barcelona as early as 1543; Denis Papin made a similar attempt at Cassel in 1707; but it was not until Watt had solved the problem of the steam-engine that the idea of the steam-boat could be developed in practice, which was done by Miller of Dalswinton in 1788. Sages and poets have frequently foreshadowed inventions of great social moment. Thus Dr. Darwin's anticipation of the locomotive, in his *Botanic Garden*, published in 1791, before any locomotive had been invented, might almost be regarded as prophetic :—

> Soon shall thy arm, unconquered Steam ! afar
> Drag the slow barge, and drive the rapid car.

Denis Papin first threw out the idea of atmospheric locomotion; and Gauthey, another Frenchman, in 1782 pro-

---

* EDOUARD FOURNIER, *Vieux-Neuf*, i. 339.

jected a method of conveying parcels and merchandise by subterraneous tubes,* after the method recently patented and brought into operation by the London Pneumatic Despatch Company. The balloon was an ancient Italian invention, revived by Mongolfier long after the original had been forgotten. Even the reaping machine is an old invention revived. Thus Barnabe Googe, the translator of a book from the German entitled 'The whole Arte and Trade of Husbandrie,' published in 1577, in the reign of Elizabeth, speaks of the reaping-machine as a worn-out invention—a thing "which was woont to be used in France. The device was a lowe kinde of carre with a couple of wheeles, and the frunt armed with sharpe syckles, whiche, forced by the beaste through the corne, did cut down al before it. This tricke," says Googe, " might be used in levell and champion countreys; but with us it wolde make but ill-favoured woorke." † The Thames Tunnel was thought an entirely new manifestation of engineering genius; but the tunnel under the Euphrates at ancient Babylon, and that under the wide mouth of the harbour at Marseilles (a much more difficult work), show that the ancients were beforehand with us in the art of tunnelling. Macadamized roads are as old as the Roman empire; and suspension bridges, though comparatively new in Europe, have been known in China for centuries.

There is every reason to believe—indeed it seems clear—that the Romans knew of gunpowder, though they only used it for purposes of fireworks; while the secret of the destructive Greek fire has been lost altogether. When gunpowder came to be used for purposes of war, invention busied itself upon instruments of destruction. When recently examining the Museum of the Arsenal at Venice, we were surprised to find numerous weapons of the fifteenth and sixteenth centuries embodying the most recent English

---

* *Mémoires de l'Académie des Sciences,* 6 Feb. 1826.

† *Farmer's Magazine,* 1817, No. lxxi. 291.

improvements in arms, such as revolving pistols, rifled muskets, and breech-loading cannon. The latter, embodying Sir William Armstrong's modern idea, though in a rude form, had been fished up from the bottom of the Adriatic, where the ship armed with them had been sunk hundreds of years ago. Even Perkins's steam-gun was an old invention revived by Leonardo da Vinci, and by him attributed to Archimedes.* The Congreve rocket is said to have an Eastern origin, Sir William Congreve having observed its destructive effects when employed by the forces under Tippoo Saib in the Mahratta war, on which he adopted and improved the missile, and brought out the invention as his own.

Coal-gas was regularly used by the Chinese for lighting purposes long before it was known amongst us. Hydropathy was generally practised by the Romans, who established baths wherever they went. Even chloroform is no new thing. The use of ether as an anæsthetic was known to Albertus Magnus, who flourished in the thirteenth century; and in his works he gives a recipe for its preparation. In 1681 Denis Papin published his *Traité des Opérations sans Douleur*, showing that he had discovered methods of deadening pain. But the use of anæsthetics is much older than Albertus Magnus or Papin; for the ancients had their nepenthe and mandragora; the Chinese their mayo, and the Egyptians their hachisch (both preparations of Cannabis Indica), the effects of which in a great measure resemble those of chloroform. What is perhaps still more surprising is the circumstance that one of the most elegant of recent inventions, that of sun-painting by the daguerreotype, was in the fifteenth century known to Leonardo da Vinci,† whose skill as an architect and engraver, and whose accomplishments as a chemist and natural philosopher, have been almost entirely overshadowed by his genius as a

---

* *Vieux-Neuf*, i. 228 ; *Inventa Nova-Antiqua*, 742.   † *Vieux-Neuf*, i. 19. See also *Inventa Nova-Antiqua*, 803.

painter.* The idea, thus early born, lay in oblivion until
1760, when the daguerreotype was again clearly indicated
in a book published in Paris, written by a certain Tiphanie
de la Roche, under the anagrammatic title of *Giphantie*. Still
later, at the beginning of the present century, we find
Thomas Wedgwood, Sir Humphry Davy, and James Watt,
making experiments on the action of light upon nitrate
of silver; and only within the last few months a silvered
copper-plate has been found amongst the old household
lumber of Matthew Boulton (Watt's partner), having on it a
representation of the old premises at Soho, apparently taken
by some such process.†

In like manner the invention of the electric telegraph,
supposed to be exclusively modern, was clearly indicated
by Schwenter in his *Délassements Physico-Mathématiques*, published in 1636; and he there pointed out how two individuals could communicate with each other by means of the
magnetic needle. A century later, in 1746, Le Monnier
exhibited a series of experiments in the Royal Gardens at
Paris, showing how electricity could be transmitted through
iron wire 950 fathoms in length; and in 1753 we find one
Charles Marshall publishing a remarkable description of
the electric telegraph in the *Scots Magazine*, under the title

---

* Mr. Hallam, in his *Introduction
to the History of Europe*, pronounces
the following remarkable eulogium on
this extraordinary genius :—" If any
doubt could be harboured, not only as
to the right of Leonardo da Vinci to
stand as the first name of the fifteenth
century, which is beyond all doubt,
but as to his originality in so many
discoveries, which probably no one
man, especially in such circumstances,
has ever made, it must be on an
hypothesis not very untenable, that
some parts of physical science had
already attained a height which mere
books do not record." " Unpublished
MSS. by Leonardo contain discoveries
and anticipations of discoveries," says
Mr. Hallam, " within the compass of
a few pages, so as to strike us with
something like the awe of preternatural
knowledge."

† The plate is now to be seen at
the Museum of Patents at South Kensington. In the account which has
been published of the above discovery
it is stated that " an old man of ninety
(recently dead or still alive) recollected,
or recollects, that Watt and others used
to take portraits of people in a dark (?)
room ; and there is a letter extant
of Sir William Beechey, begging the
Lunar Society to desist from these experiments, as, were the process to succeed, it would ruin portrait-painting."

of 'An expeditious Method of conveying Intelligence.'
Again, in 1760, we find George Louis Lesage, professor of
mathematics at Geneva, promulgating his invention of an
electric telegraph, which he eventually completed and set
to work in 1774. This instrument was composed of twenty-
four metallic wires, separate from each other and enclosed
in a non-conducting substance. Each wire ended in a
stalk mounted with a little ball of elder-wood suspended
by a silk thread. When a stream of electricity, no matter
how slight, was sent through the wire, the elder-ball at the
opposite end was repelled, such movement designating some
letter of the alphabet. A few years later we find Arthur
Young, in his *Travels in France*, describing a similar machine
invented by a M. Lomond of Paris, the action of which he
also describes.* In these and similar cases, though the idea
was born and the model of the invention was actually made,
it still waited the advent of the scientific mechanical inventor who should bring it to perfection, and embody it
in a practical working form.

Some of the most valuable inventions have descended to
us without the names of their authors having been preserved. We are the inheritors of an immense legacy of the
results of labour and ingenuity, but we know not the names

---

* "16th Oct. 1787. In the evening
to M. Lomond, a very ingenious and
inventive mechanic, who has made an
improvement of the jenny for spinning
cotton. Common machines are said
to make too hard a thread for certain
fabrics, but this forms it loose and
spongy. In electricity he has made a
remarkable discovery: you write two
or three words on a paper; he takes it
with him into a room, and turns a
machine inclosed in a cylindrical case,
at the top of which is an electrometer,
a small fine pith ball; a wire connects
with a similar cylinder and electrometer in a distant apartment; and his
wife, by remarking the corresponding
motions of the ball, writes down the
words they indicate; from which it
appears that he has formed an alphabet
of motions. As the length of the wire
makes no difference in the effect, a correspondence might be carried on at any
distance: within and without a besieged town, for instance; or for a
purpose much more worthy, and a
thousand times more harmless, between two lovers prohibited or prevented from any better connexion.
Whatever the use may be, the invention is beautiful."—Arthur Young's
Travels in France in 1787-8-9. London, 1792, 4to. ed. p. 65.

of our benefactors.   Who invented the watch as a measurer of time?   Who invented the fast and loose pulley?   Who invented the eccentric?   Who, asks a mechanical inquirer,* "invented the method of cutting screws with stocks and dies?   Whoever he might be, he was certainly a great benefactor of his species.   Yet (adds the writer) his name is not known, though the invention has been so recent."   This is not, however, the case with most modern inventions, the greater number of which are more or less disputed.   Who was entitled to the merit of inventing printing has never yet been determined.   Weber and Senefelder both laid claim to the invention of lithography, though it was merely an old German art revived.   Even the invention of the penny-postage system by Sir Rowland Hill is disputed; Dr. Gray of the British Museum claiming to be its inventor, and a French writer alleging it to be an old French invention.†   The invention of the steamboat has been claimed on behalf of Blasco de Garay, a Spaniard, Papin, a Frenchman, Jonathan Hulls, an Englishman, and Patrick Miller of Dalswinton, a Scotchman.   The invention of the spinning machine has been variously attributed to Paul, Wyatt, Hargreaves, Higley, and Arkwright.   The invention of the balance-spring was claimed by Huyghens, a Dutchman, Hautefeuille, a Frenchman, and Hooke, an Englishman.   There is scarcely a point of detail in the locomotive but is the subject of dispute.   Thus the invention of the blast-pipe is claimed for Trevithick, George Stephenson, Goldsworthy Gurney, and Timothy Hackworth;

---

* *Mechanic's Magazine*, 4th Feb. 1859.

† A writer in the *Monde* says:— " The invention of postage-stamps is far from being so modern as is generally supposed.   A postal regulation in France of the year 1653, which has recently come to light, gives notice of the creation of pre-paid tickets to be used for Paris instead of money payments.   These tickets were to be dated and attached to the letter or wrapped round it, in such a manner that the postman could remove and retain them on delivering the missive.   These franks were to be sold by the porters of the convents, prisons, colleges, and other public institutions, at the price of one sou."

that of the tubular boiler by Seguin, Stevens, Booth, and W. H. James; that of the link-motion by John Gray, Hugh Williams, and Robert Stephenson.

Indeed many inventions appear to be coincident. A number of minds are working at the same time in the same track, with the object of supplying some want generally felt; and, guided by the same experience, they not unfrequently arrive at like results. It has sometimes happened that the inventors have been separated by great distances, so that piracy on the part of either was impossible. Thus Hadley and Godfrey almost simultaneously invented the quadrant, the one in London, the other in Philadelphia; and the process of electrotyping was invented at the same time by Mr. Spencer, a working chemist at Liverpool, and by Professor Jacobi at St. Petersburg. The safety-lamp was a coincident invention, made about the same time by Sir Humphry Davy and George Stephenson; and perhaps a still more remarkable instance of a coincident discovery was that of the planet Neptune by Leverrier at Paris, and by Adams at Cambridge.

It is always difficult to apportion the due share of merit which belongs to mechanical inventors, who are accustomed to work upon each other's hints and suggestions, as well as by their own experience. Some idea of this difficulty may be formed from the fact that, in the course of our investigations as to the origin of the planing machine—one of the most useful of modern tools—we have found that it has been claimed on behalf of six inventors—Fox of Derby, Roberts of Manchester, Matthew Murray of Leeds, Spring of Aberdeen, Clement and George Rennie of London; and there may be other claimants of whom we have not yet heard. But most mechanical inventions are of a very composite character, and are led up to by the labour and the study of a long succession of workers. Thus Savary and Newcomen led up to Watt; Cugnot, Murdock, and Trevithick to the Stephensons; and Maudslay to Clement, Roberts, Nasmyth, Whitworth, and many more mechanical

inventors.   There is scarcely a process in the arts but has
in like manner engaged mind after mind in bringing it
to perfection.   "There is nothing," says Mr. Hawkshaw,
" really worth having that man has obtained, that has not
been the result of a combined and gradual process of investigation.   A gifted individual comes across some old
footmark, stumbles on a chain of previous research and
inquiry.   He meets, for instance, with a machine, the
result of much previous labour; he modifies it, pulls it to
pieces, constructs and reconstructs it, and by further trial
and experiment he arrives at the long sought-for result."*

But the making of the invention is not the sole difficulty.
It is one thing to invent, said Sir Marc Brunel, and another
thing to make the invention work.   Thus when Watt,
after long labour and study, had brought his invention to
completion, he encountered an obstacle which has stood in
the way of other inventors, and for a time prevented the
introduction of their improvements, if not led to their
being laid aside and abandoned.   This was the circumstance that the machine projected was so much in advance
of the mechanical capability of the age that it was with
the greatest difficulty it could be executed.   When labouring upon his invention at Glasgow, Watt was baffled and
thrown into despair by the clumsiness and incompetency
of his workmen.   Writing to Dr. Roebuck on one occasion,
he said, " You ask what is the principal hindrance in
erecting engines?   It is always the smith-work."   His
first cylinder was made by a whitesmith, of hammered iron
soldered together, but having used quicksilver to keep
the cylinder air-tight, it dropped through the inequalities
into the interior, and "played the devil with the solder."
Yet, inefficient though the whitesmith was, Watt could ill
spare him, and we find him writing to Dr. Roebuck almost
in despair, saying, " My old white-iron man is dead ! " feel-

---

* Inaugural Address delivered before the Institution of Civil Engineers,
14th Jan. 1862.

ing his loss to be almost irreparable. His next cylinder
was cast and bored at Carron, but it was so untrue that it
proved next to useless. The piston could not be kept steam
tight, notwithstanding the various expedients which were
adopted of stuffing it with paper, cork, putty, pasteboard,
and old hat. Even after Watt had removed to Birmingham, and he had the assistance of Boulton's best workmen,
Smeaton expressed the opinion, when he saw the engine at
work, that notwithstanding the excellence of the invention, it could never be brought into general use because of
the difficulty of getting its various parts manufactured with
sufficient precision. For a long time we find Watt, in his
letters, complaining to his partner of the failure of his
engines through "villainous bad workmanship." Sometimes
the cylinders, when cast, were found to be more than an
eighth of an inch wider at one end than the other; and under
such circumstances it was impossible the engine could act
with precision. Yet better work could not be had. First-
rate workmen in machinery did not as yet exist; they
were only in process of education. Nearly everything had
to be done by hand. The tools used were of a very imperfect kind. A few ill-constructed lathes, with some drills
and boring-machines of a rude sort, constituted the principal furniture of the workshop. Years after, when Brunel
invented his block-machines, considerable time elapsed
before he could find competent mechanics to construct
them, and even after they had been constructed he had
equal difficulty in finding competent hands to work them.*

Watt endeavoured to remedy the defect by keeping
certain sets of workmen to special classes of work, allowing them to do nothing else. Fathers were induced to
bring up their sons at the same bench with themselves,
and initiate them in the dexterity which they had acquired
by experience; and at Soho it was not unusual for the
same precise line of work to be followed by members of the

---

* BEAMISH'S *Memoir of Sir I. M. Brunel*, 79, 80.

same family for three generations. In this way as great a degree of accuracy of a mechanical kind was arrived at as practicable under the circumstances. But notwithstanding all this care, accuracy of fitting could not be secured so long as the manufacture of steam-engines was conducted mainly by hand. There was usually a considerable waste of steam, which the expedients of chewed paper and greased hat packed outside the piston were insufficient to remedy; and it was not until the invention of automatic machine-tools by the mechanical engineers about to be mentioned, that the manufacture of the steam-engine became a matter of comparative ease and certainty. Watt was compelled to rest satisfied with imperfect results, arising from imperfect workmanship. Thus, writing to Dr. Small respecting a cylinder 18 inches in diameter, he said, "at the worst place the long diameter exceeded the short by only three-eighths of an inch." How different from the state of things at this day, when a cylinder five feet wide will be rejected as a piece of imperfect workmanship if it be found to vary in any part more than the 80th part of an inch in diameter!

Not fifty years since it was a matter of the utmost difficulty to set an engine to work, and sometimes of equal difficulty to keep it going. Though fitted by competent workmen, it often would not go at all. Then the foreman of the factory at which it was made was sent for, and he would almost live beside the engine for a month or more; and after easing her here and screwing her up there, putting in a new part and altering an old one, packing the piston and tightening the valves, the machine would at length be got to work.* Now the case is altogether dif-

---

* There was the same clumsiness in all kinds of mill-work before the introduction of machine-tools. We have heard of a piece of machinery of the old school, the wheels of which, when set to work, made such a clatter that the owner feared the engine would fall to pieces. The foreman who set it agoing, after working at it until he was almost in despair, at last gave it up, saying, "I think we had better leave the cogs to settle their differences with one another: they will grind themselves right in time!"

ferent.   The perfection of modern machine-tools is such
that the utmost possible precision is secured, and the mechanical engineer can calculate on a degree of exactitude
that does not admit of a deviation beyond the thousandth
part of an inch.   When the powerful oscillating engines
of the ' Warrior' were put on board that ship, the parts,
consisting of some five thousand separate pieces, were
brought from the different workshops of the Messrs. Penn and
Sons, where they had been made by workmen who knew
not the places they were to occupy, and fitted together
with such precision that so soon as the steam was raised
and let into the cylinders, the immense machine began as
if to breathe and move like a living creature, stretching
its huge arms like a new-born giant, and then, after practising its strength a little and proving its soundness in
body and limb, it started off with the power of above a
thousand horses to try its strength in breasting the billows
of the North Sea.

Such are among the triumphs of modern mechanical engineering, due in a great measure to the perfection of the tools
by means of which all works in metal are now fashioned.
These tools are themselves among the most striking
results of the mechanical invention of the day.   They
are automata of the most perfect kind, rendering the engine
and machine-maker in a great measure independent of inferior workmen.   For the machine tools have no unsteady
hand, are not careless nor clumsy, do not work by rule of
thumb, and cannot make mistakes.   They will repeat their
operations a thousand times without tiring, or varying one
hair's breadth in their action; and will turn out, without
complaining, any quantity of work, all of like accuracy and
finish.   Exercising as they do so remarkable an influence
on the development of modern industry, we now propose,
so far as the materials at our disposal will admit, to give
an account of their principal inventors, beginning with the
school of Bramah.

CHAPTER XI.

Joseph Bramah.

" The great Inventor is one who has walked forth upon the industrial world, not from universities, but from hovels; not as clad in silks and decked with honours, but as clad in fustian and grimed with soot and oil."—Isaac Taylor, *Ultimate Civilization.*

The inventive faculty is so strong in some men that it may be said to amount to a passion, and cannot be restrained. The saying that the poet is born, not made, applies with equal force to the inventor, who, though indebted like the other to culture and improved opportunities, nevertheless invents and goes on inventing mainly to gratify his own instinct. The inventor, however, is not a creator like the poet, but chiefly a finder-out. His power consists in a great measure in quick perception and accurate observation, and in seeing and foreseeing the effects of certain mechanical combinations. He must possess the gift of insight, as well as of manual dexterity, combined with the indispensable qualities of patience and perseverance,—for though baffled, as he often is, he must be ready to rise up again unconquered even in the moment of defeat. This is the stuff of which the greatest inventors have been made. The subject of the following memoir may not be entitled to take rank as a first-class inventor, though he was a most prolific one; but, as the founder of a school from which proceeded some of the most distinguished mechanics of our time, he is entitled to a prominent place in this series of memoirs.

Joseph Bramah was born in 1748 at the village of Stain-

borough, near Barnsley in Yorkshire, where his father rented
a small farm under Lord Strafford. Joseph was the eldest
of five children, and was early destined to follow the
plough. After receiving a small amount of education at
the village school, he was set to work upon the farm.
From an early period he showed signs of constructive
skill. When a mere boy, he occupied his leisure hours in
making musical instruments, and he succeeded in executing
some creditable pieces of work with very imperfect tools.
A violin, which he made out of a solid block of wood, was
long preserved as a curiosity. He was so fortunate as to
make a friend of the village blacksmith, whose smithy
he was in the practice of frequenting. The smith was an
ingenious workman, and, having taken a liking for the
boy, he made sundry tools for him out of old files and
razor blades; and with these his fiddle and other pieces of
work were mainly executed.

Joseph might have remained a ploughman for life, but
for an accident which happened to his right ankle at the
age of 16, which unfitted him for farm-work. While confined at home disabled, he spent his time in carving and
making things in wood; and then it occurred to him that,
though he could not now be a ploughman, he might be a
mechanic. When sufficiently recovered, he was accordingly put apprentice to one Allott, the village carpenter,
under whom he soon became an expert workman. He could
make ploughs, window-frames, or fiddles, with equal dexterity. He also made violoncellos, and was so fortunate as
to sell one of his making for three guineas, which is still
reckoned a good instrument. He doubtless felt within him
the promptings of ambition, such as every good workman
feels, and at all events entertained the desire of rising in
his trade. When his time was out, he accordingly resolved
to seek work in London, whither he made the journey on
foot. He soon found work at a cabinet-maker's, and remained with him for some time, after which he set up
business in a very small way on his own account. An

accident which happened to him in the course of his daily
work, again proved his helper, by affording him a degree of
leisure which he at once proceeded to turn to some useful
account.   Part of his business consisted in putting up
water-closets, after a method invented or improved by a
Mr. Allen; but the article was still very imperfect; and
Bramah had long resolved that if he could only secure
some leisure for the purpose, he would contrive something that should supersede it altogether.   A severe fall
which occurred to him in the course of his business, and
laid him up, though very much against his will, now afforded him the leisure which he desired, and he proceeded
to make his proposed invention.   He took out a patent for
it in 1778, describing himself in the specification as " of
Cross Court, Carnaby Market [Golden Square], Middlesex,
Cabinet Maker."   He afterwards removed to a shop in
Denmark Street, St. Giles's, and while there he made a further improvement in his invention by the addition of a
water cock, which he patented in 1783.   The merits of the
machine were generally recognised, and before long it came
into extensive use, continuing to be employed, with but
few alterations, until the present day.   His circumstances
improving with the increased use of his invention, Bramah
proceeded to undertake the manufacture of the pumps,
pipes, &c., required for its construction; and, remembering
his friend the Yorkshire blacksmith, who had made his
first tools for him out of the old files and razor-blades, he
sent for him to London to take charge of his blacksmith's
department, in which he proved a most useful assistant.
As usual, the patent was attacked by pirates so soon as it
became productive, and Bramah was under the necessity,
on more than one occasion, of defending his property in the
invention, in which he was completely successful.

We next find Bramah turning his attention to the invention of a lock that should surpass all others then known.
The locks then in use were of a very imperfect character,
easily picked by dexterous thieves, against whom they af-

forded little protection. Yet locks are a very ancient invention, though, as in many other cases, the art of making them seems in a great measure to have become lost, and accordingly had to be found out anew. Thus the tumbler lock—which consists in the use of moveable impediments acted on by the proper key only, as contradistinguished from the ordinary ward locks, where the impediments are fixed—appears to have been well known to the ancient Egyptians, the representation of such a lock being found sculptured among the bas-reliefs which decorate the great temple at Karnak. This kind of lock was revived, or at least greatly improved, by a Mr. Barron in 1774, and it was shortly after this time that Bramah directed his attention to the subject. After much study and many experiments, he contrived a lock more simple, more serviceable, as well as more secure, than Barron's, as is proved by the fact that it has stood the test of nearly eighty years' experience,* and still holds its ground. For a long time, indeed, Bramah's lock was regarded as absolutely inviolable, and it remained unpicked for sixty-seven years, until Hobbs the American mastered it in 1851. A notice had long been exhibited in Bramah's shop-window in Piccadilly, offering 200*l.* to any one who should succeed in picking the patent lock. Many tried, and all failed, until Hobbs succeeded, after sixteen days' manipulation of it with various elaborate instruments.

---

* The lock invented by Bramah was patented in 1784. Mr. Bramah himself fully set forth the specific merits of the invention in his *Dissertation on the Construction of Locks.* In a second patent, taken out by him in 1798, he amended his first with the object of preventing the counterfeiting of keys, and suspending the office of the lock until the key was again in the possession of the owner. This he effected by enabling the owner so to alter the sliders as to render the lock inaccessible to such key if applied by any other person but himself, or until the sliders had been rearranged so as to admit of its proper action. We may mention in passing that the security of Bramah's locks depends on the doctrine of combinations, or multiplication of numbers into each other, which is known to increase in the most rapid proportion. Thus, a lock of five slides admits of 3,000 variations, while one of eight will have no less than 1,935,360 changes; in other words, that number of attempts at making a key, or at picking it, may be made before it can be opened.

Lathe used by Charles Babbage (*by courtesy of the Science Museum*)

Planing machine by Richard Roberts, 1817 (*by courtesy of the Science Museum*)

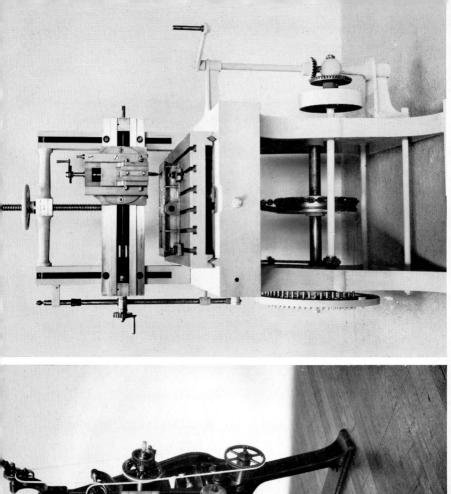

But the difficulty with which the lock was picked showed that, for all ordinary purposes, it might be pronounced impregnable.

The new locks were machines of the most delicate kind, the action of which depended in a great measure upon the precision with which the springs, sliders, levers, barrels, and other parts were finished. The merits of the invention being generally admitted, there was a considerable demand for the locks, and the necessity thus arose for inventing a series of original machine-tools to enable them to be manufactured in sufficient quantities to meet the demand. It is probable, indeed, that, but for the contrivance of such tools, the lock could never have come into general use, as the skill of hand-workmen, no matter how experienced, could not have been relied upon for turning out the article with that degree of accuracy and finish in all the parts which was indispensable for its proper action. In conducting the manufacture throughout, Bramah was greatly assisted by Henry Maudslay, his foreman, to whom he was in no small degree indebted for the contrivance of those tool-machines which enabled him to carry on the business of lock-making with advantage and profit.

Bramah's indefatigable spirit of invention was only stimulated to fresh efforts by the success of his lock ; and in the course of a few years we find him entering upon a more important and original line of action than he had yet ventured on. His patent of 1785 shows the direction of his studies. Watt had invented his steam-engine, which was coming into general use ; and the creation of motive-power in various other forms became a favourite subject of inquiry with inventors. Bramah's first invention with this object was his Hydrostatic Machine, founded on the doctrine of the equilibrium of pressure in fluids, as exhibited in the well known 'hydrostatic paradox.' In his patent of 1785, in which he no longer describes himself as 'Cabinet maker,' but 'Engine maker' of Piccadilly, he indicated many inventions, though none of them came into practical use,—such as a Hydrostatical Machine and Boiler, and the application of the power produced by them to the drawing of carriages, and the propelling of ships by a paddle-wheel fixed in the stern of the vessel, of which drawings are annexed to the specification ; but it was not until 1795 that he patented his Hydrostatic or Hydraulic Press.

Though the principle on which the Hydraulic Press is founded had long been known, and formed the subject of much curious speculation, it remained unproductive of results until a comparatively recent period, when the idea occurred of applying it to mechanical purposes. A machine of the kind was indeed proposed by Pascal, the eminent philosopher, in 1664, but more than a century elapsed before the difficulties in the way of its construction were satisfactorily overcome. Bramah's machine consists of a large and massive cylinder, in which there works an accurately-fitted solid piston or plunger. A forcing-pump of very small bore communicates with the bottom of the cylinder, and by the action of the pump-handle or lever, exceeding small quantities of water are forced in succession beneath the piston in the large cylinder, thus gradually raising it up, and compressing bodies whose bulk or volume it is intended to reduce. Hence it is most commonly used as a packing-press, being superior to every other contrivance of the kind that has yet been invented ; and though exercising a prodigious force, it is so easily managed that a boy can work it. The machine has been employed on many extraordinary occasions in preference to other methods of applying power. Thus Robert Stephenson used it to hoist the gigantic tubes of the Britannia Bridge into their bed,* and Brunel to launch the Great Eastern steamship from her cradles. It has also been used to cut bars of iron, to draw the piles driven in forming coffer dams, and to

---

* The weight raised by a single press at the Britannia Bridge was 1144 tons.

wrench up trees by the roots, all of which feats it accomplishes with comparative ease.

The principal difficulty experienced in constructing the hydraulic press before the time of Bramah arose from the tremendous pressure exercised by the pump, which forced the water through between the solid piston and the side of the cylinder in which it worked in such quantities as to render the press useless for practical purposes. Bramah himself was at first completely baffled by this difficulty. It will be observed that the problem was to secure a joint sufficiently free to let the piston slide up through it, and at the same time so water-tight as to withstand the internal force of the pump. These two conditions seemed so conflicting that Bramah was almost at his wit's end, and for a time despaired of being able to bring the machine to a state of practical efficiency. None but those who have occupied themselves in the laborious and often profitless task of helping the world to new and useful machines can have any idea of the tantalizing anxiety which arises from the apparently petty stumbling-blocks which for a while impede the realization of a great idea in mechanical invention. Such was the case with the water-tight arrangement in the hydraulic press. In his early experiments, Bramah tried the expedient of the ordinary stuffing-box for the purpose of securing the required water tightness. That is, a coil of hemp on leather washers was placed in a recess, so as to fit tightly round the moving ram or piston, and it was further held in its place by means of a compressing collar forced hard down by strong screws. The defect of this arrangement was, that, even supposing the packing could be made sufficiently tight to resist the passage of the water urged by the tremendous pressure from beneath, such was the grip which the compressed material took of the ram of the press, that it could not be got to return down after the water pressure had been removed.

In this dilemma, Bramah's ever-ready workman, Henry Maudslay, came to his rescue. The happy idea occurred to

him of employing the pressure of the water itself to give
the requisite water-tightness to the collar. It was a flash
of common-sense genius—beautiful through its very simplicity. The result was Maudslay's self-tightening collar, the
action of which a few words of description will render easily
intelligible. A collar of sound leather, the convex side upwards and the concave downwards, was fitted into the
recess turned out in the neck of the press-cylinder, at the
place formerly used as a stuffing-box. Immediately on the
high pressure water being turned on, it forced its way into
the leathern concavity and 'flapped out' the bent edges of
the collar; and, in so doing, caused the leather to apply
itself to the surface of the rising ram with a degree of
closeness and tightness so as to seal up the joint the closer
exactly in proportion to the pressure of the water in its
tendency to escape. On the other hand, the moment the
pressure was let off and the ram desired to return, the
collar collapsed and the ram slid gently down, perfectly
free and yet perfectly water-tight. Thus, the former tendency of the water to escape by the side of the piston was
by this most simple and elegant self-adjusting contrivance
made instrumental to the perfectly efficient action of the
machine; and from the moment of its invention the hydraulic press took its place as one of the grandest agents
for exercising power in a concentrated and tranquil form.

Bramah continued his useful labours as an inventor for
many years. His study of the principles of hydraulics, in
the course of his invention of the press, enabled him to
introduce many valuable improvements in pumping-machinery. By varying the form of the piston and cylinder
he was enabled to obtain a rotary motion,* which he

_____

* Dr. Thomas Young, in his article
on Bramah in the *Encyclopædia Britannica*, describes the "rotative principle" as consisting in making the
part which acts immediately on the
water in the form of a slider, sweeping
round a cylindrical cavity, and kept
in its place by means of an eccentric
groove; a contrivance which was probably Bramah's own invention, but
which had been before described, in
a form nearly similar, by Ramelli,
Canalleri, Amontons, Prince Rupert,
and Dr. Hooke.

advantageously applied to many purposes. Thus he adopted it in the well known fire-engine, the use of which has almost become universal. Another popular machine of his is the beer-pump, patented in 1797, by which the publican is enabled to raise from the casks in the cellar beneath, the various liquors sold by him over the counter. He also took out several patents for the improvement of the steam-engine, in which, however, Watt left little room for other inventors; and hence Bramah seems to have entertained a grudge against Watt, which broke out fiercely in the evidence given by him in the case of Boulton and Watt *versus* Hornblower and Maberly, tried in December 1796. On that occasion his temper seems to have got the better of his judgment, and he was cut short by the judge in the attempt which he then made to submit the contents of the pamphlet subsequently published by him in the form of a letter to the judge before whom the case was tried.* In that pamphlet he argued that Watt's specification had no definite meaning; that it was inconsistent and absurd, and could not possibly be understood; that the proposal to work steam-engines on the principle of condensation was entirely fallacious; that Watt's method of packing the piston was "monstrous stupidity;" that the engines of Newcomen (since entirely superseded) were infinitely superior, in all respects, to those of Watt;—conclusions which, we need scarcely say, have been refuted by the experience of nearly a century.

On the expiry of Boulton and Watt's patent, Bramah introduced several valuable improvements in the details of the condensing engine, which had by that time become an established power,—the most important of which was his "four-way cock," which he so arranged as to revolve continuously instead of alternately, thus insuring greater pre-

---

* *A Letter to the Right Hon. Sir James Eyre, Lord Chief Justice of the Common Pleas, on the subject of the cause Boulton and Watt v. Hornblower and Maberly, for Infringement on Mr. Watt's Patent for an Improvement of the Steam Engine.* By Joseph Bramah, Engineer. London, 1797.

cision with considerably less wear of parts. In the same
patent by which he secured this invention in 1801, he
also proposed sundry improvements in the boilers, as well
as modifications in various parts of the engine, with the
object of effecting greater simplicity and directness of
action.

In his patent of 1802, we find Bramah making another
great stride in mechanical invention, in his tools " for producing straight, smooth, and parallel surfaces on wood and
other materials requiring truth, in a manner much more
expeditious and perfect than can be performed by the use
of axes, saws, planes, and other cutting instruments used
by hand in the ordinary way." The specification describes
the object of the invention to be the saving of manual
labour, the reduction in the cost of production, and the
superior character of the work executed. The tools were
fixed on frames driven by machinery, some moving in a
rotary direction round an upright shaft, some with the
shaft horizontal like an ordinary wood-turning lathe, while
in others the tools were fixed on frames sliding in stationary grooves. A wood-planing machine * was constructed on the principle of this invention at Woolwich
Arsenal, where it still continues in efficient use. The axis
of the principal shaft was supported on a piston in a vessel
of oil, which considerably diminished the friction, and it
was so contrived as to be accurately regulated by means of
a small forcing-pump. Although the machinery described
in the patent was first applied to working on wood, it was
equally applicable to working on metals ; and in his own
shops at Pimlico Bramah employed a machine with revolving
cutters to plane metallic surfaces for his patent locks and
other articles. He also introduced a method of turning
spherical surfaces, either convex or concave, by a tool

---

* Sir Samuel Bentham and Marc
Isambard Brunel subsequently distinguished themselves by the invention of
wood-working machinery, full accounts
of which will be found in the Memoirs
of the former by Lady Bentham, and
in the Life of the latter by Mr.
Beamish.

moveable on an axis perpendicular to that of the lathe; and of cutting out concentric shells by fixing in a similar manner a curved tool of nearly the same form as that employed by common turners for making bowls. "In fact," says Mr. Mallet, "Bramah not only anticipated, but carried out upon a tolerably large scale in his own works—for the construction of the patent hydraulic press, the water-closet, and his locks—a surprisingly large proportion of our modern tools."* His remarkable predilection in favour of the use of hydraulic arrangements is displayed in his specification of the surface-planing machinery, which includes a method of running pivots entirely on a fluid, and raising and depressing them at pleasure by means of a small forcing-pump and stop-cock,—though we are not aware that any practical use has ever been made of this part of the invention.

Bramah's inventive genius displayed itself alike in small things as in great—in a tap wherewith to draw a glass of beer, and in a hydraulic machine capable of tearing up a tree by the roots. His powers of contrivance seemed inexhaustible, and were exercised on the most various subjects. When any difficulty occurred which mechanical ingenuity was calculated to remove, recourse was usually had to Bramah, and he was rarely found at a loss for a contrivance to overcome it. Thus, when applied to by the Bank of England in 1806, to construct a machine for more accurately and expeditiously printing the numbers and date lines on Bank notes, he at once proceeded to invent the requisite model, which he completed in the course of a month. He subsequently brought it to great perfection— the figures in numerical succession being changed by the action of the machine itself,—and it still continues in regular use. Its employment in the Bank of England alone saved the labour of a hundred clerks; but its chief value consisted in its greater accuracy, the perfect legibility of

---

* "Record of the International Exhibition, 1862." *Practical Mechanic's Journal*, 293.

the figures printed by it, and the greatly improved check which it afforded.

We next find him occupying himself with inventions connected with the manufacture of pens and paper. His little pen-making machine for readily making quill pens long continued in use, until driven out by the invention of the steel pen; but his patent for making paper by machinery, though ingenious, like everything he did, does not seem to have been adopted, the inventions of Fourdrinier and Donkin in this direction having shortly superseded all others. Among his other minor inventions may be mentioned his improved method of constructing and sledging carriage-wheels, and his improved method of laying water-pipes. In his specification of the last-mentioned invention, he included the application of water-power to the driving of machinery of every description, and for hoisting and lowering goods in docks and warehouses,—since carried out in practice, though in a different manner, by Sir William Armstrong.* In this, as in many other matters,

---

* In this, as in other methods of employing power, the moderns had been anticipated by the ancients; and though hydraulic machinery is a comparatively recent invention in England, it had long been in use abroad. Thus we find in Dr. Bright's *Travels in Lower Hungary* a full description of the powerful hydraulic machinery invented by M. Höll, Chief Engineer of the Imperial Mines, which had been in use since the year 1749, in pumping water from a depth of 1800 feet, from the silver and gold mines of Schemnitz and Kremnitz. A head of water was collected by forming a reservoir along the mountain side, from which it was conducted through water-tight cast-iron pipes erected perpendicularly in the mine-shaft. About forty-five fathoms down, the water descending through the pipe was forced by the weight of the column above it into the bottom of a perpendicular cylinder, in which it raised a water-tight piston. When forced up to a given point a self-acting stop-cock shut off the pressure of the descending column, while a self-acting valve enabled the water contained in the cylinder to be discharged, on which the piston again descended, and the process was repeated like the successive strokes of a steam-engine. Pump-rods were attached to this hydraulic apparatus, which were carried to the bottom of the shaft, and each worked a pump at different levels, raising the water stage by stage to the level of the main adit. The pumps of these three several stages each raised 1790 cubic feet of water from a depth of 600 feet in the hour. The regular working of the machinery was aided by the employment of a balance-beam connected by a chain with the head of the large piston and pump-rods; and

Bramah shot ahead of the mechanical necessities of his time; and hence many of his patents (of which he held at one time more than twenty) proved altogether profitless. His last patent, taken out in 1814, was for the application of Roman cement to timber for the purpose of preventing dry rot.

Besides his various mechanical pursuits, Bramah also followed to a certain extent the profession of a civil engineer, though his more urgent engagements rendered it necessary for him to refuse many advantageous offers of employment in this line. He was, however, led to carry out the new water-works at Norwich, between the years 1790 and 1793, in consequence of his having been called upon to give evidence in a dispute between the corporation of that city and the lessees, in the course of which he propounded plans which, it was alleged, could not be carried out. To prove that they could be carried out, and that his evidence was correct, he undertook the new works, and executed them with complete success; besides demonstrating in a spirited publication elicited by the controversy, the insufficiency and incongruity of the plans which had been submitted by the rival engineer.

For some time prior to his death Bramah had been employed in the erection of several large machines in his works at Pimlico for sawing stones and timber, to which he applied his hydraulic power with great success. New methods of building bridges and canal-locks, with a variety of other matters, were in an embryo state in his mind, but he did not live to complete them. He was occupied in

---

the whole of these powerful machines—by means of three of which as much as 789,840 gallons of water were pumped out of the mines every 24 hours—were set in operation and regulated merely by the turning of a stop-cock. It will be observed that the arrangement thus briefly described was equally applicable to the working of machinery of all kinds, cranes, &c., as well as pumps; and it will be noted that, notwithstanding the ingenuity of Bramah, Armstrong, and other eminent English mechanics, the Austrian engineer Höll was thus decidedly beforehand with them in the practical application of the principles of hydrostatics.

superintending the action of his hydrostatic press at Holt
Forest, in Hants—where upwards of 300 trees of the largest
dimensions were in a very short time torn up by the roots,—
when he caught a severe cold, which settled upon his
lungs, and his life was suddenly brought to a close on the
9th of December, 1814, in his 66th year.

His friend, Dr. Cullen Brown,* has said of him, that
Bramah was a man of excellent moral character, temperate
in his habits, of a pious turn of mind,† and so cheerful in
temperament, that he was the life of every company into
which he entered. To much facility of expression he

---

* Dr. Brown published a brief memoir of his friend in the *New Monthly
Magazine* for April, 1815, which has
been the foundation of all the notices
of Bramah's life that have heretofore
appeared.

† Notwithstanding his well-known
religious character, Bramah seems to
have fallen under the grievous dis-
pleasure of William Huntington, S.S.
(Sinner Saved), described by Macaulay
in his youth as " a worthless ugly lad
of the name of Hunter," and in his
manhood as " that remarkable im-
postor" (*Essays*, 1 vol. ed. 529). It
seems that Huntington sought the professional services of Bramah when re-
edifying his chapel in 1793 ; and at the
conclusion of the work, the engineer
generously sent the preacher a cheque
for 8*l.* towards defraying the necessary
expenses. Whether the sum was less
than Huntington expected, or from
whatever cause, the S. S. contemptu-
ously flung back the gift, as proceeding
from an Arian whose religion was " un-
savoury," at the same time hurling at
the giver a number of texts conveying epithets of an offensive character.
Bramah replied to the farrago of non-
sense, which he characterised as " un-
mannerly, absurd, and illiterate "—
that it must have been composed when
the writer was " intoxicated, mad, or
under the influence of Lucifer," and he

threatened that unless Huntington
apologised for his gratuitous insults,
he (Bramah) would assuredly expose
him. The mechanician nevertheless
proceeded gravely to explain and defend his " profession of faith," which
was altogether unnecessary. On this
Huntington returned to the charge,
and directed against the mechanic a
fresh volley of Scripture texts and
phraseology, not without humour, if
profanity be allowable in controversy,
as where he says, " Poor man ! he
makes a good patent lock, but cuts a
sad figure with the keys of the Kingdom
of Heaven !" " What Mr. Bramah
is," says S. S., " in respect to his character or conduct in life, as a man, a
tradesman, a neighbour, a gentleman,
a husband, friend, master, or subject, I
know not. In all these characters he
may shine as a comet for aught I
know ; but he appears to me to be as
far from any resemblance to a poor
penitent or broken-hearted sinner as
Jannes, Jambres, or Alexander the
coppersmith !" Bramah rejoined by
threatening to publish his assailant's
letters, but Huntington anticipated
him in *A Feeble Dispute with a Wise
and Learned Man*, 8vo. London,
1793, in which, whether justly or
not, Huntington makes Bramah appear to murder the king's English in
the most barbarous manner.

added the most perfect independence of opinion ; he was a benevolent and affectionate man ; neat and methodical in his habits, and knew well how to temper liberality with economy.   Greatly to his honour, he often kept his workmen employed, solely for their sake, when stagnation of trade prevented him disposing of the products of their labour.   As a manufacturer he was distinguished for his promptitude and probity, and he was celebrated for the exquisite finish which he gave to all his productions.   In this excellence of workmanship, which he was the first to introduce, he continued while he lived to be unrivalled.

Bramah was deservedly honoured and admired as the first mechanical genius of his time, and as the founder of the art of tool-making in its highest branches.   From his shops at Pimlico came Henry Maudslay, Joseph Clement, and many more first-class mechanics, who carried the mechanical arts to still higher perfection, and gave an impulse to mechanical engineering, the effects of which are still felt in every branch of industry.

The parish to which Bramah belonged was naturally proud of the distinction he had achieved in the world, and commemorated his life and career by a marble tablet erected by subscription to his memory, in the parish church of Silkstone.   In the churchyard are found the tombstones of Joseph's father, brother, and other members of the family ; and we are informed that their descendants still occupy the farm at Stainborough on which the great mechanician was born.

CHAPTER XII.

Henry Maudslay.

"The successful construction of all machinery depends on the perfection of the tools employed; and whoever is a master in the arts of toolmaking possesses the key to the construction of all machines. . . . . The contrivance and construction of tools must therefore ever stand at the head of the industrial arts."—C. Babbage, *Exposition of* 1851.

Henry Maudslay was born at Woolwich towards the end of last century, in a house standing in the court at the back of the Salutation Inn, the entrance to which is nearly opposite the Arsenal gates. His father was a native of Lancashire, descended from an old family of the same name, the head of which resided at Mawdsley Hall near Ormskirk at the beginning of the seventeenth century. The family were afterwards scattered, and several of its members became workmen. William Maudslay, the father of Henry, belonged to the neighbourhood of Bolton, where he was brought up to the trade of a joiner. His principal employment, while working at his trade in Lancashire, consisted in making the wood framing of cotton machinery, in the construction of which cast-iron had not yet been introduced. Having got into some trouble in his neighbourhood, through some alleged *liaison*, William enlisted in the Royal Artillery, and the corps to which he belonged was shortly after sent out to the West Indies. He was several times engaged in battle, and in his last action he was hit by a musket-bullet in the throat. The soldier's stock which he wore had a piece cut out of it by the ball, the direction of which was diverted, and though severely wounded, his life was saved. He brought home the stock and preserved it as a

relic, afterwards leaving it to his son. Long after, the son
would point to the stock, hung up against his wall, and say
" But for that bit of leather there would have been no Henry
Maudslay." The wounded artilleryman was invalided and
sent home to Woolwich, the headquarters of his corps,
where he was shortly after discharged. Being a handy
workman, he sought and obtained employment at the
Arsenal. He was afterwards appointed a storekeeper in
the Dockyard. It was during the former stage of William
Maudslay's employment at Woolwich, that the subject of
this memoir was born in the house in the court above
mentioned, on the 22nd of August, 1771.

The boy was early set to work. When twelve years old
he was employed as a " powder-monkey," in making and
filling cartridges. After two years, he was passed on to
the carpenter's shop where his father worked, and there
he became acquainted with tools and the art of working
in wood and iron. From the first, the latter seems to have
had by far the greatest charms for him. The blacksmiths'
shop was close to the carpenters', and Harry seized every
opportunity that offered of plying the hammer, the file, and
the chisel, in preference to the saw and the plane. Many
a cuff did the foreman of carpenters give him for absenting
himself from his proper shop and stealing off to the smithy.
His propensity was indeed so strong that, at the end of a
year, it was thought better, as he was a handy, clever boy,
to yield to his earnest desire to be placed in the smithy,
and he was removed thither accordingly in his fifteenth
year.

His heart being now in his work, he made rapid progress,
and soon became an expert smith and metal worker. He
displayed his skill especially in forging light ironwork ; and
a favourite job of his was the making of " Trivets " out
of the solid, which only the " dab hands " of the shop could
do, but which he threw off with great rapidity in first rate
style. These " Trivets " were made out of Spanish iron
bolts—rare stuff, which, though exceedingly tough, forged

like wax under the hammer. Even at the close of his life, when he had acquired eminent distinction as an inventor, and was a large employer of skilled labour, he looked back with pride to the forging of his early days in Woolwich Arsenal. He used to describe with much gusto, how the old experienced hands, with whom he was a great favourite, would crowd about him when forging his " Trivets," some of which may to this day be in use among Woolwich housewives for supporting the toast-plate before the bright fire against tea time. This was, however, entirely contraband work, done " on the sly," and strictly prohibited by the superintending officer, who used kindly to signal his approach by blowing his nose in a peculiar manner, so that all forbidden jobs might be put out of the way by the time he entered the shop.

We have referred to Maudslay's early dexterity in trivet-making—a circumstance trifling enough in itself—for the purpose of illustrating the progress which he had made in a branch of his art of the greatest importance in tool and machine making. Nothing pleased him more in his after life than to be set to work upon an unusual piece of forging, and to overcome, as none could do so cleverly as he, the difficulties which it presented. The pride of art was as strong in him as it must have been in the mediæval smiths, who turned out those beautiful pieces of workmanship, still regarded as the pride of our cathedrals and old mansions. In Maudslay's case, his dexterity as a smith was eventually directed to machinery, rather than ornamental work; though, had the latter been his line of labour, we do not doubt that he would have reached the highest distinction.

The manual skill which our young blacksmith had acquired was such as to give him considerable reputation in his craft, and he was spoken of even in the London shops as one of the most dexterous hands in the trade. It was this circumstance that shortly after led to his removal from the smithy in Woolwich Arsenal to a sphere more suitable for the development of his mechanical ability.

We have already stated in the preceding memoir, that Joseph Bramah took out the first patent for his lock in 1784, and a second for its improvement several years later; but notwithstanding the acknowledged superiority of the new lock over all others, Bramah experienced the greatest difficulty in getting it manufactured with sufficient precision, and at such a price as to render it an article of extensive commerce. This arose from the generally inferior character of the workmanship of that day, as well as the clumsiness and uncertainty of the tools then in use. Bramah found that even the best manual dexterity was not to be trusted, and yet it seemed to be his only resource; for machine-tools of a superior kind had not yet been invented. In this dilemma he determined to consult an ingenious old German artisan, then working with William Moodie, a general blacksmith in Whitechapel. This German was reckoned one of the most ingenious workmen in London at the time. Bramah had several long interviews with him, with the object of endeavouring to solve the difficult problem of how to secure precise workmanship in lock-making. But they could not solve it; they saw that without better tools the difficulty was insuperable; and then Bramah began to fear that his lock would remain a mere mechanical curiosity, and be prevented from coming into general use.

He was indeed sorely puzzled what next to do, when one of the hammermen in Moodie's shop ventured to suggest that there was a young man in the Woolwich Arsenal smithy, named Maudslay, who was so ingenious in such matters that "nothing bet him," and he recommended that Mr. Bramah should have a talk with him upon the subject of his difficulty. Maudslay was at once sent for to Bramah's workshop, and appeared before the lock-maker, a tall, strong, comely young fellow, then only eighteen years old. Bramah was almost ashamed to lay his case before such a mere youth; but necessity constrained him to try all methods of accomplishing his object, and Maudslay's suggestions in reply to his statement of the case were so modest, so sensible, and as the result proved, so practical, that the master was constrained to admit that the lad before him had an old head though set on young shoulders. Bramah decided to adopt the youth's suggestions, made him a present on the spot, and offered to give him a job if he was willing to come and work in a town shop. Maudslay gladly accepted the offer, and in due time appeared before Bramah to enter upon his duties.

As Maudslay had served no regular apprenticeship, and was of a very youthful appearance, the foreman of the shop had considerable doubts as to his ability to take rank alongside his experienced hands. But Maudslay soon set his master's and the foreman's mind at rest. Pointing to a worn-out vice-bench, he said to Bramah, " Perhaps if I can make that as good as new by six o'clock to-night, it will satisfy your foreman that I am entitled to rank as a tradesman and take my place among your men, even though I have not served a seven years' apprenticeship." There was so much self-reliant ability in the proposal, which was moreover so reasonable, that it was at once acceded to. Off went Maudslay's coat, up went his shirt sleeves, and to work he set with a will upon the old bench. The vice-jaws were re-steeled " in no time," filed up, re-cut, all the parts cleaned and made trim, and set into form again. By six o'clock, the old vice was screwed up to its place, its jaws were hardened and "let down" to proper temper, and the old bench was made to look so smart and neat that it threw all the neighbouring benches into the shade! Bramah and his foreman came round to see it, while the men of the shop looked admiringly on. It was examined and pronounced " a first-rate job." This diploma piece of work secured Maudslay's footing, and next Monday morning he came on as one of the regular hands.

He soon took rank in the shop as a first-class workman. Loving his art, he aimed at excellence in it, and succeeded. For it must be understood that the handicraftsman whose

30 James Nasmyth, 1808-1890 (by courtesy of the Science Museum)

29 Charles Babbage, 1791-1871 (by courtesy of the Science Museum)

PHOTOGRAPH of THE ORIGINAL DRAWING

OF MY STEAM HAMMER

James Nasmyt

31 A signed photograph by the inventor of James Nasmyth's original drawing of steam hammer dated November 24, 1839 (*by courtesy of the Science Museum*)

heart is in his calling, feels as much honest pride in turning out a piece of thoroughly good workmanship, as the sculptor or the painter does in executing a statue or a picture. In course of time, the most difficult and delicate jobs came to be entrusted to Maudslay; and nothing gave him greater pleasure than to be set to work upon an entirely new piece of machinery. And thus he rose, naturally and steadily, from hand to head work. For his manual dexterity was the least of his gifts. He possessed an intuitive power of mechanical analysis and synthesis. He had a quick eye to perceive the arrangements requisite to effect given purposes; and whenever a difficulty arose, his inventive mind set to work to overcome it.

His fellow-workmen were not slow to recognise his many admirable qualities, of hand, mind, and heart; and he became not only the favourite, but the hero of the shop. Perhaps he owed something to his fine personal appearance. Hence on gala-days, when the men turned out in procession, "Harry" was usually selected to march at their head and carry the flag. His conduct as a son, also, was as admirable as his qualities as a workman. His father dying shortly after Maudslay entered Bramah's concern, he was accustomed to walk down to Woolwich every Saturday night, and hand over to his mother, for whom he had the tenderest regard, a considerable share of his week's wages, and this he continued to do as long as she lived.

Notwithstanding his youth, he was raised from one post to another, until he was appointed, by unanimous consent, the head foreman of the works; and was recognised by all who had occasion to do business there as " Bramah's right-hand man." He not only won the heart of his master, but—what proved of far greater importance to him—he also won the heart of his master's pretty housemaid, Sarah Tindel by name, whom he married, and she went hand-in-hand with him through life, an admirable " help meet," in every way worthy of the noble character of the great mechanic.

Maudslay was found especially useful by his master in

devising the tools for making his patent locks; and many were the beautiful contrivances which he invented for the purpose of ensuring their more accurate and speedy manufacture, with a minimum degree of labour, and without the need of any large amount of manual dexterity on the part of the workman. The lock was so delicate a machine, that the identity of the several parts of which it was composed was found to be an absolute necessity. Mere handicraft, however skilled, could not secure the requisite precision of workmanship; nor could the parts be turned out in sufficient quantity to meet any large demand. It was therefore requisite to devise machine-tools which should not blunder, nor turn out imperfect work;—machines, in short, which should be in a great measure independent of the want of dexterity of individual workmen, but which should unerringly labour in their prescribed track, and do the work set them, even in the minutest details, after the methods designed by their inventor. In this department Maudslay was eminently successful, and to his laborious ingenuity, as first displayed in Bramah's workshops, and afterwards in his own establishment, we unquestionably owe much of the power and accuracy of our present self-acting machines.

Bramah himself was not backward in admitting that to Henry Maudslay's practical skill in contriving the machines for manufacturing his locks on a large scale, the success of his invention was in a great degree attributable. In further proof of his manual dexterity, it may be mentioned that he constructed with his own hands the identical padlock which so severely tested the powers of Mr. Hobbs in 1851. And when it is considered that the lock had been made for more than half a century, and did not embody any of the modern improvements, it will perhaps be regarded not only as creditable to the principles on which it was constructed, but to the workmanship of its maker, that it should so long have withstood the various mechanical dexterity to which it was exposed.

Besides the invention of improved machine-tools for the manufacture of locks, Maudslay was of further service to Bramah in applying the expedient to his famous Hydraulic Press, without which it would probably have remained an impracticable though a highly ingenious machine. As in other instances of great inventions, the practical success of the whole is often found to depend upon the action of some apparently trifling detail. This was especially the case with the hydraulic press; to which Maudslay added the essential feature of the self-tightening collar, above described in the memoir of Bramah. Mr. James Nasmyth is our authority for ascribing this invention to Maudslay, who was certainly quite competent to have made it; and it is a matter of fact that Bramah's specification of the press says nothing of the hollow collar,* on which its efficient action mainly depends. Mr. Nasmyth says—" Maudslay himself told me, or led me to believe, that it was he who invented the self-tightening collar for the hydraulic press, without which it would never have been a serviceable machine. As the self-tightening collar is to the hydraulic press, so is the steamblast to the locomotive. It is the one thing needful that has made it effective in practice. If Maudslay was the inventor of the collar, that one contrivance ought to immortalize him. He used to tell me of it with great gusto, and I have no reason to doubt the correctness of his statement." Whoever really struck out the idea of the collar, displayed the instinct of the true inventor, who invariably seeks to accomplish his object by the adoption of the simplest possible means.

During the time that Maudslay held the important office of manager of Bramah's works, his highest wages were not

---

* The words Bramah uses in describing this part of his patent of 1795 are these—" The piston must be made perfectly watertight by leather or other materials, as used in pump-making." He elsewhere speaks of the piston-rod " working through the stuffing-box." But in practice, as we have above shown, these methods were found to be altogether inefficient.

more than thirty shillings a-week. He himself thought
that he was worth more to his master—as indeed he was,—
and he felt somewhat mortified that he should have to
make an application for an advance; but the increasing
expenses of his family compelled him in a measure to do
so. His application was refused in such a manner as
greatly to hurt his sensitive feelings; and the result was
that he threw up his situation, and determined to begin
working on his own account.

His first start in business was in the year 1797, in a
small workshop and smithy situated in Wells Street, Oxford
Street. It was in an awful state of dirt and dilapidation
when he became its tenant. He entered the place on a
Friday, but by the Saturday evening, with the help of his
excellent wife, he had the shop thoroughly cleaned, white-
washed, and put in readiness for beginning work on the
next Monday morning. He had then the pleasure of
hearing the roar of his own forge-fire, and the cheering
ring of the hammer on his own anvil; and great was the
pride he felt in standing for the first time within his own
smithy and executing orders for customers on his own
account. His first customer was an artist, who gave him
an order to execute the iron work of a large easel, embodying some new arrangements; and the work was punc-
tually done to his employer's satisfaction. Other orders
followed, and he soon became fully employed. His fame
as a first-rate workman was almost as great as that of his
former master; and many who had been accustomed to do
business with him at Pimlico followed him to Wells Street.
Long years after, the thought of these early days of self-
dependence and hard work used to set him in a glow, and
he would dilate to his intimate friends upon his early
struggles and his first successes, which were much more
highly prized by him than those of his maturer years.

With a true love of his craft, Maudslay continued to
apply himself, as he had done whilst working as Bramah's
foreman, to the best methods of ensuring accuracy and

finish of work, so as in a measure to be independent of the carelessness or want of dexterity of the workman. With this object he aimed at the contrivance of improved machine-tools, which should be as much self-acting and self-regulating as possible ; and it was while pursuing this study that he wrought out the important mechanical invention with which his name is usually identified—that of the Slide Rest. It continued to be his special delight, when engaged in the execution of any piece of work in which he took a personal interest, to introduce a system of identity of parts, and to adapt for the purpose some one or other of the mechanical contrivances with which his fertile brain was always teeming. Thus it was from his desire to leave nothing to the chance of mere individual dexterity of hand that he introduced the slide rest in the lathe, and rendered it one of the most important of machine-tools. The first device of this kind was contrived by him for Bramah, in whose shops it continued in practical use long after he had begun business for himself. " I have seen the slide rest," says Mr. James Nasmyth, " the first that Henry Maudslay made, in use at Messrs. Bramah's workshops, and in it were all those arrangements which are to be found in the most modern slide rest of our own day,* all of which are the legitimate offspring of Maudslay's original rest. If this tool be yet extant, it ought to be preserved with the greatest care, for it was the beginning of those mechanical triumphs which give to the days in which we live so much of their distinguishing character."

A very few words of explanation will serve to illustrate the importance of Maudslay's invention. Every person is familiar with the uses of the common turning-lathe. It is

---

* In this lathe the slide rest and frame were moveable along the traversing-bar, according to the length of the work, and could be placed in any position and secured by a handle and screw underneath. The Rest, however, afterwards underwent many important modifications ; but the principle of the whole machine was there.

a favourite machine with amateur mechanics, and its employment is indispensable for the execution of all kinds of rounded work in wood and metal. Perhaps there is no contrivance by which the skill of the handicraftsman has been more effectually aided than by this machine. Its origin is lost in the shades of antiquity. Its most ancient form was probably the potter's wheel, from which it advanced, by successive improvements, to its present highly improved form. It was found that, by whatever means a substance capable of being cut could be made to revolve with a circular motion round a fixed right line as a centre, a cutting tool applied to its surface would remove the inequalities so that any part of such surface should be equidistant from that centre. Such is the fundamental idea of the ordinary turning-lathe. The ingenuity and experience of mechanics working such an instrument enabled them to add many improvements to it; until the skilful artisan at length produced not merely circular turning of the most beautiful and accurate description, but exquisite figure-work, and complicated geometrical designs, depending upon the cycloidal and eccentric movements which were from time to time added to the machine.

The artisans of the Middle Ages were very skilful in the use of the lathe, and turned out much beautiful screen and stall work, still to be seen in our cathedrals, as well as twisted and swash-work for the balusters of staircases and other ornamental purposes. English mechanics seem early to have distinguished themselves as improvers of the lathe; and in Moxon's 'Treatise on Turning,' published in 1680, we find Mr. Thomas Oldfield, at the sign of the Flower-de-Luce, near the Savoy in the Strand, named as an excellent maker of oval-engines and swash-engines, showing that such machines were then in some demand. The French writer Plumier * also mentions an ingenious modification of the lathe by means of which any kind of

---

* PLUMIER, *L'Art de Tourner*, Paris, 1754, p. 155.

reticulated form could be given to the work; and, from its being employed to ornament the handles of knives, it was called by him the "Machine à manche de Couteau d'Angleterre." But the French artisans were at that time much better skilled than the English in the use of tools, and it is most probable that we owe to the Flemish and French Protestant workmen who flocked into England in such large numbers during the religious persecutions of the sixteenth and seventeenth centuries, the improvement, if not the introduction, of the art of turning, as well as many other arts hereafter to be referred to. It is certain that at the period to which we refer numerous treatises were published in France on the art of turning, some of them of a most elaborate character. Such were the works of De la Hire,* who described how every kind of polygon might be made by the lathe; De la Condamine,† who showed how a lathe could turn all sorts of irregular figures by means of tracers; and of Grand Jean,‡ Morin,§ Plumier, Bergeron, and many other writers.

The work of Plumier is especially elaborate, entering into the construction of the lathe in its various parts, the making of the tools and cutters, and the different motions to be given to the machine by means of wheels, eccentrics, and other expedients, amongst which may be mentioned one very much resembling the slide rest and planing-machine combined.‖ From this work it appears that turning had long been a favourite pursuit in France with

---

* *Machines approuvées par l'Académie*, 1719.

† *Machines approuvées par l'Académie*, 1733.

‡ *Ibid.*

§ *L'Art de Tourner en perfection*, 49.

‖ It consisted of two parallel bars of wood or iron connected together at both extremities by bolts or keys of sufficient width to admit of the article required to be planed. A moveable frame was placed between the two bars, motion being given to it by a long cylindrical thread acting on any tool put into the sliding frame, and, consequently, causing the screw, by means of a handle at each end of it, to push or draw the point or cutting-edge of the tool either way. — Mr. George Rennie's Preface to Buchanan's *Practical Essays on Mill Work*, 3rd Ed. xli.

amateurs of all ranks, who spared no expense in the contrivance and perfection of elaborate machinery for the production of complex figures.* There was at that time a great passion for automata in France, which gave rise to many highly ingenious devices, such as Camus's miniature carriage (made for Louis XIV. when a child), Degennes' mechanical peacock, Vaucanson's duck, and Maillardet's conjuror. It had the effect of introducing among the higher order of artists habits of nice and accurate workmanship in executing delicate pieces of machinery; and the same combination of mechanical powers which made the steel spider crawl, the duck quack, or waved the tiny rod of the magician, contributed in future years to purposes of higher import,—the wheels and pinions, which in these automata almost eluded the human senses by their minuteness, reappearing in modern times in the stupendous mechanism of our self-acting lathes, spinning-mules, and steam-engines.

"In our own country," says Professor Willis, "the literature of this subject is so defective that it is very difficult to discover what progress we were making during the seventeenth and eighteenth centuries." † We believe the fact to be, that the progress made in England down to the end of last century had been very small indeed, and that

---

* Turning was a favourite amusement amongst the French nobles of last century, many of whom acquired great dexterity in the art, which they turned to account when compelled to emigrate at the Revolution. Louis XVI. himself was a very good locksmith, and could have earned a fair living at the trade. Our own George III. was a good turner, and was learned in wheels and treadles, chucks and chisels. Henry Mayhew says, on the authority of an old working turner, that, with average industry, the King might have made from 40s. to 50s. a-week as a hard wood and ivory turner. Lord John Hay, though one-armed, was an adept at the latter, and Lord Gray was another capital turner. Indeed the late Mr. Holtzapffel's elaborately illustrated treatise was written quite as much for amateurs as for working mechanics. Among other noble handicraftsmen we may mention the late Lord Douglas, who cultivated bookbinding. Lord Traquair's fancy was cutlery, and one could not come to him in a more welcome fashion than with a pair of old razors to set up.

† Professor WILLIS, *Lectures on the Results of the Great Exhibition of 1851*, 1st series, p. 306.

the lathe had experienced little or no improvement until Maudslay took it in hand. Nothing seems to have been known of the slide rest until he re-invented it, and applied it to the production of machinery of a far more elaborate character than had ever before been contemplated as possible. Professor Willis says that Bramah's, in other words Maudslay's, slide rest of 1794 is so different from that described in the French ' Encyclopédie' in 1772, that the two could not have had a common origin. We are therefore led to the conclusion that Maudslay's invention was entirely independent of all that had gone before, and that he contrived it for the special purpose of overcoming the difficulties which he himself experienced in turning out duplicate parts in large numbers. At all events, he was so early and zealous a promoter of its use, that we think he may, in the eyes of all practical mechanics, stand as the parent of its introduction to the workshops of England.

It is unquestionable that at the time when Maudslay began the improvement of machine-tools, the methods of working in wood and metals were exceedingly imperfect. Mr. William Fairbairn has stated that when he first became acquainted with mechanical engineering, about sixty years ago, there were no self-acting tools; everything was executed by hand. There were neither planing, slotting, nor shaping machines; and the whole stock of an engineering or machine establishment might be summed up in a few ill-constructed lathes, and a few drills and boring machines of rude construction.* Our mechanics were equally backward in contrivances for working in wood. Thus, when Sir Samuel Bentham made a tour through the manufacturing districts of England in 1791, he was surprised to find how little had been done to substitute the invariable accuracy of machinery for the uncertain dexterity of the human hand. Steam-power was as yet only

---

* Address delivered before the British Association at Manchester in 1861; and *Useful Information for Engineers,* 1st Series, p. 22.

employed in driving spinning-machines, rolling metals, pumping water, and such like purposes. In the working of wood no machinery had been introduced beyond the common turning-lathe and some saws, and a few boring tools used in making blocks for the navy. Even saws worked by inanimate force for slitting timber, though in extensive use in foreign countries, were nowhere to be found in Great Britain.* As everything depended on the dexterity of hand and correctness of eye of the workmen, the work turned out was of very unequal merit, besides being exceedingly costly. Even in the construction of comparatively simple machines, the expense was so great as to present a formidable obstacle to their introduction and extensive use; and but for the invention of machine-making tools, the use of the steam-engine in the various forms in which it is now applied for the production of power could never have become general.

In turning a piece of work on the old-fashioned lathe, the workman applied and guided his tool by means of muscular strength. The work was made to revolve, and the turner, holding the cutting tool firmly upon the long, straight, guiding edge of the rest, along which he carried it, and pressing its point firmly against the article to be turned, was thus enabled to reduce its surface to the required size and shape. Some dexterous turners were able, with practice and carefulness, to execute very clever pieces of work by this simple means. But when the article to be turned was of considerable size, and especially when it was of metal, the expenditure of muscular strength was so great that the workman soon became exhausted. The slightest variation in the pressure of the tool led to an irregularity of surface; and with the utmost care on the workman's part, he could not avoid occasionally cutting a little too deep, in consequence of which he must necessarily go over the surface again, to reduce the whole to

---

* *Life of Sir Samuel Bentham,* 97-8.

the level of that accidentally cut too deep ; and thus possibly the job would be altogether spoiled by the diameter
of the article under operation being made too small for its
intended purpose.

The introduction of the slide rest furnished a complete
remedy for this source of imperfection. The principle of
the invention consists in constructing and fitting the rest
so that, instead of being screwed down to one place, and
the tool in the hands of the workman travelling over it,
the rest shall itself hold the cutting tool firmly fixed in it,
and slide along the surface of the bench in a direction
exactly parallel with the axis of the work.   Before its
invention various methods had been tried with the object
of enabling the work to be turned true independent of the
dexterity of the workman.   Thus, a square steel cutter
used to be firmly fixed in a bed, along which it was
wedged from point to point of the work, and tolerable
accuracy was in this way secured.   But the slide rest was
much more easily managed, and the result was much more
satisfactory.   All that the workman had to do, after the
tool was firmly fitted into the rest, was merely to turn a
screw-handle, and thus advance the cutter along the face
of the work as required, with an expenditure of strength
so slight as scarcely to be appreciable.   And even this
labour has now been got rid of ; for, by an arrangement of
the gearing, the slide itself has been made self-acting, and
advances with the revolution of the work in the lathe,
which thus supplies the place of the workman's hand.
The accuracy of the turning done by this beautiful yet
simple arrangement is as mechanically perfect as work can
be.   The pair of steel fingers which hold the cutting tool
firmly in their grasp never tire, and it moves along the
metal to be cut with an accuracy and precision which the
human hand, however skilled, could never equal.

The effects of the introduction of the slide rest were
very shortly felt in all departments of mechanism. Though
it had to encounter some of the ridicule with which new

methods of working are usually received, and for a time was spoken of in derision as "Maudslay's Go-cart,"—its practical advantages were so decided that it gradually made its way, and became an established tool in all the best mechanical workshops. It was found alike capable of executing the most delicate and the most ponderous pieces of machinery ; and as slide-lathes could be manufactured to any extent, machinery, steam-engines, and all kinds of metal work could now be turned out in a quantity and at a price that, but for its use, could never have been practicable. In course of time various modifications of the machine were introduced—such as the planing machine, the wheel-cutting machine, and other beautiful tools on the slide-rest principle,—the result of which has been that extraordinary development of mechanical production and power which is so characteristic a feature of the age we live in.

"It is not, indeed, saying at all too much to state," says Mr. Nasmyth,* a most competent judge in such a matter, "that its influence in improving and extending the use of machinery has been as great as that produced by the improvement of the steam-engine in respect to perfecting manufactures and extending commerce, inasmuch as without the aid of the vast accession to our power of producing perfect mechanism which it at once supplied, we could never have worked out into practical and profitable forms the conceptions of those master minds who, during the last half century, have so successfully pioneered the way for mankind. The steam-engine itself, which supplies us with such unbounded power, owes its present perfection to this most admirable means of giving to metallic objects the most precise and perfect geometrical forms. How could we, for instance, have good steam-engines if we had not the means of boring out a true cylinder, or turning a true

---

* Remarks on the Introduction of the Slide Principle in Tools and Machines employed in the Production | of Machinery, in Buchanan's *Practical Essays on Mill Work and other Machinery.* 3rd ed. p. 397.

piston-rod, or planing a valve face ?   It is this alone which
has furnished us with the means of carrying into practice
the accumulated results of scientific investigation on mechanical subjects. It would be blamable indeed," continues Mr.
Nasmyth, " after having endeavoured to set forth the vast
advantages which have been conferred on the mechanical
world, and therefore on mankind generally, by the invention
and introduction of the Slide Rest, were I to suppress the
name of that admirable individual to whom we are indebted
for this powerful agent towards the attainment of mechanical perfection. I allude to Henry Maudslay, whose useful
life was enthusiastically devoted to the grand object of improving our means of producing perfect workmanship and
machinery : to him we are certainly indebted for the slide
rest, and, consequently, to say the least, we are indirectly
so for the vast benefits which have resulted from the introduction of so powerful an agent in perfecting our machinery
and mechanism generally. The indefatigable care which
he took in inculcating and diffusing among his workmen,
and mechanical men generally, sound ideas of practical
knowledge and refined views of construction, have rendered and ever will continue to render his name identified with all that is noble in the ambition of a lover of
mechanical perfection."

One of the first uses to which Mr. Maudslay applied the
improved slide rest, which he perfected shortly after beginning business in Margaret Street, Cavendish Square, was
in executing the requisite tools and machinery required by
Mr. (afterwards Sir Marc Isambard) Brunel for manufacturing ships' blocks. The career of Brunel was of a more
romantic character than falls to the ordinary lot of mechanical engineers. His father was a small farmer and post-
master, at the village of Hacqueville, in Normandy, where
Marc Isambard was born in 1769. He was early intended
for a priest, and educated accordingly. But he was much
fonder of the carpenter's shop than of the school; and
coaxing, entreaty, and punishment alike failed in making a

hopeful scholar of him.   He drew faces and plans until his
father was almost in despair.   Sent to school at Rouen, his
chief pleasure was in watching the ships along the quays;
and one day his curiosity was excited by the sight of some
large iron castings just landed.   What were they?   How
had they been made?   Where did they come from?   His
eager inquiries were soon answered.   They were parts of
an engine intended for the great Paris water-works; the
engine was to pump water by the power of steam; and the
castings had been made in England, and had just been
landed from an English ship.   " England!" exclaimed the
boy, " ah! when I am a man I will go see the country
where such grand machines are made!"   On one occasion,
seeing a new tool in a cutler's window, he coveted it so
much that he pawned his hat to possess it.   This was not
the right road to the priesthood; and his father soon saw
that it was of no use urging him further: but the boy's instinct proved truer than the father's judgment.

It was eventually determined that he should qualify
himself to enter the royal navy, and at seventeen he was
nominated to serve in a corvette as "volontaire d'hon-
neur."   His ship was paid off in 1792, and he was at Paris
during the trial of the King.   With the incautiousness of
youth he openly avowed his royalist opinions in the café
which he frequented.   On the very day that Louis was condemned to death, Brunel had an angry altercation with some
ultra-republicans, after which he called to his dog, "Viens,
citoyen!"   Scowling looks were turned upon him, and he
deemed it expedient to take the first opportunity of escaping from the house, which he did by a back-door, and made
the best of his way to Hacqueville.   From thence he went
to Rouen, and succeeded in finding a passage on board an
American ship, in which he sailed for New York, having
first pledged his affections to an English girl, Sophia
Kingdom, whom he had accidentally met at the house of
Mr. Carpentier, the American consul at Rouen.

Arrived in America, he succeeded in finding employ-

ment as assistant surveyor of a tract of land along the
Black River, near Lake Ontario.   In the intervals of his
labours he made occasional visits to New York, and it was
there that the first idea of his block-machinery occurred to
him.   He carried his idea back with him into the woods,
where it often mingled with his thoughts of Sophia Kingdom, by this time safe in England after passing through
the horrors of a French prison.   "My first thought of the
block-machinery," he once said, "was at a dinner party at
Major-General Hamilton's, in New York; my second under
an American tree, when, one day that I was carving letters
on its bark, the turn of one of them reminded me of it, and
I thought, 'Ah! my block! so it must be.'   And what do
you think were the letters I was cutting?   Of course none
other than S. K."   Brunel subsequently obtained some employment as an architect in New York, and promulgated
various plans for improving the navigation of the principal
rivers.   Among the designs of his which were carried out,
was that of the Park Theatre at New York, and a cannon
foundry, in which he introduced improvements in casting and boring big guns.   But being badly paid for his
work, and a powerful attraction drawing him constantly
towards England, he determined to take final leave of
America, which he did in 1799, and landed at Falmouth in
the following March.   There he again met Miss Kingdom,
who had remained faithful to him during his six long years
of exile, and the pair were shortly after united for life.

Brunel was a prolific inventor.   During his residence in
America, he had planned many contrivances in his mind,
which he now proceeded to work out.   The first was a
duplicate writing and drawing machine, which he patented.
The next was a machine for twisting cotton thread and
forming it into balls; but omitting to protect it by a
patent, he derived no benefit from the invention, though
it shortly came into very general use.   He then invented
a machine for trimmings and borders for muslins, lawns,
and cambrics,—of the nature of a sewing machine.   His

famous block-machinery formed the subject of his next
patent.

It may be explained that the making of the blocks em
ployed in the rigging of ships for raising and lowering
the sails, masts, and yards, was then a highly important
branch of manufacture. Some idea may be formed of the
number used in the Royal Navy alone, from the fact that a
74-gun ship required to be provided with no fewer than 1400
blocks of various sizes. The sheaved blocks used for the
running rigging consisted of the shell, the sheaves, which
revolved within the shell, and the pins which fastened them
together. The fabrication of these articles, though apparently simple, was in reality attended with much difficulty.
Every part had to be fashioned with great accuracy and
precision to ensure the easy working of the block when put
together, as any hitch in the raising or lowering of the
sails might, on certain emergencies, occasion a serious
disaster. Indeed, it became clear that mere hand-work
was not to be relied on in the manufacture of these articles,
and efforts were early made to produce them by means of
machinery of the most perfect kind that could be devised.
In 1781, Mr. Taylor, of Southampton, set up a large establishment on the river Itchen for their manufacture; and
on the expiry of his contract, the Government determined
to establish works of their own in Portsmouth Dockyard,
for the purpose at the same time of securing greater economy, and of being independent of individual makers in
the supply of an article of such importance in the equipment of ships.

Sir Samuel Bentham, who then filled the office of In-
spector-General of Naval Works, was a highly ingenious
person, and had for some years been applying his mind to
the invention of improved machinery for working in wood.
He had succeeded in introducing into the royal dock-
yards sawing-machines and planing-machines of a superior
kind, as well as block-making machines. Thus the specification of one of his patents, taken out in 1793, clearly

describes a machine for shaping the shells of the blocks, in a manner similar to that afterwards specified by Brunel. Bentham had even proceeded with the erection of a building in Portsmouth Dockyard for the manufacture of the blocks after his method, the necessary steam-engine being already provided; but with a singular degree of candour and generosity, on Brunel's method being submitted to him, Sir Samuel at once acknowledged its superiority to his own, and promised to recommend its adoption by the authorities in his department.

The circumstance of Mrs. Brunel's brother being Under-Secretary to the Navy Board at the time, probably led Brunel in the first instance to offer his invention to the Admiralty. A great deal, however, remained to be done before he could bring his ideas of the block-machinery into a definite shape; for there is usually a wide interval between the first conception of an intricate machine and its practical realization. Though Brunel had a good knowledge of mechanics, and was able to master the intricacies of any machine, he laboured under the disadvantage of not being a practical mechanic; and it is probable that but for the help of some one possessed of this important qualification, his invention, ingenious and important though it was, would have borne no practical fruits. It was at this juncture that he was so fortunate as to be introduced to Henry Maudslay, the inventor of the sliderest.

It happened that a M. de Bacquancourt, one of the French émigrés, of whom there were then so many in London, was accustomed almost daily to pass Maudslay's little shop in Wells-street, and being himself an amateur turner, he curiously inspected the articles from time to time exhibited in the window of the young mechanic. One day a more than ordinarily nice piece of screw-cutting made its appearance, on which he entered the shop to make inquiries as to the method by which it had been executed. He had a long conversation with Maudslay, with whom he was greatly pleased; and he was afterwards accustomed to look in upon him occasionally to see what new work was going on. Bacquancourt was also on intimate terms with Brunel, who communicated to him the difficulty he had experienced in finding a mechanic of sufficient dexterity to execute his design of the block-making machinery. It immediately occurred to the former that Henry Maudslay was the very man to execute work of the elaborate character proposed, and he described to Brunel the new and beautiful tools which Maudslay had contrived for the purpose of ensuring accuracy and finish. Brunel at once determined to call upon Maudslay, and it was arranged that Bacquancourt should introduce him, which he did, and after the interview which took place Brunel promised to call again with the drawings of his proposed model.

A few days passed, and Brunel called with the first drawing, done by himself; for he was a capital draughtsman, and used to speak of drawing as the "alphabet of the engineer." The drawing only showed a little bit of the intended machine, and Brunel did not yet think it advisable to communicate to Maudslay the precise object he had in view; for inventors are usually very chary of explaining their schemes to others, for fear of being anticipated. Again Brunel appeared at Maudslay's shop with a further drawing, still not explaining his design; but at the third visit, immediately on looking at the fresh drawings he had brought, Maudslay exclaimed, "Ah! now I see what you are thinking of; you want machinery for making blocks." At this Brunel became more communicative, and explained his designs to the mechanic, who fully entered into his views, and went on from that time forward striving to his utmost to work out the inventor's conceptions and embody them in a practical machine.

While still occupied on the models, which were begun in 1800, Maudslay removed his shop from Wells-street, where he was assisted by a single journeyman, to Margaret-street, Cavendish-square, where he had greater room for carrying on his trade, and was also enabled to increase

the number of his hands. The working models were ready
for inspection by Sir Samuel Bentham and the Lords of
the Admiralty in 1801, and having been fully approved
by them, Brunel was authorized to proceed with the execution of the requisite machinery for the manufacture of
the ships' blocks required for the Royal Navy. The whole
of this machinery was executed by Henry Maudslay ; it occupied him very fully for nearly six years, so that the
manufacture of blocks by the new process was not begun
until September, 1808.

We despair of being able to give any adequate description in words of the intricate arrangements and mode of
action of the block-making machinery. Let any one attempt to describe the much more simple and familiar process by which a shoemaker makes a pair of shoes, and he will
find how inadequate mere words are to describe any mechanical operation.* Suffice it to say, that the machinery was
of the most beautiful manufacture and finish, and even at
this day will bear comparison with the most perfect
machines which can be turned out with all the improved
appliances of modern tools. The framing was of cast-
iron, while the parts exposed to violent and rapid action
were all of the best hardened steel. In turning out the
various parts, Maudslay found his slide rest of indispensable
value. Indeed, without this contrivance, it is doubtful
whether machinery of so delicate and intricate a character
could possibly have been executed. There was not one,
but many machines in the series, each devoted to a special
operation in the formation of a block. Thus there were
various sawing-machines,—the Straight Cross-Cutting Saw,
the Circular Cross-Cutting Saw, the Reciprocating Ripping-
Saw, and the Circular Ripping-Saw. Then there were the

---

* So far as words and drawings can serve to describe the block-making machinery, it will be found very ably described by Mr. Farey in his article under this head in Rees's *Cyclopædia*, and by Dr. Brewster in the *Edinburgh Cyclopædia*. A very good account will also be found in Tomlinson's *Cyclopædia of the Useful Arts*, Art. " Block."

Boring Machines, and the Mortising Machine, of beautiful
construction, for cutting the sheave-holes, furnished with
numerous chisels, each making from 110 to 150 strokes a
minute, and cutting at every stroke a chip as thick as pasteboard with the utmost precision. In addition to these were
the Corner-Saw for cutting off the corners of the block,
the Shaping Machine for accurately forming the outside
surfaces, the Scoring Engine for cutting the groove round
the longest diameter of the block for the reception of the
rope, and various other machines for drilling, riveting, and
finishing the blocks, besides those for making the sheaves.

The total number of machines employed in the various operations of making a ship's block by the new method
was forty-four; and after being regularly employed in
Portsmouth Dockyard for upwards of fifty years, they are
still as perfect in their action as on the day they were
erected. They constitute one of the most ingenious and
complete collections of tools ever invented for making
articles in wood, being capable of performing most of the
practical operations of carpentry with the utmost accuracy
and finish. The machines are worked by a steam-engine
of 32-horse power, which is also used for various other
dockyard purposes. Under the new system of block-making it was found that the articles were better made, supplied with much greater rapidity, and executed at a greatly
reduced cost. Only ten men, with the new machinery,
could perform the work which before had required a
hundred and ten men to execute, and not fewer than
160,000 blocks of various kinds and sizes could be turned
out in a year, worth not less than 541,000l.*

---

* The remuneration paid to Mr.
Brunel for his share in the invention
was only one year's savings, which,
however, were estimated by Sir Samuel
Bentham at 17,663l.; besides which
a grant of 5000l. was afterwards made
to Brunel when labouring under pecuniary difficulties. But the *annual*
saving to the nation by the adoption
of the block-making machinery was
probably more than the entire sum
paid to the engineer. Brunel afterwards invented other wood-working
machinery, but none to compare in
merit and excellence with the above.
For further particulars of his career,
see BEAMISH's *Memoirs of Sir Marc
Isambard Brunel, C.E.* London, 1862.

The satisfactory execution of the block-machinery brought Maudslay a large accession of fame and business; and the premises in Margaret Street proving much too limited for his requirements, he again resolved to shift his quarters. He found a piece of ground suitable for his purpose in Westminster Road, Lambeth. Little more than a century since it formed part of a Marsh, the name of which is still retained in the adjoining street; its principal productions being bulrushes and willows, which were haunted in certain seasons by snipe and waterfowl. An enterprising riding-master had erected some premises on a part of the marsh, which he used for a riding-school; but the speculation not answering, they were sold, and Henry Maudslay became the proprietor. Hither he removed his machinery from Margaret Street in 1810, adding fresh plant from time to time as it was required; and with the aid of his late excellent partner he built up the far-famed establishment of Maudslay, Field, and Co. There he went on improving his old tools and inventing new ones, as the necessity for them arose, until the original slide-lathes used for making the block-machinery became thrown into the shade by the comparatively gigantic machine-tools of the modern school. Yet the original lathes are still to be found in the collection of the firm in Westminster Road, and continue to do their daily quota of work with the same precision as they did when turned out of the hands of their inventor and maker some sixty years ago.

It is unnecessary that we should describe in any great detail the further career of Henry Maudslay. The rest of his life was full of useful and profitable work to others as well as to himself. His business embraced the making of flour and saw mills, mint machinery, and steam-engines of all kinds. Before he left Margaret Street, in 1807, he took out a patent for improvements in the steam-engine, by which he much simplified its parts, and secured greater directness of action. His new engine was called the Pyramidal, because of its form, and was the first move towards what are now called Direct-acting Engines, in which the lateral movement of the piston is communicated by connecting-rods to the rotatory movement of the crank-shaft. Mr. Nasmyth says of it, that " on account of its great simplicity and *get-at-ability* of parts, its compactness and self-contained steadiness, this engine has been the parent of a vast progeny, all more or less marked by the distinguishing features of the original design, which is still in as high favour as ever."   Mr. Maudslay also directed his attention in like manner to the improvement of the marine engine, which he made so simple and effective as to become in a great measure the type of its class; and it has held its ground almost unchanged for nearly thirty years.   The ' Regent,' which was the first steamboat that plied between London and Margate, was fitted with engines by Maudslay in 1816; and it proved the forerunner of a vast number of marine engines, the manufacture of which soon became one of the most important branches of mechanical engineering.

Another of Mr. Maudslay's inventions was his machine for punching boiler-plates, by which the production of iron-work of many kinds was greatly facilitated.   This improvement originated in the contract which he held for some years for supplying the Royal Navy with iron plates for ships' tanks.   The operations of shearing and punching had before been very imperfectly done by hand, with great expenditure of labour.   To improve the style of the work and lessen the labour, Maudslay invented the machine now in general use, by which the holes punched in the iron plate are exactly equidistant, and the subsequent operation of riveting is greatly facilitated.   One of the results of the improved method was the great saving which was at once effected in the cost of preparing the plates to receive the rivets, the price of which was reduced from seven shillings per tank to ninepence.

He continued to devote himself to the last to the improvement of the lathe,—in his opinion the master-machine, the life and soul of engine-turning, of which the planing, screw-cutting, and other machines in common use, are but modifications.   In one of the early lathes which he contrived and made, the mandrill was nine inches in diameter; it was driven by wheel-gearing like a crane motion, and adapted to different speeds.   Some of his friends, on first looking at it, said he was going "too fast;" but he lived to see work projected on so large a scale as to prove that his conceptions were just, and that he had merely anticipated by a few years the mechanical progress of his time.   His large removeable bar-lathe was a highly important tool of the same kind.   It was used to turn surfaces many feet in diameter.   While it could be used for boring wheels, or the side-rods of marine engines, it could turn a roller or cylinder twice or three times the diameter of its own centres from the ground-level, and indeed could drive round work of any diameter that would clear the roof of the shop.   This was therefore an almost universal tool, capable of very extensive uses.   Indeed much of the work now executed by means of special tools, such as the planing or slotting machine, was then done in the lathe, which was used as a cutter-shaping machine, fitted with various appliances according to the work.

Maudslay's love of accuracy also led him from an early period to study the subject of improved screw-cutting. The importance of this department of mechanism can scarcely be overrated, the solidity and permanency of most mechanical structures mainly depending on the employment of the screw, at the same time that the parts can be readily separated for renewal or repair.   Any one can form an idea of the importance of the screw as an element in mechanical construction by examining say a steam-engine, and counting the number of screws employed in holding it together.   Previous to the time at which the subject occupied the attention of our mechanic, the tools used for making screws were of the most rude and inexact kind.   The screws were for the most part cut by hand: the

small by filing, the larger by chipping and filing. In consequence of the great difficulty of making them, as few were
used as possible; and cotters, cotterils, or forelocks, were
employed in stead. Screws, however, were to a certain
extent indispensable; and each manufacturing establishment made them after their own fashion. There was an
utter want of uniformity. No system was observed as to
" pitch," *i. e.* the number of threads to the inch, nor was
any rule followed as to the form of those threads. Every
bolt and nut was a sort of specialty in itself, and neither
owed nor admitted of any community with its neighbours.
To such an extent was this irregularity carried, that all
bolts and their corresponding nuts had to be marked as
belonging to each other; and any mixing of them together
led to endless trouble, hopeless confusion, and enormous
expense. Indeed none but those who lived in the comparatively early days of machine-manufacture can form an adequate idea of the annoyance occasioned by the want of
system in this branch of detail, or duly appreciate the
services rendered by Maudslay to mechanical engineering
by the practical measures which he was among the first to
introduce for its remedy. In his system of screw-cutting
machinery, his taps and dies, and screw-tackle generally,
he laid the foundations of all that has since been done in
this essential branch of machine-construction, in which he
was so ably followed up by several of the eminent mechanics brought up in his school, and more especially by
Joseph Clement and Joseph Whitworth. One of his earliest
self-acting screw lathes, moved by a guide-screw and wheels
after the plan followed by the latter engineer, cut screws
of large diameter and of any required pitch. As an illustration of its completeness and accuracy, we may mention
that by its means a screw five feet in length, and two inches
in diameter, was cut with fifty threads to the inch; the nut
to fit on to it being twelve inches long, and containing six
hundred threads. This screw was principally used for dividing scales for astronomical purposes; and by its means

divisions were produced so minute that they could not be detected without the aid of a magnifier. The screw, which was sent for exhibition to the Society of Arts, is still carefully preserved amongst the specimens of Maudslay's handicraft at the Lambeth Works, and is a piece of delicate work which every skilled mechanic will thoroughly appreciate. Yet the tool by which this fine piece of turning was produced was not an exceptional tool, but was daily employed in the ordinary work of the manufactory.

Like every good workman who takes pride in his craft, he kept his tools in first-rate order, clean, and tidily arranged, so that he could lay his hand upon the thing he wanted at once, without loss of time. They are still preserved in the state in which he left them, and strikingly illustrate his love of order, "nattiness," and dexterity. Mr. Nasmyth says of him that you could see the man's character in whatever work he turned out; and as the connoisseur in art will exclaim at sight of a picture, "That is Turner," or "That is Stansfield," detecting the hand of the master in it, so the experienced mechanician, at sight of one of his machines or engines, will be equally ready to exclaim, "That is Maudslay;" for the characteristic style of the master-mind is as clear to the experienced eye in the case of the finished machine as the touches of the artist's pencil are in the case of the finished picture. Every mechanical contrivance that became the subject of his study came forth from his hand and mind rearranged, simplified, and made new, with the impress of his individuality stamped upon it. He at once stripped the subject of all unnecessary complications; for he possessed a wonderful faculty of *knowing what to do without*—the result of his clearness of insight into mechanical adaptations, and the accurate and well-defined notions he had formed of the precise object to be accomplished. "Every member or separate machine in the system of block-machinery," says Mr. Nasmyth, "is full of Maudslay's presence; and in that machinery, as constructed by him, is to be found the parent of every engineering tool by the aid of which we are now achieving such great things in mechanical construction. To the tools of which Maudslay furnished the prototypes are we mainly indebted for the perfection of our textile machinery, our locomotives, our marine engines, and the various implements of art, of agriculture, and of war. If any one who can enter into the details of this subject will be at the pains to analyse, if I may so term it, the machinery of our modern engineering workshops, he will find in all of them the strongly-marked features of Maudslay's parent machine, the slide rest and slide system — whether it be a planing machine, a slotting machine, a slide-lathe, or any other of the wonderful tools which are now enabling us to accomplish so much in mechanism."

One of the things in which Mr. Maudslay took just pride was in the excellence of his work. In designing and executing it, his main object was to do it in the best possible style and finish, altogether irrespective of the probable pecuniary results. This he regarded in the light of a duty he could not and would not evade, independent of its being a good investment for securing a future reputation ; and the character which he thus obtained, although at times purchased at great cost, eventually justified the soundness of his views. As the eminent Mr. Penn, the head of the great engineering firm, is accustomed to say, " I cannot afford to turn out second-rate work," so Mr. Maudslay found both character and profit in striving after the highest excellence in his productions. He was particular even in the minutest details. Thus one of the points on which he insisted—apparently a trivial matter, but in reality of considerable importance in mechanical construction—was the avoidance of sharp interior angles in ironwork, whether wrought or cast; for he found that in such interior angles cracks were apt to originate ; and when the article was a tool, the sharp angle was less pleasant to the hand as well as to the eye. In the application of his favourite round or hollow corner system—as, for instance, in the case of the points of junction of the arms of a wheel with its centre and rim—he used to illustrate its superiority by holding up his hand and pointing out the nice rounded hollow at the junction of the fingers, or by referring to the junction of the branches to the stem of a tree. Hence he made a point of having all the angles of his machine frame-work nicely rounded off on their exterior, and carefully hollowed in their interior angles. In forging such articles he would so shape his metal before bending that the result should be the right hollow or rounded corner when bent; the anticipated external angle falling into its proper place when the bar so shaped was brought to its ultimate form. In all such matters of detail he was greatly assisted by his early dexterity as a blacksmith; and he used to say that to be a good smith you must be able to *see* in the bar of iron the object proposed to be got out of it by the hammer or the tool, just as the sculptor is supposed to see in the block of stone the statue which he proposes to bring forth from it by his mind and his chisel.

Mr. Maudslay did not allow himself to forget his skill in the use of the hammer, and to the last he took pleasure in handling it, sometimes in the way of business, and often through sheer love of his art. Mr. Nasmyth says, " It was one of my duties, while acting as assistant in his beautiful little workshop, to keep up a stock of handy bars of lead which he had placed on a shelf under his work-bench, which was of thick slate for the more ready making of his usual illustrative sketches of machinery in chalk. His love of iron-forging led him to take delight in forging the models of work to be ultimately done in iron; and cold lead being of about the same malleability as red-hot iron, furnished a convenient material for illustrating the method to be adopted with the large work. I well remember the smile of satisfaction that lit up his honest face when he met with a good excuse for ' having a go at ' one of the bars of lead with hammer and anvil as if it were a bar of iron; and

how, with a few dexterous strokes, punchings of holes, and
rounded notches, he would give the rough bar or block its
desired form. He always aimed at working it out of the
solid as much as possible, so as to avoid the risk of any
concealed defect, to which ironwork built up of welded
parts is so liable ; and when he had thus cleverly finished
his model, he used forthwith to send for the foreman of
smiths, and show him how he was to instruct his men as
to the proper forging of the desired object."   One of Mr.
Maudslay's old workmen, when informing us of the skilful
manner in which he handled the file, said, "It was a pleasure
to see him handle a tool of any kind, but he was *quite
splendid* with an eighteen-inch file!"   The vice at which
he worked was constructed by himself, and it was perfect
of its kind.   It could be turned round to any position on
the bench ; the jaws would turn from the horizontal to the
perpendicular or any other position—upside-down if necessary—and they would open twelve inches parallel.

Mr. Nasmyth furnishes the following further recollections of Mr. Maudslay, which will serve in some measure
to illustrate his personal character.   "Henry Maudslay,"
he says, "lived in the days of snuff-taking, which unhappily, as I think, has given way to the cigar-smoking
system.   He enjoyed his occasional pinch very much.
It generally preceded the giving out of a new notion or
suggestion for an improvement or alteration of some job in
hand.   As with most of those who enjoy their pinch, about
three times as much was taken between the fingers as was
utilized by the nose, and the consequence was that a large
unconsumed surplus collected in the folds of the master's
waistcoat as he sat working at his bench.   Sometimes a
file, or a tool, or some small piece of work would drop, and
then it was my duty to go down on my knees and fetch it
up.   On such occasions, while waiting for the article, he
would take the opportunity of pulling down his waistcoat
front, which had become disarranged by his energetic
working at the bench ; and many a time have I come up

with the dropped article, half-blinded by the snuff jerked into my eyes from off his waistcoat front.

"All the while he was at work he would be narrating some incident in his past life, or describing the progress of some new and important undertaking, in illustrating which he would use the bit of chalk ready to his hand upon the slate bench before him, which was thus in almost constant use. One of the pleasures he indulged in while he sat at work was Music, of which he was very fond,—more particularly of melodies and airs which took a lasting hold on his mind. Hence he was never without an assortment of musical boxes, some of which were of a large size. One of these he would set agoing on his library table, which was next to his workshop, and with the door kept open, he was thus enabled to enjoy the music while he sat working at his bench. Intimate friends would frequently call upon him and sit by the hour, but though talking all the while he never dropped his work, but continued employed on it with as much zeal as if he were only beginning life. His old friend Sir Samuel Bentham was a frequent caller in this way, as well as Sir Isambard Brunel while occupied with his Thames Tunnel works,* and Mr. Chantrey, who was accustomed to consult him about the casting of his bronze statuary. Mr. Barton of the Royal Mint, and Mr. Donkin the engineer, with whom Mr. Barton was associated in ascertaining and devising a correct system of dividing the Standard Yard, and many others, had like audience of Mr. Maudslay in his little workshop, for friendly converse, for advice, or on affairs of business.

"It was a special and constant practice with him on a workman's holiday, or on a Sunday morning, to take a walk through his workshops when all was quiet, and then

---

* Among the last works executed by the firm during Mr. Maudslay's lifetime was the famous Shield employed by his friend Brunel in carrying forward the excavation of the Thames Tunnel. He also supplied the pumping-engines for the same great work, the completion of which he did not live to see.

and there examine the various jobs in hand. On such occasions he carried with him a piece of chalk, with which, in a neat and very legible hand, he would record his remarks in the most pithy and sometimes caustic terms. Any evidence of want of correctness in setting things square, or in 'flat filing,' which he held in high esteem, or untidiness in not sweeping down the bench and laying the tools in order, was sure to have a record in chalk made on the spot. If it was a mild case, the reproof was recorded in gentle terms, simply to show that the master's eye was on the workman; but where the case deserved hearty approbation or required equally hearty reproof, the words employed were few, but went straight to the mark. These chalk jottings on the bench were held in the highest respect by the workmen themselves, whether they conveyed praise or blame, as they were sure to be deserved; and when the men next assembled, it soon became known all over the shop who had received the honour or otherwise of one of the master's bench memoranda in chalk."

The vigilant, the critical, and yet withal the generous eye of the master being over all his workmen, it will readily be understood how Maudslay's works came to be regarded as a first-class school for mechanical engineers. Every one felt that the quality of his workmanship was fully understood; and, if he had the right stuff in him, and was determined to advance, that his progress in skill would be thoroughly appreciated. It is scarcely necessary to point out how this feeling, pervading the establishment, must have operated, not only in maintaining the quality of the work, but in improving the character of the workmen. The results were felt in the increased practical ability of a large number of artisans, some of whom subsequently rose to the highest distinction. Indeed it may be said that what Oxford and Cambridge are in letters, workshops such as Maudslay's and Penn's are in mechanics. Nor can Oxford and Cambridge men be prouder of the connection with their respective colleges than mechanics such as Whitworth,

Nasmyth, Roberts, Muir, and Lewis, are of their connection with the school of Maudslay. For all these distinguished engineers at one time or another formed part of his working staff, and were trained to the exercise of their special abilities under his own eye. The result has been a development of mechanical ability the like of which perhaps is not to be found in any age or country.

Although Mr. Maudslay was an unceasing inventor, he troubled himself very little about patenting his inventions. He considered that the superiority of his tools and the excellence of his work were his surest protection. Yet he had sometimes the annoyance of being threatened with actions by persons who had patented the inventions which he himself had made.* He was much beset by inventors, sometimes sadly out at elbows, but always with a boundless fortune looming before them. To such as applied to him for advice in a frank and candid spirit, he did not hesitate to speak freely, and communicate the results of his great experience in the most liberal manner; and to poor and deserving men of this class he was often found as ready to help them with his purse as with his still more valuable advice. He had a singular way of estimating the abilities of those who thus called upon him about their projects. The highest order of man was marked in his own mind at 100°; and by this ideal standard he measured others, setting them down at 90°, 80°, and so on. A very first-rate man he would set down at 95°, but men of this rank were exceedingly rare. After an interview with one of the applicants to him for advice, he would say to

---

* His principal patents were—two, taken out in 1805 and 1808, while in Margaret Street, for printing calicoes (Nos. 2872 and 3117); one taken out in 1806, in conjunction with Mr. Donkin, for lifting heavy weights (2948); one taken out in 1807, while still in Margaret Street, for improvements in the steam-engine, reducing its parts and rendering it more compact and portable (3050); another, taken out in conjunction with Robert Dickinson in 1812, for sweetening water and other liquids (3538); and, lastly, a patent taken out in conjunction with Joshua Field in 1824 for preventing concentration of brine in boilers (5021).

his pupil Nasmyth, " Jem, I think that man may be set down at 45°, but he might be *worked up to* 60°"—a common enough way of speaking of the working of a steam-engine, but a somewhat novel though by no means an inexpressive method of estimating the powers of an individual.

But while he had much toleration for modest and meritorious inventors, he had a great dislike for secret-mongers, —schemers of the close, cunning sort,—and usually made short work of them. He had an almost equal aversion for what he called the " fiddle-faddle inventors," with their omnibus patents, into which they packed every possible thing that their noddles could imagine. " Only once or twice in a century," said he, " does a great inventor appear, and yet here we have a set of fellows each taking out as many patents as would fill a cart,— some of them embodying not a single original idea, but including in their specifications all manner of modifications of well-known processes, as well as anticipating the arrangements which may become practicable in the progress of mechanical improvement." Many of these " patents " he regarded as mere pit-falls to catch the unwary ; and he spoke of such " inventors " as the pests of the profession.

The personal appearance of Henry Maudslay was in correspondence with his character. He was of a commanding presence, for he stood full six feet two inches in height, a massive and portly man. His face was round, full, and lit up with good humour. A fine, large, and square forehead, of the grand constructive order, dominated over all, and his bright keen eye gave energy and life to his countenance. He was thoroughly " jolly " and good-natured, yet full of force and character. It was a positive delight to hear his cheerful, ringing laugh. He was cordial in manner, and his frankness set everybody at their ease who had occasion to meet him, even for the first time. No one could be more faithful and consistent in his friendships, nor more firm in the hour of adversity. In fine, Henry Maudslay was, as described by his friend

Mr. Nasmyth, the very beau ideal of an honest, upright, straight-forward, hard-working, intelligent Englishman.

A severe cold which he caught on his way home from one of his visits to France, was the cause of his death, which occurred on the 14th of February, 1831. The void which his decease caused was long and deeply felt, not only by his family and his large circle of friends, but by his workmen, who admired him for his industrial skill, and loved him because of his invariably manly, generous, and upright conduct towards them. He directed that he should be buried in Woolwich parish-churchyard, where a cast-iron tomb, made to his own design, was erected over his remains. He had ever a warm heart for Woolwich, where he had been born and brought up. He often returned to it, sometimes to carry his mother a share of his week's wages while she lived, and afterwards to refresh himself with a sight of the neighbourhood with which he had been so familiar when a boy. He liked its green common, with the soldiers about it; Shooter's Hill, with its out-look over Kent and down the valley of the Thames; the river busy with shipping, and the royal craft loading and unloading their armaments at the dockyard wharves. He liked the clangour of the Arsenal smithy where he had first learned his art, and all the busy industry of the place. It was natural, therefore, that, being proud of his early connection with Woolwich, he should wish to lie there; and Woolwich, on its part, let us add, has equal reason to be proud of Henry Maudslay.

CHAPTER XIII.

Joseph Clement.

> "It is almost impossible to over-estimate the importance of these inventions. The Greeks would have elevated their authors among the gods; nor will the enlightened judgment of modern times deny them the place among their fellow-men which is so undeniably their due."—*Edinburgh Review.*

THAT skill in mechanical contrivance is a matter of education and training as well as of inborn faculty, is clear from the fact of so many of our distinguished mechanics undergoing the same kind of practical discipline, and perhaps still more so from the circumstance of so many of them passing through the same workshops. Thus Maudslay and Clement were trained in the workshops of Bramah; and Roberts, Whitworth, Nasmyth, and others, were trained in those of Maudslay.

Joseph Clement was born at Great Ashby in Westmoreland, in the year 1779. His father was a hand-loom weaver, and a man of remarkable culture considering his humble station in life. He was an ardent student of natural history, and possessed a much more complete knowledge of several sub-branches of that science than was to have been looked for in a common working-man. One of the departments which he specially studied was Entomology. In his leisure hours he was accustomed to traverse the country searching the hedge-bottoms for beetles and other insects, of which he formed a remarkably complete collection; and the capture of a rare specimen was quite an event in his life. In order more deliberately to study the habits of the bee tribe, he had a number of hives constructed for the purpose of enabling him to watch their proceedings without leaving his work; and the pursuit was a source of the greatest pleasure to him. He was a lover of all dumb creatures; his cottage was haunted by birds which flew in and out at his door, and some of them became so tame as to hop up to him and feed out of his hand. " Old Clement " was also a bit of a mechanic, and such of his leisure moments as he did not devote to insect-hunting, were employed in working a lathe of his own construction, which he used to turn his bobbins on, and also in various kinds of amateur mechanics.

His boy Joseph, like other poor men's sons, was early set to work. He received very little education, and learnt only the merest rudiments of reading and writing at the village school. The rest of his education he gave to himself as he grew older. His father needed his help at the loom, where he worked with him for some years; but, as handloom weaving was gradually being driven out by improved mechanism, the father prudently resolved to put his son to a better trade. They have a saying in Cumberland that when the bairns reach a certain age, they are thrown on to the house-rigg, and that those who stick on are made thatchers of, while those who fall off are sent to St. Bees to be made parsons of. Joseph must have been one of those that stuck on—at all events his father decided to make him a thatcher, afterwards a slater, and he worked at that trade for five years, between eighteen and twenty-three.

The son, like the father, had a strong liking for mechanics, and as the slating trade did not keep him in regular employment, especially in winter time, he had plenty of opportunity for following the bent of his inclinations. He made a friend of the village blacksmith, whose smithy he was accustomed to frequent, and there he learned to work at the forge, to handle the hammer and file, and in a short time to shoe horses with considerable expertness. A cousin of his named Farer, a clock and watchmaker by trade,

having returned to the village from London, brought with
him some books on mechanics, which he lent to Joseph to
read; and they kindled in him an ardent desire to be a
mechanic instead of a slater.   He nevertheless continued
to maintain himself by the latter trade for some time
longer, until his skill had grown; and, by way of cultivating it, he determined, with the aid of his friend the village
blacksmith, to make a turning-lathe.   The two set to work,
and the result was the production of an article in every
way superior to that made by Clement's father, which was
accordingly displaced to make room for the new machine.
It was found to work very satisfactorily, and by its means
Joseph proceeded to turn fifes, flutes, clarinets, and haut-
boys; for to his other accomplishments he joined that of
music, and could play upon the instruments that he made.
One of his most ambitious efforts was the making of a
pair of Northumberland bagpipes, which he finished to his
satisfaction, and performed upon to the great delight of the
villagers.   To assist his father in his entomological studies,
he even contrived, with the aid of the descriptions given in
the books borrowed from his cousin the watchmaker, to
make for him a microscope, from which he proceeded to
make a reflecting telescope, which proved a very good
instrument.   At this early period (1804) he also seems to
have directed his attention to screw-making—a branch of
mechanics in which he afterwards became famous; and he
proceeded to make a pair of very satisfactory die-stocks,
though it is said that he had not before seen or even heard
of such a contrivance for making screws.

So clever a workman was not likely to remain long a
village slater.   Although the ingenious pieces of work
which he turned out by his lathe did not bring him in
much money, he liked the occupation so much better than
slating that he was gradually giving up that trade.   His
father urged him to stick to slating as "a safe thing;" but
his own mind was in favour of following his instinct to be
a mechanic; and at length he determined to leave his village

and seek work in a new line. He succeeded in finding
employment in a small factory at Kirby Stephen, a town
some thirteen miles from Great Ashby, where he worked
at making power-looms. From an old statement of account
against his employer which we have seen, in his own
handwriting, dated the 6th September, 1805, it appears that
his earnings at such work as "fitting the first set of iron
loames," "fitting up shittles," and "making moddles," were
3s. 6d. a day; and he must, during the same time, have
lived with his employer, who charged him as a set-off "14
weaks bord at 8s. per weak." He afterwards seems to have
worked at piece-work in partnership with one Andrew
Camble—supplying the materials as well as the workmanship for the looms and shuttles. His employer, Mr. George
Dickinson, also seems to have bought his reflecting telescope from him for the sum of 12l.

From Kirby Stephen Clement removed to Carlisle, where
he was employed by Forster and Sons during the next
two years at the same description of work; and he conducted himself, according to their certificate on his leaving
their employment to proceed to Glasgow in 1807, "with
great sobriety and industry, entirely to their satisfaction."
While working at Glasgow as a turner, he took lessons in
drawing from Peter Nicholson, the well-known writer on
carpentry—a highly ingenious man. Nicholson happened
to call at the shop at which Clement worked in order to
make a drawing of a power-loom; and Clement's expres-
sions of admiration at his expertness were so enthusiastic,
that Nicholson, pleased with the youth's praise, asked if he
could be of service to him in any way. Emboldened by
the offer, Clement requested, as the greatest favour he
could confer upon him, to have the loan of the drawing he
had just made, in order that he might copy it. The request
was at once complied with; and Clement, though very poor
at the time, and scarcely able to buy candle for the long
winter evenings, sat up late every night until he had
finished it. Though the first drawing he had ever made,

he handed it back to Nicholson instead of the original, and at first the draughtsman did not recognise that the drawing was not his own. When Clement told him that it was only the copy, Nicholson's brief but emphatic praise was— "Young man, *you'll do!*" Proud to have such a pupil, Nicholson generously offered to give him gratuitous lessons in drawing, which were thankfully accepted; and Clement, working at nights with great ardour, soon made rapid progress, and became an expert draughtsman.

Trade being very slack in Glasgow at the time, Clement, after about a year's stay in the place, accepted a situation with Messrs. Leys, Masson, and Co., of Aberdeen, with whom he began at a guinea and a half a week, from which he gradually rose to two guineas, and ultimately to three guineas. His principal work consisted in designing and making power-looms for his employers, and fitting them up in different parts of the country. He continued to devote himself to the study of practical mechanics, and made many improvements in the tools with which he worked. While at Glasgow he had made an improved pair of die-stocks for screws; and, at Aberdeen, he made a turning-lathe with a sliding mandrill and guide-screws, for cutting screws, furnished also with the means for correcting guide-screws. In the same machine he introduced a small slide rest, into which he fixed the tool for cutting the screws,—having never before seen a slide rest, though it is very probable he may have heard of what Maudslay had already done in the same direction. Clement continued during this period of his life an industrious self-cultivator, occupying most of his spare hours in mechanical and landscape drawing, and in various studies. Among the papers left behind him we find a ticket to a course of instruction on Natural Philosophy given by Professor Copland in the Marischal College at Aberdeen, which Clement attended in the session of 1812-13; and we do not doubt that our mechanic was among the most diligent of his pupils.

Towards the end of 1813, after saving about 100*l.* out of

his wages, Clement resolved to proceed to London for the purpose of improving himself in his trade and pushing his way in the world.   The coach by which he travelled set him down in Snow Hill, Holborn; and his first thought was of finding work.   He had no friend in town to consult on the matter, so he made inquiry of the coach-guard whether he knew of any person in the mechanical line in that neighbourhood.   The guard said, "Yes; there was Alexander Galloway's show shop, just round the corner, and he employed a large number of hands."   Running round the corner, Clement looked in at Galloway's window, through which he saw some lathes and other articles used in machine shops.   Next morning he called upon the owner of the shop to ask employment.   "What can you do?" asked Galloway.   "I can work at the forge," said Clement. "Anything else?"   "I can turn."   "What else?"   "I can draw."   "What!" said Galloway, "can you draw? Then I will engage you."   A man who could draw or work to a drawing in those days was regarded as a superior sort of mechanic.   Though Galloway was one of the leading tradesmen of his time, and had excellent opportunities for advancement, he missed them all.   As Clement afterwards said of him, "He was only a mouthing common-council man, the height of whose ambition was to be an alderman;" and, like most corporation celebrities, he held a low rank in his own business.   He very rarely went into his work-shops to superintend or direct his workmen, leaving this to his foremen—a sufficient indication of the causes of his failure as a mechanic.*

---

* On one occasion Galloway had a cast-iron roof made for his workshop, so flat and so independent of ties that the wonder was that it should have stood an hour.   One day Peter Keir, an engineer much employed by the government — a clever man, though somewhat eccentric—was taken into the shop by Galloway to admire the new roof.   Keir, on glancing up at it, immediately exclaimed, "Come outside, and let us speak about it there!" All that he could say to Galloway respecting the unsoundness of its construction was of no avail.   The fact was that, however Keir might argue about its not being able to stand, there it was actually standing, and that was

On entering Galloway's shop, Clement was first employed in working at the lathe; but finding the tools so bad that it was impossible to execute satisfactory work with them, he at once went to the forge, and began making a new set of tools for himself. The other men, to whom such a proceeding was entirely new, came round him to observe his operations, and they were much struck with his manual dexterity. The tools made, he proceeded to use them, displaying what seemed to the other workmen an unusual degree of energy and intelligence; and some of the old hands did not hesitate already to pronounce Clement to be the best mechanic in the shop. When Saturday night came round, the other men were curious to know what wages Galloway would allow the new hand; and when he had been paid, they asked him. "A guinea," was the reply. "A guinea! Why, you are worth two if you are worth a shilling," said an old man who came out of the rank—an excellent mechanic, who, though comparatively worthless through his devotion to drink, knew Clement's money value to his employer better than any man there; and he added, "Wait for a week or two, and if you are not better paid than this, I can tell you of a master who will give you a fairer wage." Several Saturdays came round, but no advance was made on the guinea a week; and then the old workman recommended Clement to offer himself to Bramah at Pimlico, who was always on the look out for first-rate mechanics.

Clement acted on the advice, and took with him some

---

enough for Galloway. Keir went home, his mind filled with Galloway's most unprincipled roof. "If that stands," said he to himself, "all that I have been learning and doing for thirty years has been wrong." That night he could not sleep for thinking about it. In the morning he strolled up Primrose Hill, and returned home still muttering to himself about "that roof." "What," said his wife to him, "are you thinking of Galloway's roof?" "Yes," said he. "Then you have seen the papers?" "No — what about them?" "Galloway's roof has fallen in this morning, and killed eight or ten of the men!" Keir immediately went to bed, and slept soundly till next morning.

of his drawings, at sight of which Bramah immediately engaged him for a month; and at the end of that time he had given so much satisfaction, that it was agreed he should continue for three months longer at two guineas a week. Clement was placed in charge of the tools of the shop, and he showed himself so apt at introducing improvements in them, as well as in organizing the work with a view to despatch and economy, that at the end of the term Bramah made him a handsome present, adding, " If I had secured your services five years since, I would now have been a richer man by many thousands of pounds." A formal agreement for a term of five years was then entered into between Bramah and Clement, dated the 1st of April, 1814, by which the latter undertook to fill the office of chief-draughtsman and superintendent of the Pimlico Works, in consideration of a salary of three guineas a week, with an advance of four shillings a week in each succeeding year of the engagement. This arrangement proved of mutual advantage to both. Clement devoted himself with increased zeal to the improvement of the mechanical arrangements of the concern, exhibiting his ingenuity in many ways, and taking a genuine pride in upholding the character of his master for turning out first-class work.

On the death of Bramah, his sons returned from college and entered into possession of the business. They found Clement the ruling mind there, and grew jealous of him to such an extent that his situation became uncomfortable; and by mutual consent he was allowed to leave before the expiry of his term of agreement. He had no difficulty in finding employment; and was at once taken on as chief draughtsman at Maudslay and Field's, where he was of much assistance in proportioning the early marine engines, for the manufacture of which that firm were becoming celebrated. After a short time, he became desirous of beginning business on his own account as a mechanical engineer. He was encouraged to do this by the Duke of

Northumberland, who, being a great lover of mechanics and himself a capital turner, used often to visit Maudslay's, and thus became acquainted with Clement, whose expertness as a draughtsman and mechanic he greatly admired. Being a man of frugal and sober habits, always keeping his expenditure very considerably within his income, Clement had been enabled to accumulate about 500*l.*, which he thought would be enough for his purpose; and he accordingly proceeded, in 1817, to take a small workshop in Prospect Place, Newington Butts, where he began business as a mechanical draughtsman and manufacturer of small machinery requiring first-class workmanship.

From the time when he took his first gratuitous lessons in drawing from Peter Nicholson, at Glasgow, in 1807, he had been steadily improving in this art, the knowledge of which is indispensable to whoever aspires to eminence as a mechanical engineer,—until by general consent Clement was confessed to stand unrivalled as a draughtsman. Some of the very best drawings contained in the Transactions of the Society of Arts, from the year 1817 downwards,—especially those requiring the delineation of any unusually elaborate piece of machinery,—proceeded from the hand of Clement. In some of these, he reached a degree of truth in mechanical perspective which has never been surpassed.* To facilitate his labours, he invented an extremely ingenious instrument, by means of which ellipses of all proportions, as well as circles and right lines, might be geometrically drawn on paper or on copper. He took his idea of this instrument from the trammel used by car-

---

* See more particularly *The Transactions of the Society for the Encouragement of Arts*, vol. xxxiii. (1817), at pp. 74, 157, 160, 175, 208 (an admirable drawing of Mr. James Allen's Theodolite); vol. xxxvi. (1818), pp. 28, 176 (a series of remarkable illustrations of Mr. Clement's own invention of an Instrument for Drawing Ellipses); vol. xliii. (1825), containing an illustration of the Drawing Table invented by him for large drawings; vol. xlvi. (1828), containing a series of elaborate illustrations of his Prize Turning Lathe; and xlviii. (1829), containing illustrations of his Self-adjusting Double Driver Centre Chuck.

penters for drawing imperfect ellipses; and when he had
succeeded in avoiding the crossing of the points, he proceeded to invent the straight-line motion.   For this invention the Society of Arts awarded him their gold medal
in 1818.   Some years later, he submitted to the same
Society his invention of a stand for drawings of large size.
He had experienced considerable difficulty in making such
drawings, and with his accustomed readiness to overcome
obstacles, he forthwith set to work and brought out his
new drawing-table.

As with many other original-minded mechanics, invention became a habit with him, and by study and labour
he rarely failed in attaining the object which he had bent
his mind upon accomplishing.   Indeed, nothing pleased
him better than to have what he called " a tough job;" as
it stimulated his inventive faculty, in the exercise of which
he took the highest pleasure.   Hence mechanical schemers
of all kinds were accustomed to resort to Clement for
help when they had found an idea which they desired to
embody in a machine.   If there was any value in their
idea, none could be more ready than he to recognise its
merit, and to work it into shape; but if worthless, he spoke
out his mind at once, dissuading the projector from wasting
upon it further labour or expense.

One of the important branches of practical mechanics to
which Clement continued through life to devote himself,
was the improvement of self-acting tools, more especially
of the slide-lathe.   He introduced various improvements in
its construction and arrangement, until in his hands it
became as nearly perfect as it was possible to be.   In 1818,
he furnished the lathe with a slide rest twenty-two inches
long, for the purpose of cutting screws, provided with the
means of self-correction; and some years later, in 1827,
the Society of Arts awarded him their gold Isis medal for
his improved turning-lathe, which embodied many ingenious contrivances calculated to increase its precision and
accuracy in large surface-turning.

The beautiful arrangements embodied in Mr. Clement's improved lathe can with difficulty be described in words; but its ingenuity may be inferred from a brief statement of the defects which it was invented to remedy, and which it successfully overcame. When the mandrill of a lathe, having a metal plate fixed to it, turns round with a uniform motion, and the slide rest which carries the cutter is moving from the circumference of the work to the centre, it will be obvious that the quantity of metal passing over the edge of the cutter at each revolution, and therefore at equal intervals of time, is continually diminishing, in exact proportion to the spiral line described by the cutter on the face of the work. But in turning metal plates it is found very inexpedient to increase the speed of the work beyond a certain quantity; for when this happens, and the tool passes the work at too great a velocity, it heats, softens, and is ground away, the edge of the cutter becomes dull, and the surface of the plate is indented and burnished, instead of being turned. Hence loss of time on the part of the workman, and diminished work on the part of the tool, results which, considering the wages of the one and the capital expended on the construction of the other, are of no small importance ; for the prime objects of all improvement of tools are, economy of time and economy of capital—to minimize labour and cost, and maximize result.

The defect to which we have referred was almost the only remaining imperfection in the lathe, and Mr. Clement overcame it by making the machine self-regulating; so that, whatever might be the situation of the cutter, equal quantities of metal should pass over it in equal times,—the speed at the centre not exceeding that suited to the work at the circumference,—while the workman was enabled to convert the varying rate of the mandrill into a uniform one whenever he chose. Thus the expedients of wheels, riggers, and drums, of different diameters, by which it had been endeavoured to alter the speed of the lathe-mandrill, according to the hardness of the metal and the diameter of the thing to be turned, were effectually disposed of. These, though answering very well where cylinders of equal diameter had to be bored, and a uniform motion was all that was required, were found very inefficient where a plane surface had to be turned; and it was in such cases that Mr. Clement's lathe was found so valuable. By its means surfaces of unrivalled correctness were produced, and the slide-lathe, so improved, became recognised and adopted as the most accurate and extensively applicable of all machine-tools.

The year after Mr. Clement brought out his improved turning-lathe, he added to it his self-adjusting double driving centre-chuck, for which the Society of Arts awarded him their silver medal in 1828. In introducing this invention to the notice of the Society, Mr. Clement said, " Although I have been in the habit of turning and making turning-lathes and other machinery for upwards of thirty-five years, and have examined the best turning-lathes in the principal manufactories throughout Great Britain, I find it universally regretted by all practical men that they cannot turn anything perfectly true between the centres of the lathe." It was found by experience, that there was a degree of eccentricity, and consequently of imperfection, in the figure of any long cylinder turned while suspended between the centres of the lathe, and made to revolve by the action of a single driver. Under such circumstances the pressure of the tool tended to force the work out of the right line and to distribute the strain between the driver and the adjacent centre, so that one end of the cylinder became eccentric with respect to the other. By Mr. Clement's invention of the two-armed driver, which was self-adjusting, the strain was taken from the centre and divided between the two arms, which being equidistant from the centre, effectually corrected all eccentricity in the work. This invention was found of great importance in ensuring the true turning of large machinery, which before had been found a matter of considerable difficulty.

In the same year (1828) Mr. Clement began the making of fluted taps and dies, and he established a mechanical practice with reference to the pitch of the screw, which proved of the greatest importance in the economics of manufacture. Before his time, each mechanical engineer adopted a thread of his own; so that when a piece of work came under repair, the screw-hob had usually to be drilled out, and a new thread was introduced according to the usage which prevailed in the shop in which the work was executed. Mr. Clement saw a great waste of labour in this practice, and he promulgated the idea that every screw of a particular length ought to be furnished with its appointed number of threads of a settled pitch. Taking the inch as the basis of his calculations, he determined the number of threads in each case; and the practice thus initiated by him, recommended as it was by convenience and economy, was very shortly adopted throughout the trade. It may be mentioned that one of Clement's ablest journeymen, Mr. Whitworth, has, since his time, been mainly instrumental in establishing the settled practice; and Whitworth's thread (initiated by Clement) has become recognised throughout the mechanical world. To carry out his idea, Clement invented his screw-engine lathe, with gearing, mandrill, and sliding-table wheel-work, by means of which he first cut the inside screw-tools from the left-handed hobs—the reverse mode having before been adopted,—while in shaping machines he was the first to use the revolving cutter attached to the slide rest. Then, in 1828, he fluted the taps for the first time with a revolving cutter,—other makers having up to that time only notched them. Among his other inventions in screws may be mentioned his headless tap, which, according to Mr. Nasmyth, is so valuable an invention, that, "if he had done nothing else, it ought to immortalize him among mechanics. It passed right through the hole to be tapped, and was thus enabled to do the duty of three ordinary screws." By these improvements much greater precision was secured in the manufacture of tools and machinery, accompanied by a greatly reduced cost of production; the results of which are felt to this day.

Another of Mr. Clement's ingenious inventions was his Planing Machine, by means of which metal plates of large dimensions were planed with perfect truth and finished with beautiful accuracy. There is perhaps scarcely a machine about which there has been more controversy than this; and we do not pretend to be able to determine the respective merits of the many able mechanics who have had a hand in its invention. It is exceedingly probable that others besides Clement worked out the problem in their own way, by independent methods; and this is confirmed by the circumstance that though the results achieved by the respective inventors were the same, the methods employed by them were in many respects different. As regards Clement, we find that previous to the year 1820 he had a machine in regular use for planing the triangular bars of lathes and the sides of weaving-looms. This instrument was found so useful and so economical in its working, that Clement proceeded to elaborate a planing machine of a more complete kind, which he finished and set to work in the year 1825. He prepared no model of it, but made it direct from the working drawings; and it was so nicely constructed, that when put together it went without a hitch, and has continued steadily working for more than thirty years down to the present day.

Clement took out no patent for his invention, relying for protection mainly on his own and his workmen's skill in using it. We therefore find no specification of his machine at the Patent Office, as in the case of most other capital inventions; but a very complete account of it is to be found in the Transactions of the Society of Arts for 1832, as described by Mr. Varley. The practical value of the Planing Machine induced the Society to apply to Mr. Clement for liberty to publish a full description of it; and

Mr. Varley's paper was the result.* It may be briefly stated that this engineer's plane differs greatly from the carpenter's plane, the cutter of which is only allowed to project so far as to admit of a thin shaving to be sliced off,—the plane working flat in proportion to the width of the tool, and its length and straightness preventing the cutter from descending into any hollows in the wood. The engineer's plane more resembles the turning-lathe, of which indeed it is but a modification, working upon the same principle, on flat surfaces. The tools or cutters in Clement's machine were similar to those used in the lathe, varying in like manner, but performing their work in right lines,—the tool being stationary and the work moving under it, the tool only travelling when making lateral cuts. To save time two cutters were mounted, one to cut the work while going, the other while returning, both being so arranged and held as to be presented to the work in the firmest manner, and with the least possible friction. The bed of the machine, on which the work was laid, passed under the cutters on perfectly true rollers or wheels, lodged and held in their bearings as accurately as the best mandrill could be, and having set-screws acting against their ends totally preventing all end-motion. The machine was bedded on a massive and solid foundation of masonry in heavy blocks, the support at all points being so complete as effectually to destroy all tendency to vibration, with the object of securing full, round, and quiet cuts. The rollers on which the planing-machine travelled were so true, that Clement himself used to say of them, "If you were to put but a paper shaving under one of the rollers, it would at once stop all the rest." Nor was this any exaggeration—the entire mechanism, notwithstanding its great size, being as true and accurate as that of a watch.

---

* *Transactions of the Society for the Encouragement of Arts*, vol. xlix. p. 157.

By an ingenious adaptation of the apparatus, which will also be found described in the Society of Arts paper, the planing machine might be fitted with a lathe-bed, either to hold two centres, or a head with a suitable mandrill. When so fitted, the machine was enabled to do the work of a turning-lathe, though in a different way, cutting cylinders or cones in their longitudinal direction perfectly straight, as well as solids or prisms of any angle, either by the longitudinal or lateral motion of the cutter; whilst by making the work revolve, it might be turned as in any other lathe. This ingenious machine, as contrived by Mr. Clement, therefore represented a complete union of the turning-lathe with the planing machine and dividing engine, by which turning of the most complicated kind might readily be executed. For ten years after it was set in motion, Clement's was the only machine of the sort available for planing large work; and being consequently very much in request, it was often kept going night and day,—the earnings by the planing machine alone during that time forming the principal income of its inventor. As it took in a piece of work six feet square, and as his charge for planing was three-halfpence the square inch, or eighteen shillings the square foot, he could thus earn by his machine alone some ten pounds for every day's work of twelve hours. We may add that since planing machines in various forms have become common in mechanical workshops, the cost of planing does not amount to more than three-halfpence the square foot.

The excellence of Mr. Clement's tools, and his well-known skill in designing and executing work requiring unusual accuracy and finish, led to his being employed by Mr. Babbage to make his celebrated Calculating or Difference Engine. The contrivance of a machine that should work out complicated sums in arithmetic with perfect precision, was, as may readily be imagined, one of the most difficult feats of the mechanical intellect. To do this was in an especial sense to stamp matter with the im-

press of mind, and render it subservient to the highest
thinking faculty. Attempts had been made at an early
period to perform arithmetical calculations by mechanical
aids more rapidly and precisely than it was possible to do
by the operations of the individual mind. The preparation
of arithmetical tables of high numbers involved a vast deal
of labour, and even with the greatest care errors were
unavoidable and numerous. Thus in a multiplication-table
prepared by a man so eminent as Dr. Hutton for the Board
of Longitude, no fewer than forty errors were discovered
in a single page taken at random. In the tables of the
Nautical Almanac, where the greatest possible precision was
desirable and necessary, more than five hundred errors were
detected by one person; and the Tables of the Board of
Longitude were found equally incorrect. But such errors
were impossible to be avoided so long as the ordinary modes
of calculating, transcribing, and printing continued in use.

The earliest and simplest form of calculating apparatus
was that employed by the schoolboys of ancient Greece,
called the Abacus; consisting of a smooth board with
a narrow rim, on which they were taught to compute
by means of progressive rows of pebbles, bits of bone or
ivory, or pieces of silver coin, used as counters. The same
board, strewn over with sand, was used for teaching
the rudiments of writing and the principles of geometry.
The Romans subsequently adopted the Abacus, dividing
it by means of perpendicular lines or bars, and from the
designation of calculus which they gave to each pebble
or counter employed on the board, we have derived our
English word to *calculate*. The same instrument continued to be employed during the middle ages, and the
table used by the English Court of Exchequer was but a
modified form of the Greek Abacus, the chequered lines
across it giving the designation to the Court, which still
survives. Tallies, from the French word *tailler* to cut,
were another of the mechanical methods employed to
record computations, though in a very rude way. Step

by step improvements were made; the most important being that invented by Napier of Merchiston, the inventor of logarithms, commonly called *Napier's bones*, consisting of a number of rods divided into ten equal squares and numbered, so that the whole when placed together formed the common multiplication table.   By these means various operations in multiplication and division were performed. Sir Samuel Morland, Gunter, and Lamb introduced other contrivances, applicable to trigonometry; Gunter's scale being still in common use.   The calculating machines of Gersten and Pascal were of a different kind, working out arithmetical calculations by means of trains of wheels and other arrangements; and that contrived by Lord Stanhope for the purpose of verifying his calculations with respect to the National Debt was of like character.   But none of these will bear for a moment to be compared with the machine designed by Mr. Babbage for performing arithmetical calculations and mathematical analyses, as well as for recording the calculations when made, thereby getting rid entirely of individual error in the operations of calculation, transcription, and printing.

The French government, in their desire to promote the extension of the decimal system, had ordered the construction of logarithmical tables of vast extent; but the great labour and expense involved in the undertaking prevented the design from being carried out.   It was reserved for Mr. Babbage to develope the idea by means of a machine which he called the Difference Engine.   This machine is of so complicated a character that it would be impossible for us to give any intelligible description of it in words. Although Dr. Lardner was unrivalled in the art of describing mechanism, he occupied twenty-five pages of the ' Edinburgh Review ' (vol. 59) in endeavouring to describe its action, and there were several features in it which he gave up as hopeless.   Some parts of the apparatus and modes of action are indeed extraordinary — and perhaps none more so than that for ensuring accuracy in the calcu-

lated results,—the machine actually correcting itself, and
rubbing itself back into accuracy, when the disposition to
err occurs, by the friction of the adjacent machinery!
When an error is made, the wheels become locked and
refuse to proceed; thus the machine must go rightly or
not at all,—an arrangement as nearly resembling volition
as anything that brass and steel are likely to accomplish.

This intricate subject was taken up by Mr. Babbage in
1821, when he undertook to superintend for the British
government the construction of a machine for calculating
and printing mathematical and astronomical tables. The
model first constructed to illustrate the nature of his invention produced figures at the rate of 44 a minute. In
1823 the Royal Society was requested to report upon the
invention, and after full inquiry the committee recommended it as one highly deserving of public encouragement. A sum of 1500*l.* was then placed at Mr. Babbage's disposal by the Lords of the Treasury for the
purpose of enabling him to perfect his invention. It was
at this time that he engaged Mr. Clement as draughtsman
and mechanic to embody his ideas in a working machine.
Numerous tools were expressly contrived by the latter for
executing the several parts, and workmen were specially
educated for the purpose of using them. Some idea of the
elaborate character of the drawings may be formed from
the fact that those required for the calculating machinery
alone—not to mention the printing machinery, which was
almost equally elaborate—covered not less than four hundred square feet of surface! The cost of executing the
calculating machine was of course very great, and the progress of the work was necessarily slow. The consequence
was that the government first became impatient, and then
began to grumble at the expense. At the end of seven
years the engineer's bills alone were found to amount to
nearly 7200*l.*, and Mr. Babbage's costs out of pocket to
7000*l.* more. In order to make more satisfactory progress,
it was determined to remove the works to the neighbour-

hood of Mr. Babbage's own residence; but as Clement's claims for conducting the operations in the new premises were thought exorbitant, and as he himself considered that the work did not yield him the average profit of ordinary employment in his own trade, he eventually withdrew from the enterprise, taking with him the tools which he had constructed for executing the machine.   The government also shortly after withdrew from it, and from that time the scheme was suspended, the Calculating Engine remaining a beautiful but unfinished fragment of a great work.   Though originally intended to go as far as twenty figures, it was only completed to the extent of being capable of calculating to the depth of five figures, and two orders of differences; and only a small part of the proposed printing machinery was ever made.   The engine was placed in the museum of King's College in 1843, enclosed in a glass case, until the year 1862, when it was removed for a time to the Great Exhibition, where it formed perhaps the most remarkable and beautifully executed piece of mechanism— the combined result of intellectual and mechanical contrivance—in the entire collection.*

---

* A complete account of the calculating machine, as well as of an analytical engine afterwards contrived by Mr. Babbage, of still greater power than the other, will be found in the *Bibliothèque Universelle de Genève*, of which a translation into English, with copious original notes, by the late Lady Lovelace, daughter of Lord Byron, was published in the 3rd vol. of Taylor's *Scientific Memoirs* (London, 1843). A history of the machine, and of the circumstances connected with its construction, will also be found in Weld's *History of the Royal Society*, vol. ii. 369-391.   It remains to be added, that the perusal by Messrs. Scheutz of Stockholm of Dr. Lardner's account of Mr. Babbage's engine in the *Edinburgh Review*, led those clever mechanics to enter upon the scheme of constructing and completing it, and the result is, that their machine not only calculates the tables, but prints the results.   It took them nearly twenty years to perfect it, but when completed the machine seemed to be almost capable of thinking. The original was exhibited at the Paris Exhibition of 1855.   A copy of it has since been secured by the English government at a cost of 1200*l.*, and it is now busily employed at Somerset House in working out annuity and other tables for the Registrar-General. The copy was constructed, with several admirable improvements, by the Messrs. Donkin, the well-known mechanical engineers, after the working drawings of the Messrs. Scheutz.

Clement was on various other occasions invited to undertake work requiring extra skill, which other mechanics were unwilling or unable to execute. He was thus always full of employment, never being under the necessity of canvassing for customers. He was almost constantly in his workshop, in which he took great pride. His dwelling was over the office in the yard, and it was with difficulty he could be induced to leave the premises. On one occasion Mr. Brunel of the Great Western Railway called upon him to ask if he could supply him with a superior steam-whistle for his locomotives, the whistles which they were using giving forth very little sound. Clement examined the specimen brought by Brunel, and pronounced it to be " mere tallow-chandler's work." He undertook to supply a proper article, and after his usual fashion he proceeded to contrive a machine or tool for the express purpose of making steam-whistles. They were made and supplied, and when mounted on the locomotive the effect was indeed " screaming." They were heard miles off, and Brunel, delighted, ordered a hundred. But when the bill came in, it was found that the charge made for them was very high—as much as 40l. the set. The company demurred at the price,—Brunel declaring it to be six times more than the price they had before been paying. " That may be; " rejoined Clement, " but mine are more than six times better. You ordered a first-rate article, and you must be content to pay for it." The matter was referred to an arbitrator, who awarded the full sum claimed. Mr. Weld mentions a similar case of an order which Clement received from America to make a large screw of given dimensions " in the best possible manner," and he accordingly proceeded to make one with the greatest mathematical accuracy. But his bill amounted to some hundreds of pounds, which completely staggered the American, who did not calculate on having to pay more than 20l. at the utmost for the screw. The matter was, however, referred to arbitrators, who gave their decision, as in the former case, in favour of the mechanic.*

One of the last works which Clement executed as a matter of pleasure, was the building of an organ for his own use. It will be remembered that when working as a slater at Great Ashby, he had made flutes and clarinets, and now in his old age he determined to try his skill at making an organ—in his opinion the king of musical instruments. The building of it became his hobby, and his greatest delight was in superintending its progress. It cost him about two thousand pounds in labour alone, but he lived to finish it, and we have been informed that it was pronounced a very excellent instrument.

Clement was a heavy-browed man, without any polish of manner or speech; for to the last he continued to use his strong Westmoreland dialect. He was not educated in a literary sense; for he read but little, and could write with difficulty. He was eminently a mechanic, and had achieved his exquisite skill by observation, experience, and reflection. His head was a complete repertory of inventions, on which he was constantly drawing for the improvement of mechanical practice. Though he had never more than thirty workmen in his factory, they were all of the first class; and the example which Clement set before them of extreme carefulness and accuracy in execution rendered his shop one of the best schools of its time for the training of thoroughly accomplished mechanics. Mr. Clement died in 1844, in his sixty-fifth year; after which his works were carried on by Mr. Wilkinson, one of his nephews; and his planing machine still continues in useful work.

---

* *History of the Royal Society*, ii. 374.

CHAPTER XIV.

Fox of Derby — Murray of Leeds — Roberts and Whitworth of Manchester.

———

" Founders and senators of states and cities, lawgivers, extirpers of tyrants, fathers of the people, and other eminent persons in civil government, were honoured but with titles of Worthies or demi-gods ; whereas, such as were inventors and authors of new arts, endowments, and commodities towards man's life, were ever consecrated amongst the gods themselves."—BACON, *Advancement of Learning.*

———

WHILE such were the advances made in the arts of toolmaking and engine-construction through the labours of Bramah, Maudslay, and Clement, there were other mechanics of almost equal eminence who flourished about the same time and subsequently in several of the northern manufacturing towns. Among these may be mentioned James Fox of Derby; Matthew Murray and Peter Fairbairn of Leeds; Richard Roberts, Joseph Whitworth, James Nasmyth, and William Fairbairn of Manchester; to all of whom the manufacturing industry of Great Britain stands in the highest degree indebted.

James Fox, the founder of the Derby firm of mechanical engineers, was originally a butler in the service of the Rev. Thomas Gisborne, of Foxhall Lodge, Staffordshire. Though a situation of this kind might not seem by any means favourable for the display of mechanical ability, yet the butler's instinct for handicraft was so strong that it could not be repressed; and his master not only encouraged him in the handling of tools in his leisure hours, but had so genuine an admiration of his skill as well as his excellent qualities of character, that he eventually furnished him with the means of beginning business on his own account.

The growth and extension of the cotton, silk, and lace trades, in the neighbourhood of Derby, furnished Fox with sufficient opportunities for the exercise of his mechanical skill; and he soon found ample scope for its employment. His lace machinery became celebrated, and he supplied it largely to the neighbouring town of Nottingham; he also obtained considerable employment from the great firms of Arkwright and Strutt—the founders of the modern cotton manufacture.   Mr. Fox also became celebrated for his lathes, which were of excellent quality, still maintaining their high reputation; and besides making largely for the supply of the home demand, he exported much machinery abroad, to France, Russia, and the Mauritius.

The present Messrs. Fox of Derby, who continue to carry on the business of the firm, claim for their grandfather, its founder, that he made the first planing machine in 1814,* and they add that the original article continued in use until quite recently. We have been furnished by Samuel Hall, formerly a workman at the Messrs. Fox's, with the following description of the machine :—" It was essentially the same in principle as the planing machine now in general use, although differing in detail.   It had a self-acting ratchet motion for moving the slides of a compound slide rest, and a self-acting reversing tackle, consisting of three bevel wheels, one a stud, one loose on the driving shaft, and another on a socket, with a pinion on the opposite end of the driving shaft running on the socket. The other end was the place for the driving pulley.   A clutch box was placed between the two opposite wheels, which was made to slide on a feather, so that by means of another shaft containing levers and a tumbling ball, the box on reversing was carried from one bevel wheel to the opposite one."   The same James Fox is also said at a very

---

* *Engineer*, Oct. 10th, 1862.

early period to have invented a screw-cutting machine, an engine for accurately dividing and cutting the teeth of wheels, and a self-acting lathe. But the evidence as to the dates at which these several inventions are said to have been made is so conflicting that it is impossible to decide with whom the merit of making them really rests. The same idea is found floating at the same time in many minds, the like necessity pressing upon all, and the process of invention takes place in like manner: hence the contemporaneousness of so many inventions, and the disputes that arise respecting them, as described in a previous chapter.

There are still other claimants for the merit of having invented the planing machine; among whom may be mentioned more particularly Matthew Murray of Leeds, and Richard Roberts of Manchester. We are informed by Mr. March, the present mayor of Leeds, head of the celebrated tool-manufacturing firm of that town, that when he first went to work at Matthew Murray's, in 1814, a planing machine of his invention was used to plane the circular part or back of the D valve, which he had by that time introduced in the steam-engine. Mr. March says, " I recollect it very distinctly, and even the sort of framing on which it stood. The machine was not patented, and like many inventions in those days, it was kept as much a secret as possible, being locked up in a small room by itself, to which the ordinary workmen could not obtain access. The year in which I remember it being in use was, so far as I am aware, long before any planing-machine of a similar kind had been invented."

Matthew Murray was born at Stockton-on-Tees in the year 1763. His parents were of the working class, and Matthew, like the other members of the family, was brought up with the ordinary career of labour before him. When of due age his father apprenticed him to the trade of a blacksmith, in which he very soon acquired considerable expertness. He married before his term had expired; after which, trade being slack at Stockton, he found it necessary to look for work elsewhere.   Leaving his wife behind him, he set out for Leeds with his bundle on his back, and after a long journey on foot, he reached that town with not enough money left in his pocket to pay for a bed at the Bay Horse inn, where he put up.   But telling the landlord that he expected work at Marshall's, and seeming to be a respectable young man, the landlord trusted him ; and he was so fortunate as to obtain the job which he sought at Mr. Marshall's, who was then beginning the manufacture of flax, for which the firm has since become so famous.

Mr. Marshall was at that time engaged in improving the method of manufacture,* and the young blacksmith was so fortunate or rather so dexterous as to be able to suggest several improvements in the machinery which secured the approval of his employer, who made him a present of 20*l.*, and very shortly promoted him to be the first mechanic in the workshop.   On this stroke of good fortune Murray took a house at the neighbouring village of Beeston, sent to Stockton for his wife, who speedily joined him, and he now felt himself fairly started in the world.   He remained with Mr. Marshall for about twelve years, during which he introduced numerous improvements in the machinery for spinning flax, and obtained the reputation of being a first-rate mechanic.   This induced Mr. James Fenton and Mr. David Wood to offer to join him in the establishment

---

* We are informed in Mr. Longstaffe's *Annals and Characteristics of Darlington*, that the spinning of flax by machinery was first begun by one John Kendrew, an ingenious self-taught mechanic of that town, who invented a machine for the purpose, for which he took out a patent in 1787. Mr. Marshall went over from Leeds to see his machine, and agreed to give him so much per spindle for the right to use it. But ceasing to pay the patent right, Kendrew commenced an action against him for a sum of nine hundred pounds alleged to be due under the agreement. The claim was disputed, and Kendrew lost his action ; and it is added in Longstaffe's Annals, that even had he succeeded, it would have been of no use ; for Mr. Marshall declared that he had not then the money wherewith to pay him. It is possible that Matthew Murray may have obtained some experience of flax-machinery in working for Kendrew, which afterwards proved of use to him in Mr. Marshall's establishment.

of an engineering and machine-making factory at Leeds, which he agreed to, and operations were commenced at Holbeck in the year 1795.

As Mr. Murray had obtained considerable practical knowledge of the steam-engine while working at Mr. Marshall's, he took principal charge of the engine-building department, while his partner Wood directed the machine-making. In the branch of engine-building Mr. Murray very shortly established a high reputation, treading close upon the heels of Boulton and Watt—so close, indeed, that that firm became very jealous of him, and purchased a large piece of ground close to his works with the object of preventing their extension.* His additions to the steam-engine were of great practical value, one of which, the self-acting apparatus attached to the boiler for the purpose of regulating the intensity of fire under it, and consequently the production of steam, is still in general use. This was invented by him as early as 1799. He also subsequently invented the D slide valve, or at least greatly improved it, while he added to the power of the air-pump, and gave a new arrangement to the other parts, with a view to the simplification of the powers of the engine. To make the D valve work efficiently, it was found necessary to form two perfectly plane surfaces, to produce which he invented his planing machine. He was also the first to adopt the practice of placing the piston in a horizontal position in the common condensing engine. Among his other modifications in the steam-engine, was his improvement of the locomotive as invented by Trevithick; and it ought to be remembered to his honour that he made the first locomotive that regularly worked upon any railway.

---

* The purchase of this large piece of ground, known as Camp Field, had the effect of "plugging up" Matthew Murray for a time; and it remained disused, except for the deposit of dead dogs and other rubbish, for more than half a century. It has only been enclosed during the present year, and now forms part of the works of Messrs. Smith, Beacock, and Tannet, the eminent tool-makers.

This was the engine erected by him for Blenkinsop, to work the Middleton colliery railway near Leeds, on which it began to run in 1812, and continued in regular use for many years. In this engine he introduced the double cylinder—Trevithick's engine being provided with only one cylinder, the defects of which were supplemented by the addition of a fly-wheel to carry the crank over the dead points.

But Matthew Murray's most important inventions, considered in their effects on manufacturing industry, were those connected with the machinery for heckling and spinning flax, which he very greatly improved. His heckling machine obtained for him the prize of the gold medal of the Society of Arts; and this as well as his machine for wet flax-spinning by means of sponge weights proved of the greatest practical value. At the time when these inventions were made the flax trade was on the point of expiring, the spinners being unable to produce yarn to a profit; and their almost immediate effect was to reduce the cost of production, to improve immensely the quality of the manufacture, and to establish the British linen trade on a solid foundation. The production of flax-machinery became an important branch of manufacture at Leeds, large quantities being made for use at home as well as for exportation, giving employment to an increasing number of highly skilled mechanics.* Mr. Murray's faculty for organising work, perfected by experience, enabled him also to introduce many valuable improvements in the mechanics of manufacturing. His pre-eminent skill in mill-gearing became generally acknowledged, and the effects of his labours are felt to this day in the extensive and still thriving branches of industry which his ingenuity and ability mainly contributed to establish. All the machine-

---

* Among more recent improvers of flax-machinery, the late Sir Peter Fairbairn is entitled to high merit: the work turned out by him being of first-rate excellence, embodying numerous inventions and improvements of great value and importance.

tools used in his establishment were designed by himself, and he was most careful in the personal superintendence of all the details of their construction. Mr. Murray died at Leeds in 1826, in his sixty-third year.

We have not yet exhausted the list of claimants to the invention of the Planing Machine, for we find still another in the person of Richard Roberts of Manchester, one of the most prolific of modern inventors. Mr. Roberts has indeed achieved so many undisputed inventions, that he can readily afford to divide the honour in this case with others. He has contrived things so various as the self-acting mule and the best electro-magnet, wet gas-meters and dry planing machines, iron billiard-tables and turret-clocks, the centrifugal railway and the drill slotting-machine, an apparatus for making cigars and machinery for the propulsion and equipment of steamships; so that he may almost be regarded as the Admirable Crichton of modern mechanics.

Richard Roberts was born in 1789, at Carreghova in the parish of Llanymynech. His father was by trade a shoemaker, to which he occasionally added the occupation of toll-keeper. The house in which Richard was born stood upon the border line which then divided the counties of Salop and Montgomery; the front door opening in the one county, and the back door in the other. Richard, when a boy, received next to no education, and as soon as he was of fitting age was put to common labouring work. For some time he worked in a quarry near his father's dwelling; but being of an ingenious turn, he occupied his leisure in making various articles of mechanism, partly for amusement and partly for profit. One of his first achievements, while working as a quarryman, was a spinning-wheel, of which he was very proud, for it was considered "a good job." Thus he gradually acquired dexterity in handling tools, and he shortly came to entertain the ambition of becoming a mechanic.

There were several ironworks in the neighbourhood,

and thither he went in search of employment. He succeeded in finding work as a pattern-maker at Bradley, near Bilston, under John Wilkinson, the famous ironmaster—a man of great enterprise as well as mechanical skill; for he was the first man, as already stated, that Watt could find capable of boring a cylinder with any approach to truth, for the purposes of his steam-engines. After acquiring some practical knowledge of the art of working in wood as well as iron, Roberts proceeded to Birmingham, where he passed through different shops, gaining further experience in mechanical practice. He tried his hand at many kinds of work, and acquired considerable dexterity in each. He was regarded as a sort of jack-of-all-trades; for he was a good turner, a tolerable wheel-wright, and could repair mill-work at a pinch.

He next moved northward to the Horsley ironworks, Tipton, where he was working as a pattern-maker when he had the misfortune to be drawn in his own county for the militia. He immediately left his work and made his way homeward to Llanymynech, determined not to be a soldier or even a militiaman. But home was not the place for him to rest in, and after bidding a hasty adieu to his father, he crossed the country northward on foot and reached Liverpool, in the hope of finding work there. Failing in that, he set out for Manchester and reached it at dusk, very weary and very miry in consequence of the road being in such a wretched state of mud and ruts. He relates that, not knowing a person in the town, he went up to an apple-stall ostensibly to buy a pennyworth of apples, but really to ask the stall-keeper if he knew of any person in want of a hand. Was there any turner in the neighbourhood? Yes, round the corner. Thither he went at once, found the wood-turner in, and was promised a job on the following morning. He remained with the turner for only a short time, after which he found a job in Salford at lathe and tool-making. But hearing that the militia warrant-officers were still searching for him, he became uneasy and determined to take refuge in London.

He trudged all the way on foot to that great hiding-place, and first tried Holtzapffel's, the famous tool-maker's, but failing in his application he next went to Maudslay's and succeeded in getting employment. He worked there for some time, acquiring much valuable practical knowledge in the use of tools, cultivating his skill by contact with first-class workmen, and benefiting by the spirit of active contrivance which pervaded the Maudslay shops. His manual dexterity greatly increased, and his inventive ingenuity fully stimulated, he determined on making his way back to Manchester, which, even more than London itself, at that time presented abundant openings for men of mechanical skill. Hence we find so many of the best mechanics trained at Maudslay's and Clement's—Nasmyth, Lewis, Muir, Roberts, Whitworth, and others—shortly rising into distinction there as leading mechanicians and tool-makers.

The mere enumeration of the various results of Mr. Roberts's inventive skill during the period of his settlement at Manchester as a mechanical engineer, would occupy more space than we can well spare. But we may briefly mention a few of the more important. In 1816, while carrying on business on his own account in Deansgate, he invented his improved sector for correctly sizing wheels in blank previously to their being cut, which is still extensively used. In the same year he invented his improved screw-lathe ; and in the following year, at the request of the boroughreeve and constables of Manchester, he contrived an oscillating and rotating wet gas meter of a new kind, which enabled them to sell gas by measure. This was the first meter in which a water lute was applied to prevent the escape of gas by the index shaft, the want of which, as well as its great complexity, had prevented the only other gas meter then in existence from working satisfactorily. The water lute was immediately adopted by the patentee of that meter. The planing machine, though claimed, as we have seen, by many inventors, was constructed by Mr. Roberts after an original plan of his own in 1817, and became the tool most generally employed in mechanical workshops—acting by means of a chain and rack—though it has since been superseded to some extent by the planing machine of Whitworth, which works both ways upon an endless screw. Improvements followed in the slide-lathe (giving a large range of speed with increased diameters for the same size of headstocks, &c.), in the wheel-cutting engine, in the scalebeam (by which, with a load of 2 oz. on each end, the fifteen-hundredth part of a grain could be indicated), in the broaching-machine, the slotting-machine, and other engines.

But the inventions by which his fame became most extensively known arose out of circumstances connected with the cotton manufactures of Manchester and the neighbourhood. The great improvements which he introduced in the machine for making weavers' reeds, led to the formation of the firm of Sharp, Roberts, and Co., of which Mr. Roberts was the acting mechanical partner for many years. Not less important were his improvements in power-looms for weaving fustians, which were extensively adopted. But by far the most famous of his inventions was unquestionably his Self-acting Mule, one of the most elaborate and beautiful pieces of machinery ever contrived. Before its invention, the working of the entire machinery of the cotton-mill, as well as the employment of the piecers, cleaners, and other classes of operatives, depended upon the spinners, who, though receiving the highest rates of pay, were by much the most given to strikes; and they were frequently accustomed to turn out in times when trade was brisk, thereby bringing the whole operations of the manufactories to a standstill, and throwing all the other operatives out of employment. A long-continued strike of this sort took place in 1824, when the idea occurred to the masters that it might be possible to make the spinning-mules run out and in at the proper speed by means of self-acting machinery, and thus render them in some measure independent of the more refractory class of their workmen. It seemed, however, to be so very difficult a problem, that they were by no means sanguine of success in its solution. Some time passed before they could find any mechanic willing so much as to consider the subject. Mr. Ashton of Staley-bridge made every effort with this object, but the answer he got was uniformly the same. The thing was declared to be impracticable and impossible. Mr. Ashton, accompanied by two other leading spinners, called on Sharp, Roberts, and Co., to seek an interview with Mr. Roberts. They introduced the subject to him, but he would scarcely listen to their explanations, cutting them short with the remark that he knew nothing whatever about cotton-spinning. They insisted, nevertheless, on explaining to him what they required, but they went away without being able to obtain from him any promise of assistance in bringing out the required machine.

The strike continued, and the manufacturers again called upon Mr. Roberts, but with no better result. A third time they called and appealed to Mr. Sharp, the capitalist of the firm, who promised to use his best endeavours to induce his mechanical partner to take the matter in hand. But Mr. Roberts, notwithstanding his reticence, had been occupied in carefully pondering the subject since Mr. Ashton's first interview with him. The very difficulty of the problem to be solved had tempted him boldly to grapple with it, though he would not hold out the slightest expectation to the cotton-spinners of his being able to help them in their emergency until he saw his way perfectly clear. That time had now come; and when Mr. Sharp introduced the subject, he said he had turned the matter over and thought he could construct the required self-acting machinery. It was arranged that he should proceed with it at once, and after a close study of four months he brought out the machine now so extensively known as the self-acting mule. The invention was patented in 1825, and was perfected by subsequent additions, which were also patented.

Like so many other inventions, the idea of the self-acting mule was not new. Thus Mr. William Strutt of Derby, the father of Lord Belper, invented a machine of this sort at an early period; Mr. William Kelly, of the New Lanark Mills, invented a second; and various other projectors tried their skill in the same direction; but none of these inventions came into practical use. In such cases it has become generally admitted that the real inventor is not the person who suggests the idea of the invention, but he who first works it out into a practicable process, and so makes it of practical and commercial value. This was accomplished by Mr. Roberts, who, working out the idea after his own independent methods, succeeded in making the first self-acting mule that would really act as such; and he is therefore fairly entitled to be regarded as its inventor.

By means of this beautiful contrivance, spindle-carriages, bearing hundreds of spindles, run themselves out and in by means of automatic machinery, at the proper speed, without a hand touching them; the only labour required being that of a few boys and girls to watch them and mend the broken threads when the carriage recedes from the roller beam, and to stop it when the cop is completely formed, as is indicated by the bell of the counter attached to the working gear. Mr. Baines describes the self-acting mule while at work as " drawing out, twisting, and winding up many thousand threads, with unfailing precision and indefatigable patience and strength—a scene as magical to the eye which is not familiarized with it, as the effects have been marvellous in augmenting the wealth and population of the country." *

Mr. Roberts's great success with the self-acting mule led to his being often appealed to for help in the mechanics

---

* EDWARD BAINES, Esq., M.P., *History of the Cotton Manufacture*, 212.

of manufacturing. In 1826, the year after his patent was taken out, he was sent for to Mulhouse, in Alsace, to design and arrange the machine establishment of André Koechlin and Co.; and in that and the two subsequent years he fairly set the works a-going, instructing the workmen in the manufacture of spinning-machinery, and thus contributing largely to the success of the French cotton manufacture. In 1832 he patented his invention of the Radial Arm for "winding on" in the self-acting mule, now in general use; and in future years he took out sundry patents for roving, slubbing, spinning, and doubling cotton and other fibrous materials; and for weaving, beetling, and mangling fabrics of various sorts.

A considerable branch of business carried on by the firm of Sharp, Roberts, and Co. was the manufacture of iron billiard-tables, which were constructed with almost perfect truth by means of Mr. Roberts's planing-machine, and became a large article of export. But a much more important and remunerative department was the manufacture of locomotives, which was begun by the firm shortly after the opening of the Liverpool and Manchester Railway had marked this as one of the chief branches of future mechanical engineering. Mr. Roberts adroitly seized the opportunity presented by this new field of invention and enterprise, and devoted himself for a time to the careful study of the locomotive and its powers. As early as the year 1829 we find him presenting to the Manchester Mechanics' Institute a machine exhibiting the nature of friction upon railroads, in solution of the problem then under discussion in the scientific journals. In the following year he patented an arrangement for communicating power to both driving-wheels of the locomotive, at all times in the exact proportions required when turning to the right or left,—an arrangement which has since been adopted in many road locomotives and agricultural engines. In the same patent will be found embodied his invention of the steam-brake, which was also a favourite idea of George

Stephenson, since elaborated by Mr. MacConnell of the London and North-Western Railway.   In 1834, Sharp, Roberts, and Co. began the manufacture of locomotives on a large scale; and the compactness of their engines, the excellence of their workmanship, and the numerous original improvements introduced in them, speedily secured for the engines of the Atlas firm a high reputation and a very large demand.   Among Mr. Roberts's improvements may be mentioned his method of manufacturing the crank axle, of welding the rim and tyres of the wheels, and his arrangement and form of the wrought-iron framing and axle-guards.   His system of templets and gauges, by means of which every part of an engine or tender corresponded with that of every other engine or tender of the same class, was as great an improvement as Maudslay's system of uniformity of parts in other descriptions of machinery.

In connection with the subject of railways, we may allude in passing to Mr. Roberts's invention of the Jacquard punching machine—a self-acting tool of great power, used for punching any required number of holes, of any pitch and to any pattern, with mathematical accuracy, in bridge or boiler plates.   The origin of this invention was somewhat similar to that of the self-acting mule.   The contractors for the Conway Tubular Bridge while under construction, in 1848, were greatly hampered by combinations amongst the workmen, and they despaired of being able to finish the girders within the time specified in the contract.   The punching of the iron plates by hand was a tedious and expensive as well as an inaccurate process; and the work was proceeding so slowly that the contractors found it absolutely necessary to adopt some new method of punching if they were to finish the work in time.   In their emergency they appealed to Mr. Roberts, and endeavoured to persuade him to take the matter up.   He at length consented to do so, and evolved the machine in question during his evening's leisure—for the most part while quietly sipping his tea.   The machine was produced, the

contractors were enabled to proceed with the punching of
the plates independent of the refractory men, and the work
was executed with a despatch, accuracy, and excellence
that would not otherwise have been possible. Only a few
years since Mr. Roberts added a useful companion to the
Jacquard punching machine, in his combined self-acting
machine for shearing iron and punching both webs of
angle or T iron simultaneously to any required pitch;
though this machine, like others which have proceeded
from his fertile brain, is ahead even of this fast-manufac-
turing age, and has not yet come into general use, but is
certain to do so before many years have elapsed.

These inventions were surely enough for one man to have
accomplished; but we have not yet done. The mere enumeration of his other inventions would occupy several
pages. We shall merely allude to a few of them. One
was his Turret Clock, for which he obtained the medal
at the Great Exhibition of 1851. Another was his Prize
Electro-Magnet of 1845. When this subject was first mentioned to him, he said he did not know anything of the
theory or practice of electro-magnetism, but he would try
and find out. The result of his trying was that he won the
prize for the most powerful electro-magnet: one is placed
in the museum at Peel Park, Manchester, and another
with the Scottish Society of Arts, Edinburgh. In 1846 he
perfected an American invention for making cigars by
machinery; enabling a boy, working one of his cigar-
engines, to make as many as 5000 in a day. In 1852 he
patented improvements in the construction, propelling, and
equipment of steamships, which have, we believe, been
adopted to a certain extent by the Admiralty; and a few
years later, in 1855, we find him presenting the Secretary
of War with plans of elongated rifle projectiles to be used
in smooth-bore ordnance with a view to utilize the old-
pattern gun. His head, like many inventors of the time,
being full of the mechanics of war, he went so far as to
wait upon Louis Napoleon, and laid before him a plan by

which Sebastopol was to be blown down.   In short, upon whatever subject he turned his mind, he left the impress of his inventive faculty.   If it was imperfect, he improved it; if incapable of improvement, and impracticable, he in-vented something entirely new, superseding it altogether. But with all his inventive genius, in the exercise of which Mr. Roberts has so largely added to the productive power of the country, we regret to say that he is not gifted with the commercial faculty.   He has helped others in their difficulties, but forgotten himself.   Many have profited by his inventions, without even acknowledging the obliga-tions which they owed to him.   They have used his brains and copied his tools, and the "sucked orange" is all but forgotten.   There may have been a want of worldly wisdom on his part, but it is lamentable to think that one of the most prolific and useful inventors of his time should in his old age be left to fight with poverty.

Mr. Whitworth is another of the first-class tool-makers of Manchester who has turned to excellent account his training in the workshops of Maudslay and Clement.   He has carried fully out the system of uniformity in Screw Threads which they initiated; and he has still further improved the mechanism of the planing machine, enabling it to work both backwards and forwards by means of a screw and roller motion.   His "Jim Crow Machine," so called from its peculiar motion in reversing itself and working both ways, is an extremely beautiful tool, adapted alike for horizontal, vertical, or angular motions.   The minute accuracy of Mr. Whitworth's machines is not the least of their merits; and nothing will satisfy him short of perfect truth.   At the meeting of the Institute of Mecha-nical Engineers at Glasgow in 1856 he read a paper on the essential importance of possessing a true plane as a standard of reference in mechanical constructions, and he described elaborately the true method of securing it,—namely, by scraping, instead of by the ordinary process of grinding. At the same meeting he exhibited a machine of his invention by which he stated that a difference of *the millionth part* of an inch in length could at once be detected. He also there urged his favourite idea of uniformity, and proper gradations of size of parts, in all the various branches of the mechanical arts, as a chief means towards economy of production—a principle, as he showed, capable of very extensive application. To show the progress of tools and machinery in his own time, Mr. Whitworth cited the fact that thirty years since the cost of labour for making a surface of cast-iron true—one of the most important operations in mechanics—by chipping and filing by the hand, was 12*s.* a square foot; whereas it is now done by the planing machine at a cost for labour of less than a penny. Then in machinery, pieces of 74 reed printing-cotton cloth of 29 yards each could not be produced at less cost than 30*s.* 6*d.* per piece; whereas the same description is now sold for 3*s.* 9*d.* Mr. Whitworth has been among the most effective workers in this field of improvement, his tools taking the first place in point of speed, accuracy, and finish of work, in which respects they challenge competition with the world. Mr. Whitworth has of late years been applying himself with his accustomed ardour to the development of the powers of rifled guns and projectiles,—a branch of mechanical science in which he confessedly holds a foremost place, and in perfecting which he is still occupied.

CHAPTER XV.

JAMES NASMYTH.

———

" By Hammer and Hand
All Arts doth stand."
Hammermen's Motto.

———

THE founder of the Scotch family of Naesmyth is said to
have derived his name from the following circumstance.
In the course of the feuds which raged for some time
between the Scotch kings and their powerful subjects the
Earls of Douglas, a rencontre took place one day on the
outskirts of a Border village, when the king's adherents
were worsted. One of them took refuge in the village
smithy, where, hastily disguising himself, and donning a
spare leathern apron, he pretended to be engaged in assist-
ing the smith with his work, when a party of the Douglas
followers rushed in. They glanced at the pretended workman at the anvil, and observed him deliver a blow upon
it so unskilfully that the hammer-shaft broke in his hand.
On this one of the Douglas men rushed at him, calling
out, " Ye're nae smyth!" The assailed man seized his
sword, which lay conveniently at hand, and defended himself so vigorously that he shortly killed his assailant, while
the smith brained another with his hammer ; and, a party
of the king's men having come to their help, the rest were
speedily overpowered. The royal forces then rallied, and
their temporary defeat was converted into a victory. The
king bestowed a grant of land on his follower " Nae Smyth,"
who assumed for his arms a sword between two hammers

with broken shafts, and the motto " Non arte sed Marte,"
as if to disclaim the art of the Smith, in which he had
failed, and to emphasize the superiority of the warrior.
Such is said to be the traditional origin of the family of
Naesmyth of Posso in Peeblesshire, who continue to bear
the same name and arms.

It is remarkable that the inventor of the steam-hammer
should have so effectually contradicted the name he bears
and reversed the motto of his family ; for so far from
being " Nae Smyth," he may not inappropriately be designated the very Vulcan of the nineteenth century. His
hammer is a tool of immense power and pliancy, but for
which we must have stopped short in many of those gigantic
engineering works which are among the marvels of the
age we live in. It possesses so much precision and delicacy that it will chip the end of an egg resting in a glass
on the anvil without breaking it, while it delivers a blow
of ten tons with such a force as to be felt shaking the
parish. It is therefore with a high degree of appropriate-
ness that Mr. Nasmyth has discarded the feckless hammer
with the broken shaft, and assumed for his emblem his own
magnificent steam-hammer, at the same time reversing the
family motto, which he has converted into " Non Marte
sed Arte."

James Nasmyth belongs to a family whose genius in art
has long been recognised. His father, Alexander Nasmyth
of Edinburgh, was a landscape-painter of great eminence,
whose works are sometimes confounded with those of his son
Patrick, called the English Hobbema, though his own
merits are peculiar and distinctive. The elder Nasmyth
was also an admirable portrait painter, as his head of
Burns—the best ever painted of the poet—bears ample
witness. His daughters, the Misses Nasmyth, were highly
skilled painters of landscape, and their works are well
known and much prized. James, the youngest of the
family, inherits the same love of art, though his name is
more extensively known as a worker and inventor in iron.

He was born at Edinburgh, on the 19th of August, 1808 ; and his attention was early directed to mechanics by the circumstance of this being one of his father's hobbies. Besides being an excellent painter, Mr. Nasmyth had a good general knowledge of architecture and civil engineering, and could work at the lathe and handle tools with the dexterity of a mechanic. He employed nearly the whole of his spare time in a little workshop which adjoined his studio, where he encouraged his youngest son to work with him in all sorts of materials. Among his visitors at the studio were Professor Leslie, Patrick Miller of Dalswinton, and other men of distinction. He assisted Mr. Miller in his early experiments with paddle-boats, which eventually led to the invention of the steamboat. It was a great advantage for the boy to be trained by a father who so loved excellence in all its forms, and could minister to his love of mechanics by his own instruction and practice. James used to drink in with pleasure and profit the conversation which passed between his father and his visitors on scientific and mechanical subjects ; and as he became older, the resolve grew stronger in him every day that he would be a mechanical engineer, and nothing else. At a proper age, he was sent to the High School, then as now celebrated for the excellence of its instruction, and there he laid the foundations of a sound and liberal education. But he has himself told the simple story of his early life in such graphic terms that we feel we cannot do better than quote his own words :—*

"I had the good luck," he says, "to have for a school companion the son of an iron founder. Every spare hour that I could command was devoted to visits to his father's iron foundry, where I delighted to watch the various pro-

---

* Originally prepared for John Hick, Esq., C.E., of Bolton, and embodied by him in his lectures on "Self Help," delivered before the Holy Trinity Working Men's Association of that town, on the 18th and 20th March, 1862 ; the account having been kindly corrected by Mr. Nasmyth for the present publication.

cesses of moulding, iron-melting, casting, forging, pattern-making, and other smith and metal work; and although I was only about twelve years old at the time, I used to lend a hand, in which hearty zeal did a good deal to make up for want of strength. I look back to the Saturday after-noons spent in the workshops of that small foundry, as an important part of my education. I did not trust to reading about such and such things; I saw and handled them; and all the ideas in connection with them became permanent in my mind. I also obtained there—what was of much value to me in after life—a considerable acquaint-ance with the nature and characters of workmen. By the time I was fifteen, I could work and turn out really re-spectable jobs in wood, brass, iron, and steel : indeed, in the working of the latter inestimable material, I had at a very early age (eleven or twelve) acquired considerable proficiency. As that was the pre-lucifer match period, the possession of a steel and tinder box was quite a patent of nobility among boys. So I used to forge old files into ' steels ' in my father's little workshop, and harden them and produce such first-rate, neat little articles in that line, that I became quite famous amongst my school com-panions; and many a task have I had excused me by bribing the monitor, whose grim sense of duty never could withstand the glimpse of a steel.

" My first essay at making a steam engine was when I was fifteen. I then made a real working steam-engine, 1¾ diameter cylinder, and 8 in. stroke, which not only could act, but really did some useful work; for I made it grind the oil colours which my father required for his painting. Steam engine models, now so common, were exceedingly scarce in those days, and very difficult to be had; and as the demand for them arose, I found it both delightful and profitable to make them; as well as sectional models of steam engines, which I introduced for the purpose of ex-hibiting the movements of all the parts, both exterior and interior. With the results of the sale of such models I was enabled to pay the price of tickets of admission to the lectures on natural philosophy and chemistry delivered in the University of Edinburgh. About the same time (1826) I was so happy as to be employed by Professor Leslie in making models and portions of apparatus required by him for his lectures and philosophical investigations, and I had also the inestimable good fortune to secure his friendship. His admirably clear manner of communicating a knowledge of the fundamental principles of mechanical science rendered my intercourse with him of the utmost importance to myself. A hearty, cheerful, earnest desire to toil in his service, caused him to take pleasure in instructing me by occasional explanations of what might otherwise have remained obscure.

" About the years 1827 and 1828, the subject of steam-carriages for common roads occupied much of the attention of the public. Many tried to solve the problem. I made a working model of an engine which performed so well that some friends determined to give me the means of making one on a larger scale. This I did; and I shall never forget the pleasure and the downright hard work I had in producing, in the autumn of 1828, at an outlay of 60l., a complete steam-carriage, that ran many a mile with eight persons on it. After keeping it in action two months, to the satisfaction of all who were interested in it, my friends allowed me to dispose of it, and I sold it a great bargain, after which the engine was used in driving a small factory. I may mention that in that engine I employed the waste steam to cause an increased draught by its discharge up the chimney. This important use of the waste steam had been introduced by George Stephenson some years before, though entirely unknown to me.

" The earnest desire which I cherished of getting forward in the real business of life induced me to turn my attention to obtaining employment in some of the great engineering establishments of the day, at the head of which, in my fancy as well as in reality, stood that of Henry

Maudslay, of London. It was the summit of my ambition to get work in that establishment; but as my father had not the means of paying a premium, I determined to try what I could do towards attaining my object by submitting to Mr. Maudslay actual specimens of my capability as a young workman and draughtsman. To this end I set to work and made a small steam-engine, every part of which was the result of my own handiwork, including the casting and the forging of the several parts. This I turned out in such a style as I should even now be proud of. My sample drawings were, I may say, highly respectable. Armed with such means of obtaining the good opinion of the great Henry Maudslay, on the 19th of May, 1829, I sailed for London in a Leith smack, and after an eight days' voyage saw the metropolis for the first time. I made bold to call on Mr. Maudslay, and told him my simple tale. He desired me to bring my models for him to look at. I did so, and when he came to me I could see by the expression of his cheerful, well-remembered countenance, that I had attained my object. He then and there appointed me to be his own private workman, to assist him in his little paradise of a workshop, furnished with the models of improved machinery and engineering tools of which he has been the great originator. He left me to arrange as to wages with his chief cashier, Mr. Robert Young, and on the first Saturday evening I accordingly went to the counting-house to enquire of him about my pay. He asked me what would satisfy me. Knowing the value of the situation I had obtained, and having a very modest notion of my worthiness to occupy it, I said, that if he would not consider 10s. a week too much, I thought I could do very well with that. I suppose he concluded that I had some means of my own to live on besides the 10s. a week which I asked. He little knew that I had determined not to cost my father another farthing when I left home to begin the world on my own account. My proposal was at once acceded to. And well do I remember the pride and delight I felt when I carried to my three shillings a week lodging that night my first wages. Ample they were in my idea; for I knew how little I could live on, and was persuaded that by strict economy I could easily contrive to make the money support me. To help me in this object, I contrived a small cooking apparatus, which I forthwith got made by a tinsmith in Lambeth, at a cost of 6s., and by its aid I managed to keep the eating and drinking part of my private account within 3s. 6d. per week, or 4s. at the outside. I had three meat dinners a week, and generally four rice and milk dinners, all of which were cooked by my little apparatus, which I set in action after breakfast. The oil cost not quite a halfpenny per day. The meat dinners consisted of a stew of from a half to three quarters of a lb. of leg of beef, the meat costing 3½d. per lb., which, with sliced potatoes and a little onion, and as much water as just covered all, with a sprinkle of salt and black pepper, by the time I returned to dinner at half-past six furnished a repast in every respect as good as my appetite. For breakfast I had coffee and a due proportion of quartern loaf. After the first year of my employment under Mr. Maudslay, my wages were raised to 15s. a week, and I then, but not till then, indulged in the luxury of butter to my bread. I am the more particular in all this, to show you that I was a thrifty housekeeper, although only a lodger in a 3s. room. I have the old apparatus by me yet, and I shall have another dinner out of it ere I am a year older, out of regard to days that were full of the real romance of life.

" On the death of Henry Maudslay in 1831, I passed over to the service of his worthy partner, Mr. Joshua Field, and acted as his draughtsman, much to my advantage, until the end of that year, when I returned to Edinburgh, to construct a small stock of engineering tools for the purpose of enabling me to start in business on my own account. This occupied me until the spring of 1833, and during the interval I was accustomed to take in jobs to execute in my little workshop in Edinburgh, so as to obtain the means of

completing my stock of tools.*　In June, 1834, I went to
Manchester, and took a flat of an old mill in Dale Street,
where I began business.　In two years my stock had so
increased as to overload the floor of the old building to
such an extent that the landlord, Mr. Wrenn, became
alarmed, especially as the tenant below me—a glass-cutter
—had a visit from the end of a 20-horse engine beam one
morning among his cut tumblers.　To set their anxiety at
rest, I went out that evening to Patricroft and took a look
at a rather choice bit of land bounded on one side by the
canal, and on the other by the Liverpool and Manchester
Railway.　By the end of the week I had secured a lease
of the site for 999 years; by the end of the month my
wood sheds were erected; the ring of the hammer on the
smith's anvil was soon heard all over the place; and the
Bridgewater Foundry was fairly under way.　There I toiled
right heartily until December 31st, 1856, when I retired
to enjoy in active leisure the reward of a laborious life,
during which, with the blessing of God, I enjoyed much
true happiness through the hearty love which I always had
for my profession; and I trust I may be allowed to say,
without undue vanity, that I have left behind me some
useful results of my labours in those inventions with which
my name is identified, which have had no small share in
the accomplishment of some of the greatest mechanical
works of our age."

If Mr. Nasmyth had accomplished nothing more than
the invention of his steam-hammer, it would have been

---

* Most of the tools with which he
began business in Manchester were made
by his own hands in his father's little
workshop at Edinburgh.　He was on
one occasion "hard up" for brass with
which to make a wheel for his planing
machine.　There was a row of old-
fashioned brass candlesticks standing in
bright array on the kitchen mantel-
piece which he greatly coveted for the
purpose.　His father was reluctant to
give them up; "for," said he, "I have
had many a crack with Burns when
these candlesticks were on the table."
But his mother at length yielded;
when the candlesticks were at once
recast, and made into the wheel of the
planing machine, which is still at work
in Manchester.

enough to found a reputation. Professor Tomlinson describes it as "one of the most perfect of artificial machines and noblest triumphs of mind over matter that modern English engineers have yet developed."* The hand-hammer has always been an important tool, and, in the form of the stone celt, it was perhaps the first invented. When the hammer of iron superseded that of stone, it was found practicable in the hands of a "cunning" workman to execute by its means metal work of great beauty and even delicacy. But since the invention of cast-iron, and the manufacture of wrought-iron in large masses, the art of hammer-working has almost become lost; and great artists, such as Matsys of Antwerp and Rukers of Nuremberg were,† no longer think it worth their while to expend time and skill in working on so humble a material as wrought-iron. It is evident from the marks of care and elaborate design which many of these early works exhibit, that the workman's heart was in his work, and that his object was not merely to get it out of hand, but to execute it in first-rate artistic style.

When the use of iron extended and larger ironwork came to be forged, for cannon, tools, and machinery, the ordinary hand-hammer was found insufficient, and the helve or forge-hammer was invented. This was usually driven by a water-wheel, or by oxen or horses. The tilt-hammer was another form in which it was used, the smaller kinds being worked by the foot. Among Watt's various inventions, was a tilt-hammer of considerable power, which he at first worked by means of a water-wheel, and afterwards by a steam-

---

* *Cyclopædia of Useful Arts*, ii. 739.

† Matsys' beautiful wrought-iron well cover, still standing in front of the cathedral at Antwerp, and Rukers's steel or iron chair exhibited at South Kensington in 1862, are examples of the beautiful hammer work turned out by the artisans of the middle ages. The railings of the tombs of Henry VII. and Queen Eleanor in Westminster Abbey, the hinges and iron work of Lincoln Cathedral, of St. George's Chapel at Windsor, and of some of the Oxford colleges, afford equally striking illustrations of the skill of our English blacksmiths several centuries ago.

engine regulated by a fly-wheel. His first hammer of this kind was 120 lbs. in weight; it was raised eight inches before making each blow. Watt afterwards made a tilt-hammer for Mr. Wilkinson of Bradley Forge, of 7½ cwt., and it made 300 blows a minute. Other improvements were made in the hammer from time to time, but no material alteration was made in the power by which it was worked until Mr. Nasmyth took it in hand, and applying to it the force of steam, at once provided the worker in iron with the most formidable of machine-tools. This important invention originated as follows :—

In the early part of 1837, the directors of the Great Western Steam-Ship Company sent Mr. Francis Humphries, their engineer, to consult Mr. Nasmyth as to some engineering tools of unusual size and power, which were required for the construction of the engines of the "Great Britain" steamship. They had determined to construct those engines on the vertical trunk-engine principle, in accordance with Mr. Humphries' designs; and very complete works were erected by them at their Bristol dockyard for the execution of the requisite machinery, the most important of the tools being supplied by Nasmyth and Gaskell. The engines were in hand, when a difficulty arose with respect to the enormous paddle-shaft of the vessel, which was of such a size of forging as had never before been executed. Mr. Humphries applied to the largest engineering firms throughout the country for tenders of the price at which they would execute this part of the work, but to his surprise and dismay he found that not one of the firms he applied to would undertake so large a forging. In this dilemma he wrote to Mr. Nasmyth on the 24th November, 1838, informing him of this unlooked-for difficulty. "I find," said he, "there is not a forge-hammer in England or Scotland powerful enough to forge the paddle-shaft of the engines for the 'Great Britain!' What am I to do? Do you think I might dare to use cast-iron?"

This letter immediately set Mr. Nasmyth a-thinking.

How was it that existing hammers were incapable of forging a wrought-iron shaft of thirty inches diameter? Simply because of their want of compass, or range and fall, as well as power of blow. A few moments' rapid thought satisfied him that it was by rigidly adhering to the old traditional form of hand-hammer—of which the tilt, though driven by steam, was but a modification—that the difficulty had arisen. When even the largest hammer was tilted up to its full height, its range was so small, that when a piece of work of considerable size was placed on the anvil, the hammer became "gagged," and, on such an occasion, where the forging required the most powerful blow, it received next to no blow at all,—the clear space for fall being almost entirely occupied by the work on the anvil.

The obvious remedy was to invent some method, by which a block of iron should be lifted to a sufficient height above the object on which it was desired to strike a blow, and let the block fall down upon the work,—guiding it in its descent by such simple means as should give the required precision in the percussive action of the falling mass. Following out this idea, Mr. Nasmyth at once sketched on paper his steam-hammer, having it clearly before him in his mind's eye a few minutes after receiving Mr. Humphries' letter narrating his unlooked-for difficulty.   The hammer, as thus sketched, consisted of, first an anvil on which to rest the work; second, a block of iron constituting the hammer or blow-giving part; third, an inverted steam-cylinder to whose piston-rod the block was attached. All that was then required to produce by such means a most effective hammer, was simply to admit steam in the cylinder so as to act on the under side of the piston, and so raise the block attached to the piston-rod, and by a simple contrivance to let the steam escape and so permit the block rapidly to descend by its own gravity upon the work then on the anvil. Such, in a few words, is the rationale of the steam-hammer.

By the same day's post, Mr. Nasmyth wrote to Mr.

Humphries, inclosing a sketch of the invention by which he proposed to forge the "Great Britain" paddle-shaft. Mr. Humphries showed it to Mr. Brunel, the engineer-in-chief of the company, to Mr. Guppy, the managing director, and to others interested in the undertaking, by all of whom it was heartily approved. Mr. Nasmyth gave permission to communicate his plans to such forge proprietors as might feel disposed to erect such a hammer to execute the proposed work,—the only condition which he made being, that in the event of his hammer being adopted, he was to be allowed to supply it according to his own design.

The paddle-shaft of the "Great Britain" was, however, never forged. About that time, the substitution of the Screw for the Paddle-wheel as a means of propulsion of steam-vessels was attracting much attention; and the performances of the "Archimedes" were so successful as to induce Mr. Brunel to recommend his Directors to adopt the new power. They yielded to his entreaty. The great engines which Mr. Humphries had designed were accordingly set aside; and he was required to produce fresh designs of engines suited for screw propulsion. The result was fatal to Mr. Humphries. The labour, the anxiety, and perhaps the disappointment, proved too much for him, and a brain-fever carried him off; so that neither his great paddle-shaft nor Mr. Nasmyth's steam-hammer to forge it was any longer needed.

The hammer was left to bide its time. No forge-master would take it up. The inventor wrote to all the great firms, urging its superiority to every other tool for working malleable iron into all kinds of forge work. Thus he wrote and sent illustrative sketches of his hammer to Accramans and Morgan of Bristol, to the late Benjamin Hick and Rushton and Eckersley of Bolton, to Howard and Ravenhill of Rotherhithe, and other firms; but unhappily bad times for the iron trade had set in; and although all to whom he communicated his design were much struck with its simplicity and obvious advantages, the answer usually given was—" We have not orders enough to keep in work the forge-hammers we already have, and we do not desire at present to add any new ones, however improved." At that time no patent had been taken out for the invention. Mr. Nasmyth had not yet saved money enough to enable him to do so on his own account; and his partner declined to spend money upon a tool that no engineer would give the firm an order for. No secret was made of the invention, and, excepting to its owner, it did not seem to be worth one farthing.

Such was the unpromising state of affairs, when M. Schneider, of the Creusot Iron Works in France, called at the Patricroft works together with his practical mechanic M. Bourdon, for the purpose of ordering some tools of the firm. Mr. Nasmyth was absent on a journey at the time, but his partner, Mr. Gaskell, as an act of courtesy to the strangers, took the opportunity of showing them all that was new and interesting in regard to mechanism about the works. And among other things, Mr. Gaskell brought out his partner's sketch or " Scheme book," which lay in a drawer in the office, and showed them the design of the Steam Hammer, which no English firm would adopt. They were much struck with its simplicity and practical utility; and M. Bourdon took careful note of its arrangements. Mr. Nasmyth on his return was informed of the visit of MM. Schneider and Bourdon, but the circumstance of their having inspected the design of his steam-hammer seems to have been regarded by his partner as too trivial a matter to be repeated to him; and he knew nothing of the circumstance until his visit to France in April, 1840. When passing through the works at Creusot with M. Bourdon, Mr. Nasmyth saw a crank shaft of unusual size, not only forged in the piece, but punched. He immediately asked, "How did you forge that shaft?" M. Bourdon's answer was, " Why, with your hammer, to be sure!" Great indeed was Nasmyth's surprise; for he had

never yet seen the hammer, except in his own drawing!
A little explanation soon cleared all up. M. Bourdon said
he had been so much struck with the ingenuity and simplicity of the arrangement, that he had no sooner returned
than he set to work, and had a hammer made in general
accordance with the design Mr. Gaskell had shown him;
and that its performances had answered his every expectation. He then took Mr. Nasmyth to see the steam-hammer;
and great was his delight at seeing the child of his brain
in full and active work. It was not, according to Mr.
Nasmyth's ideas, quite perfect, and he readily suggested
several improvements, conformable with the original design, which M. Bourdon forthwith adopted.

On reaching England, Mr. Nasmyth at once wrote to his
partner telling him what he had seen, and urging that the
taking out of a patent for the protection of the invention
ought no longer to be deferred. But trade was still very
much depressed, and as the Patricroft firm needed all their
capital to carry on their business, Mr. Gaskell objected to
lock any of it up in engineering novelties. Seeing himself
on the brink of losing his property in the invention, Mr.
Nasmyth applied to his brother-in-law, William Bennett,
Esq., who advanced him the requisite money for the
purpose—about 280*l.*,—and the patent was secured in
June 1840. The first hammer, of 30 cwt., was made for
the Patricroft works, with the consent of the partners; and
in the course of a few weeks it was in full work. The
precision and beauty of its action—the perfect ease with
which it was managed, and the untiring force of its percussive blows—were the admiration of all who saw it; and
from that moment the steam-hammer became a recognised
power in modern mechanics. The variety or gradation of
its blows was such, that it was found practicable to mani-
pulate a hammer of ten tons as easily as if it had only been
of ten ounces weight. It was under such complete control
that while descending with its greatest momentum, it

could be arrested at any point with even greater ease than any instrument used by hand.   While capable of forging an Armstrong hundred-pounder, or the sheet-anchor for a ship of the line, it could hammer a nail, or crack a nut without bruising the kernel.   When it came into general use, the facilities which it afforded for executing all kinds of forging had the effect of greatly increasing the quantity of work done, at the same time that expense was saved.   The cost of making anchors was reduced by at least 50 per cent., while the quality of the forging was improved.   Before its invention the manufacture of a shaft of 15 or 20 cwt. required the concentrated exertions of a large establishment, and its successful execution was regarded as a great triumph of skill; whereas forgings of 20 and 30 tons weight are now things of almost every-day occurrence.   Its advantages were so obvious, that its adoption soon became general, and in the course of a few years Nasmyth steam-hammers were to be found in every well-appointed workshop both at home and abroad.   Many modifications have been made in the tool, by Condie, Morrison, Naylor, Rigby, and others; but Nasmyth's was the father of them all, and still holds its ground.*

Among the important uses to which this hammer has of late years been applied, is the manufacture of iron plates for covering our ships of war, and the fabrication of the immense wrought-iron ordnance of Armstrong, Whitworth, and Blakely.   But for the steam-hammer, indeed, it is doubtful whether such weapons could have been made.   It is also used for the re-manufacture of iron in various other forms, to say nothing of the greatly extended use which it

---

* Mr. Nasmyth has lately introduced, with the assistance of Mr. Wilson of the Low Moor Iron Works, a new, exceedingly ingenious, and very simple contrivance for working the hammer. By this application any length of stroke, any amount of blow, and any amount of variation can be given by the operation of a single lever; and by this improvement the machine has attained a rapidity of action and change of motion suitable to the powers of the engine, and the form or consistency of the articles under the hammer.—Mr. Fairbairn's *Report on the Paris Universal Exhibition of* 1855, p. 100.

has been the direct means of effecting in wrought-iron and steel forgings in every description of machinery, from the largest marine steam-engines to the most nice and delicate parts of textile mechanism. "It is not too much to say," observes a writer in the *Engineer*, "that, without Nasmyth's steam-hammer, we must have stopped short in many of those gigantic engineering works which, but for the decay of all wonder in us, would be the perpetual wonder of this age, and which have enabled our modern engineers to take rank above the gods of all mythologies. There is one use to which the steam-hammer is now becoming extensively applied by some of our manufacturers that deserves especial mention, rather for the prospect which it opens to us than for what has already been actually accomplished. We allude to the manufacture of large articles in *dies*. At one manufactory in the country, railway wheels, for example, are being manufactured with enormous economy by this means. The various parts of the wheels are produced in quantity either by rolling or by dies under the hammer; these parts are brought together in their relative positions in a mould, heated to a welding heat, and then by a blow of the steam hammer, furnished with dies, are stamped into a complete and all but finished wheel. It is evident that wherever wrought-iron articles of a manageable size have to be produced in considerable quantities, the same process may be adopted, and the saving effected by the substitution of this for the ordinary forging process will doubtless ere long prove incalculable. For this, as for the many other advantageous uses of the steam-hammer, we are primarily and mainly indebted to Mr. Nasmyth. It is but right, therefore, that we should hold his name in honour. In fact, when we think of the universal service which this machine is rendering us, we feel that some special expression of our indebtedness to him would be a reasonable and grateful service. The benefit which he has conferred upon us is so great as to justly entitle him to stand side by side with the few men who have gained name and fame as great inventive engineers, and to whom we have testified our gratitude—usually, unhappily, when it was too late for them to enjoy it."

Mr. Nasmyth subsequently applied the principle of the steam-hammer in the pile driver, which he invented in 1845. Until its production, all piles had been driven by means of a small mass of iron falling upon the head of the pile with great velocity from a considerable height,—the raising of the iron mass by means of the "monkey" being an operation that occupied much time and labour, with which the results were very incommensurate. Pile-driving was, in Mr. Nasmyth's words, conducted on the artillery or cannon-ball principle; the action being excessive and the mass deficient, and adapted rather for destructive than impulsive action. In his new and beautiful machine, he applied the elastic force of steam in raising the ram or driving block, on which, the block being disengaged, its whole weight of three tons descended on the head of the pile, and the process being repeated eighty times in the minute, the pile was sent home with a rapidity that was quite marvellous compared with the old-fashioned system. In forming coffer-dams for the piers and abutments of bridges, quays, and harbours, and in piling the foundations of all kinds of masonry, the steam pile driver was found of invaluable use by the engineer. At the first experiment made with the machine, Mr. Nasmyth drove a 14-inch pile fifteen feet into hard ground at the rate of 65 blows a minute. The driver was first used in forming the great steam dock at Devonport, where the results were very strik-ing; and it was shortly after employed by Robert Stephenson in piling the foundations of the great High Level Bridge at Newcastle, and the Border Bridge at Berwick, as well as in several other of his great works. The saving of time effected by this machine was very remarkable, the ratio being as 1 to 1800; that is, a pile could be driven in four minutes that before required twelve hours. One of the peculiar features of the invention was that of employ-

ing the pile itself as the support of the steam-hammer part
of the apparatus while it was being driven, so that the pile
had the percussive action of the dead weight of the hammer
as well as its lively blows to induce it to sink into the
ground.   The steam - hammer sat as it were on the
shoulders of the pile, while it dealt forth its ponderous
blows on the pile-head at the rate of 80 a minute, and as
the pile sank, the hammer followed it down with never
relaxing activity until it was driven home to the required
depth.   One of the most ingenious contrivances employed
in the driver, which was also adopted in the hammer, was
the use of steam as a buffer in the upper part of the cylinder, which had the effect of a recoil spring, and greatly
enhanced the force of the downward blow.

In 1846, Mr. Nasmyth designed a form of steam-engine
after that of his steam-hammer, which has been extensively
adopted all over the world for screw-ships of all sizes.
The pyramidal form of this engine, its great simplicity and
get-at-ability of parts, together with the circumstance that
all the weighty parts of the engine are kept low, have rendered it a universal favourite.   Among the other labour-
saving tools invented by Mr. Nasmyth, may be mentioned
the well-known planing machine for small work, called
" Nasmyth's Steam Arm," now used in every large workshop.
It was contrived for the purpose of executing a large order
for locomotives received from the Great Western Railway,
and was found of great use in accelerating the work, especially in planing the links, levers, connecting rods, and
smaller kinds of wrought-iron work in those engines.   His
circular cutter for toothed wheels was another of his handy
inventions, which shortly came into general use.   In iron-
founding also he introduced a valuable practical improvement.   The old mode of pouring the molten metal into the
moulds was by means of a large ladle with one or two cross
handles and levers ; but many dreadful accidents occurred
through a slip of the hand, and Mr. Nasmyth resolved, if
possible, to prevent them.   The plan he adopted was to fix

a worm-wheel on the side of the ladle, into which a worm
was geared, and by this simple contrivance one man was
enabled to move the largest ladle on its axis with perfect
ease and safety.   By this means the work was more
promptly performed, and accidents entirely avoided.

Mr. Nasmyth's skill in invention was backed by great
energy and a large fund of common sense—qualities not
often found united.   These proved of much service to the
concern of which he was the head, and indeed constituted
the vital force.   The firm prospered as it deserved; and
they executed orders not only for England, but for most
countries in the civilized world.   Mr. Nasmyth had the
advantage of being trained in a good school—that of Henry
Maudslay—where he had not only learnt handicraft under
the eye of that great mechanic, but the art of organizing
labour, and (what is of great value to an employer) knowledge of the characters of workmen.   Yet the Nasmyth firm
were not without their troubles as respected the mechanics
in their employment, and on one occasion they had to pass
through the ordeal of a very formidable strike.   The manner in which the inventor of the steam-hammer literally
" Scotched" this strike was very characteristic.

A clever young man employed by the firm as a brass
founder, being found to have a peculiar capacity for skilled
mechanical work, had been advanced to the lathe.   The
other men objected to his being so employed on the ground
that it was against the rules of the trade.   "But he is
a first-rate workman," replied the employers, "and we
think it right to advance a man according to his conduct
and his merits."   "No matter," said the workmen, "it is
against the rules, and if you do not take the man from the
lathe, we must turn out."   "Very well; we hold to our
right of selecting the best men for the best places, and we
will not take the man from the lathe."   The consequence
was a general turn out.   Pickets were set about the works,
and any stray men who went thither to seek employment
were waylaid, and if not induced to turn back, were mal-

treated or annoyed until they were glad to leave. The works were almost at a standstill. This state of things could not be allowed to go on, and the head of the firm bestirred himself accordingly with his usual energy. He went down to Scotland, searched all the best mechanical workshops there, and after a time succeeded in engaging sixty-four good hands. He forbade them coming by driblets, but held them together until there was a full freight; and then they came, with their wives, families, chests of drawers, and eight-day clocks, in a steamboat specially hired for their transport from Greenock to Liverpool. From thence they came by special train to Patricroft, where houses were in readiness for their reception. The arrival of so numerous, well-dressed, and respectable a corps of workmen and their families was an event in the neighbourhood, and could not fail to strike the " pickets " with surprise. Next morning the sixty-four Scotchmen assembled in the yard at Patricroft, and after giving " three cheers," went quietly to their work. The " picketing " went on for a little while longer, but it was of no use against a body of strong men who stood " shouther to shouther," as the new hands did. It was even bruited about that there were " more trains to follow ! " It very soon became clear that the back of the strike was broken. The men returned to their work, and the clever brass founder continued at his turning-lathe, from which he speedily rose to still higher employment.

Notwithstanding the losses and suffering occasioned by strikes, Mr. Nasmyth holds the opinion that they have on the whole produced much more good than evil. They have served to stimulate invention in an extraordinary degree. Some of the most important labour-saving processes now in common use are directly traceable to them. In the case of many of our most potent self-acting tools and machines, manufacturers could not be induced to adopt them until compelled to do so by strikes. This was the case with the self-acting mule, the wool-combing machine, the planing machine, the slotting machine, Nasmyth's steam arm, and many others. Thus, even in the mechanical world, there may be " a soul of goodness in things evil."

Mr. Nasmyth retired from business in December, 1856. He had the moral courage to come out of the groove which he had so laboriously made for himself, and to leave a large and prosperous business, saying, " I have now enough of this world's goods ; let younger men have their chance." He settled down at his rural retreat in Kent, but not to lead a life of idle ease. Industry had become his habit, and active occupation was necessary to his happiness. He fell back upon the cultivation of those artistic tastes which are the heritage of his family. When a boy at the High School of Edinburgh, he was so skilful in making pen and ink illustrations on the margins of the classics, that he thus often purchased from his monitors exemption from the lessons of the day. Nor had he ceased to cultivate the art during his residence at Patricroft, but was accustomed to fall back upon it for relaxation and enjoyment amid the pursuits of trade. That he possesses remarkable fertility of imagination, and great skill in architectural and land-scape drawing, as well as in the much more difficult art of delineating the human figure, will be obvious to any one who has seen his works,—more particularly his " City of St. Ann's," " The Fairies," and " Everybody for ever ! " which last was exhibited in Pall Mall, among the recent collection of works of Art by amateurs and others, for relief of the Lancashire distress. He has also brought his common sense to bear on such unlikely subjects as the origin of the cuneiform character. The possession of a brick from Baby-lon set him a thinking. How had it been manufactured ? Its under side was clearly marked by the sedges of the Euphrates upon which it had been laid to dry and bake in the sun. But how about those curious cuneiform characters ? How had writing assumed so remarkable a form? His sur-mise was this : that the brickmakers, in telling their tale of bricks, used the triangular corner of another brick, and by pressing it down upon the soft clay, left behind it the triangular mark which the cuneiform character exhibits. Such marks repeated, and placed in different relations to each other, would readily represent any number. From the use of the corner of a brick in writing, the transition was easy to a pointed stick with a triangular end, by the use of which all the cuneiform characters can readily be produced upon the soft clay. This curious question formed the subject of an interesting paper read by Mr. Nasmyth before the British Association at Cheltenham.

But the most engrossing of Mr. Nasmyth's later pursuits has been the science of astronomy, in which, by bringing a fresh, original mind to the observation of celestial phenomena, he has succeeded in making some of the most remarkable discoveries of our time. Astronomy was one of his favourite pursuits at Patricroft, and on his retirement became his serious study. By repeated observations with a powerful reflecting telescope of his own construction, he succeeded in making a very careful and minute painting of the craters, cracks, mountains, and valleys in the moon's surface, for which a Council Medal was awarded him at the Great Exhibition of 1851. But the most striking discovery which he has made by means of his telescope—the result of patient, continuous, and energetic observation—has been that of the nature of the sun's surface, and the character of the extraordinary light-giving bodies, apparently possessed of voluntary motion, moving across it, sometimes forming spots or hollows of more than a hundred thousand miles in diameter.

The results of these observations were of so novel a character that astronomers for some time hesitated to receive them as facts.* Yet so eminent an astronomer as Sir John Herschel does not hesitate now to describe them as " a most wonderful discovery." " According to Mr.

---

* See *Memoirs of the Literary and Philosophical Society of Manchester*, 3rd series, vol. i. 407.

Nasmyth's observations," says he, " made with a very fine telescope of his own making, the bright surface of the sun consists of separate, insulated, individual objects or things, all nearly or exactly of one certain definite size and shape, which is more like that of a willow leaf, as he describes them, than anything else. These leaves or scales are not arranged in any order (as those on a butterfly's wing are), but lie crossing one another in all directions, like what are called spills in the game of spillikins; except at the borders of a spot, where they point for the most part inwards towards the middle of the spot,* presenting much the sort of appearance that the small leaves of some water-plants or sea-weeds do at the edge of a deep hole of clear water. The exceedingly definite shape of these objects, their exact similarity one to another, and the way in which they lie across and athwart each other (except where they form a sort of bridge across a spot, in which case they seem to affect a common direction, that, namely, of the bridge itself),—all these characters seem quite repugnant to the notion of their being of a vaporous, a cloudy, or a fluid nature. Nothing remains but to consider them as separate and independent sheets, flakes, or scales, having some sort of solidity. And these flakes, be they what they may, and whatever may be said about the dashing of meteoric stones into the sun's atmosphere, &c., are evidently *the immediate sources of the solar light and heat*, by whatever mechanism or whatever processes they may be enabled to develope and, as it were, elaborate these elements from the bosom of the non-luminous fluid in which

---

* Sir John Herschel adds, " Spots of not very irregular, and what may be called compact form, covering an area of between seven and eight hundred millions of square miles, are by no means uncommon. One spot which I measured in the year 1837 occupied no less than three thousand seven hundred and eighty millions, taking in all the irregularities of its form; and the black space or nucleus in the middle of one very nearly round one would have allowed the earth to drop through it, leaving a thousand clear miles on either side; and many instances of much larger spots than these are on record."

they appear to float.   Looked at in this point of view, we cannot refuse to regard them as organisms of some peculiar and amazing kind ; and though it would be too daring to speak of such organization as partaking of the nature of life, yet we do know that vital action *is* competent to develop heat and light, as well as electricity.   These wonderful objects have been seen by others as well as Mr. Nasmyth, so that there is no room to doubt of their reality." *

Such is the marvellous discovery made by the inventor of the steam-hammer, as described by the most distinguished astronomer of the age.   A writer in the *Edinburgh Review*, referring to the subject in a recent number, says it shows him " to possess an intellect as profound as it is expert."   Doubtless his training as a mechanic, his habits of close observation and his ready inventiveness, which conferred so much power on him as an engineer, proved of equal advantage to him when labouring in the domain of physical science.   Bringing a fresh mind, of keen perception, to his new studies, and uninfluenced by preconceived opinions, he saw them in new and original lights ; and hence the extraordinary discovery above described by Sir John Herschel.

Some two hundred years since, a member of the Nasmyth family, Jean Nasmyth of Hamilton, was burnt for a witch —one of the last martyrs to ignorance and superstition in Scotland—because she read her Bible with two pairs of spectacles.   Had Mr. Nasmyth himself lived then, he might, with his two telescopes of his own making, which bring the sun and moon into his chamber for him to examine and paint, have been taken for a sorcerer.   But fortunately for him, and still more so for us, Mr. Nasmyth stands before the public of this age as not only one of its ablest mechanics, but as one of the most accomplished and original of scientific observers.

------

* SIR JOHN HERSCHEL in *Good Words* for April, 1863.

CHAPTER XVI.

William Fairbairn.

" In science there is work for all hands, more or less skilled ; and he is usually the most fit to occupy the higher posts who has risen from the ranks, and has experimentally acquainted himself with the nature of the work to be done in each and every, even the humblest department."
J. D. Forbes.

The development of the mechanical industry of England has been so rapid, especially as regards the wonders achieved by the machine-tools above referred to, that it may almost be said to have been accomplished within the life of the present generation. " When I first entered this city," said Mr. Fairbairn, in his inaugural address as President of the British Association at Manchester in 1861, " the whole of the machinery was executed by hand. There were neither planing, slotting, nor shaping machines; and, with the exception of very imperfect lathes and a few drills, the preparatory operations of construction were effected entirely by the hands of the workmen. Now, everything is done by machine-tools with a degree of accuracy which the unaided hand could never accomplish. The automaton or self-acting machine-tool has within itself an almost creative power; in fact, so great are its powers of adaptation, that there is no operation of the human hand that it does not imitate." In a letter to the author, Mr. Fairbairn says, " The great pioneers of machine-tool-making were Maudslay, Murray of Leeds, Clement and Fox of Derby, who were ably followed by Nasmyth, Roberts, and Whitworth, of Manchester, and Sir Peter Fairbairn of Leeds;" and Mr. Fairbairn might

well have added, by himself,—for he has been one of the
most influential and successful of mechanical engineers.

William Fairbairn was born at Kelso on the 19th of
February, 1787. His parents occupied a humble but respectable position in life. His father, Andrew Fairbairn,
was the son of a gardener in the employment of Mr. Baillie
of Mellerston, and lived at Smailholm, a village lying a few
miles west of Kelso. Tracing the Fairbairns still further
back, we find several of them occupying the station of
"portioners," or small lairds, at Earlston on the Tweed,
where the family had been settled since the days of the
Solemn League and Covenant. By his mother's side, the
subject of our memoir is supposed to be descended from
the ancient Border family of Douglas.

While Andrew Fairbairn (William's father) lived at
Smailholm, Walter Scott was living with his grandmother
in Smailholm or Sandyknowe Tower, whither he had been
sent from Edinburgh in the hope that change of air would
help the cure of his diseased hip-joint; and Andrew,
being nine years his senior, and a strong youth for his
age, was accustomed to carry the little patient about in
his arms, until he was able to walk by himself. At a
later period, when Miss Scott, Walter's aunt, removed
from Smailholm to Kelso, the intercourse between the
families was renewed. Scott was then an Edinburgh advocate, engaged in collecting materials for his Minstrelsy
of the Scottish Border, or, as his aunt described his pursuit, "running after the auld wives of the country gatherin'
havers." He used frequently to read over by the fireside
in the evening the results of his curious industry, which,
however, were not very greatly appreciated by his nearest
relatives; and they did not scruple to declare that for the
"Advocate" to go about collecting "ballants" was mere
waste of time as well as money.

William Fairbairn's first schoolmaster was a decrepit
old man who went by the name of "Bowed Johnnie Ker,"
—a Cameronian, with a nasal twang, which his pupils

learnt much more readily than they did his lessons in reading and arithmetic, notwithstanding a liberal use of "the tawse." Yet Johnnie had a taste for music, and taught his pupils to *sing* their reading lessons, which was reckoned quite a novelty in education. After a short time our scholar was transferred to the parish-school of the town, kept by a Mr. White, where he was placed under the charge of a rather severe helper, who, instead of the tawse, administered discipline by means of his knuckles, hard as horn, which he applied with a peculiar jerk to the crania of his pupils. At this school Willie Fairbairn lost the greater part of the singing accomplishments which he had acquired under " Bowed Johnnie," but he learnt in lieu of them to read from Scott and Barrow's collections of prose and poetry, while he obtained some knowledge of arithmetic, in which he proceeded as far as practice and the rule of three. This constituted his whole stock of school-learning up to his tenth year. Out of school-hours he learnt to climb the ruined walls of the old abbey of the town, and there was scarcely an arch, or tower, or cranny of it with which he did not become familiar.

When in his twelfth year, his father, who had been brought up to farm-work, and possessed considerable practical knowledge of agriculture, was offered the charge of a farm at Moy in Ross-shire, belonging to Lord Seaforth of Brahan Castle. The farm was of about 300 acres, situated on the banks of the river Conan, some five miles from the town of Dingwall. The family travelled thither in a covered cart, a distance of 200 miles, through a very wild and hilly country, arriving at their destination at the end of October, 1799. The farm, when reached, was found overgrown with whins and brushwood, and covered in many places with great stones and rocks ; it was, in short, as nearly in a state of nature as it was possible to be. The house intended for the farmer's reception was not finished, and Andrew Fairbairn, with his wife and five children, had to take temporary refuge in a miserable hovel, very unlike the comfortable house which they had quitted at Kelso. By next spring, however, the new house was ready; and Andrew Fairbairn set vigorously to work at the reclamation of the land. After about two years' labours it exhibited an altogether different appearance, and in place of whins and stones there were to be seen heavy crops of barley and turnips. The barren years of 1800 and 1801, however, pressed very hardly on Andrew Fairbairn as on every other farmer of arable land. About that time, Andrew's brother Peter, who acted as secretary to Lord Seaforth, and through whose influence the former had obtained the farm, left Brahan Castle for the West Indies with his Lordship, who—notwithstanding his being both deaf and dumb—had been appointed to the Governorship of Barbadoes; and in consequence of various difficulties which occurred shortly after his leaving, Andrew Fairbairn found it necessary to give up his holding, whereupon he engaged as steward to Mackenzie of Allengrange, with whom he remained for two years.

While the family lived at Moy, none of the boys were put to school. They could not be spared from the farm and the household. Those of them that could not work afield were wanted to help to nurse the younger children at home. But Andrew Fairbairn possessed a great treasure in his wife, who was a woman of much energy of character, setting before her children an example of patient industry, thrift, discreetness, and piety, which could not fail to exercise a powerful influence upon them in after-life; and this, of itself, was an education which probably far more than compensated for the boys' loss of school-culture during their life at Moy. Mrs. Fairbairn span and made all the children's clothes, as well as the blankets and sheeting; and, while in the Highlands, she not only made her own and her daughters' dresses, and her sons' jackets and trowsers, but her husband's coats and waistcoats; besides helping her neighbours to cut out their clothing for family wear.

One of William's duties at home was to nurse his younger

brother Peter, then a delicate child under two years old; and to relieve himself of the labour of carrying him about, he began the construction of a little waggon in which to wheel him. This was, however, a work of some difficulty, as all the tools he possessed were only a knife, a gimlet, and an old saw. With these implements, a piece of thin board, and a few nails, he nevertheless contrived to make a tolerably serviceable waggon-body. His chief difficulty consisted in making the wheels, which he contrived to surmount by cutting sections from the stem of a small alder-tree, and with a red-hot poker he bored the requisite holes in their centres to receive the axle. The waggon was then mounted on its four wheels, and to the great joy of its maker was found to answer its purpose admirably. In it he wheeled his little brother—afterwards well known as Sir Peter Fairbairn, mayor of Leeds—in various directions about the farm, and sometimes to a considerable distance from it; and the vehicle was regarded on the whole as a decided success. His father encouraged him in his little feats of construction of a similar kind, and he proceeded to make and rig miniature boats and ships, and then miniature wind and water mills, in which last art he acquired such expertness that he had sometimes five or six mills going at a time. The machinery was all made with a knife, the water-spouts being formed by the bark of a tree, and the millstones represented by round discs of the same material. Such were the first constructive efforts of the future millwright and engineer.

When the family removed to Allengrange in 1801, the boys were sent to school at Munlachy, about a mile and a half distant from the farm. The school was attended by about forty barefooted boys in tartan kilts, and about twenty girls, all of the poorer class. The schoolmaster was one Donald Frazer, a good teacher, but a severe disciplinarian. Under him, William made some progress in reading, writing, and arithmetic; and though he himself has often lamented the meagreness of his school instruction, it is clear, from what he has since been enabled to accomplish, that these early lessons were enough at all events to set him fairly on the road of self-culture, and proved the fruitful seed of much valuable intellectual labour, as well as of many excellent practical books.

After two years' trial of his new situation, which was by no means satisfactory, Andrew Fairbairn determined again to remove southward with his family; and, selling off everything, they set sail from Cromarty for Leith in June, 1803. Having seen his wife and children temporarily settled at Kelso, he looked out for a situation, and shortly after proceeded to undertake the management of Sir William Ingleby's farm at Ripley in Yorkshire. Meanwhile William was placed for three months under the charge of his uncle William, the parish schoolmaster of Galashiels, for the purpose of receiving instruction in book-keeping and land-surveying, from which he derived considerable benefit. He could not, however, remain longer at school; for being of the age of fourteen, it was thought necessary that he should be set to work without further delay. His first employment was on the fine new bridge at Kelso, then in course of construction after the designs of Mr. Rennie; but in helping one day to carry a handbarrow-load of stone, his strength proving insufficient, he gave way under it, and the stones fell upon him, one of them inflicting a serious wound on his leg, which kept him a cripple for months. In the mean time his father, being dissatisfied with his prospects at Ripley, accepted the appointment of manager of the Percy Main Colliery Company's farm in the neighbourhood of Newcastle-on-Tyne, whither he proceeded with his family towards the end of 1803, William joining them in the following February, when the wound in his leg had sufficiently healed to enable him to travel.

Percy Main is situated within two miles of North Shields, and is one of the largest collieries in that district. William was immediately set to work at the colliery, his first employment being to lead coals from behind the screen to the pitmen's houses.   His Scotch accent, and perhaps his awkwardness, exposed him to much annoyance from the " pit lads," who were a very rough and profligate set; and as boxing was a favourite pastime among them, our youth had to fight his way to their respect, passing through a campaign of no less than seventeen pitched battles.   He was several times on the point of abandoning the work altogether, rather than undergo the buffetings and insults to which he was almost a daily martyr, when a protracted contest with one of the noted boxers of the colliery, in which he proved the victor, at length relieved him from further persecution.

In the following year, at the age of sixteen, he was articled as an engineer for five years to the owners of Percy Main, and was placed under the charge of Mr. Robinson, the engine-wright of the colliery.   His wages as apprentice were 8s. a week; but by working over-hours, making wooden wedges used in pit-work, and blocking out segments of solid oak required for walling the sides of the mine, he considerably increased his earnings, which enabled him to add to the gross income of the family, who were still struggling with the difficulties of small means and increasing expenses.   When not engaged upon over-work in the evenings, he occupied himself in self-education.   He drew up a scheme of daily study with this object, to which he endeavoured to adhere as closely as possible,— devoting the evenings of Mondays to mensuration and arithmetic; Tuesdays to history and poetry; Wednesdays to recreation, novels, and romances; Thursdays to algebra and mathematics; Fridays to Euclid and trigonometry; Saturdays to recreation; and Sundays to church, Milton, and recreation.   He was enabled to extend the range of his reading by the help of the North Shields Subscription Library, to which his father entered him a subscriber. Portions of his spare time were also occasionally devoted to mechanical construction, in which he cultivated the useful art of handling tools.   One of his first attempts was

the contrivance of a piece of machinery worked by a weight
and a pendulum, that should at the same time serve for a
timepiece and an orrery; but his want of means, as well as
of time, prevented him prosecuting this contrivance to completion.   He was more successful with the construction of
a fiddle, on which he was ambitious to become a performer.
It must have been a tolerable instrument, for a professional
player offered him 20s. for it.   But though he succeeded in
making a fiddle, and for some time persevered in the attempt to play upon it, he did not succeed in producing any
satisfactory melody, and at length gave up the attempt,
convinced that nature had not intended him for a musician.*

In due course of time our young engineer was removed
from the workshop, and appointed to take charge of the
pumps of the mine and the steam-engine by which they
were kept in work.   This employment was more to his
taste, gave him better " insight," and afforded him greater
opportunities for improvement.   The work was, however,
very trying, and at times severe, especially in winter, the

---

* Long after, when married and
settled at Manchester, the fiddle, which
had been carefully preserved, was taken
down from the shelf for the amusement
of the children; but though they were
well enough pleased with it, the instrument was never brought from its place
without creating alarm in the mind of
their mother lest anybody should hear
it.   At length a dancing-master, who
was giving lessons in the neighbourhood, borrowed the fiddle, and, to the
great relief of the family, it was never returned.   Many years later Mr. Fairbairn
was present at the starting of a cotton
mill at Wesserling in Alsace belonging
to Messrs. Gros, Deval, and Co., for
which his Manchester firm had provided the mill-work and water-wheel
(the first erected in France on the suspension principle), when the event was
followed by an entertainment.   During
dinner Mr. Fairbairn had been explaining to M. Gros, who spoke a little
English, the nature of home-brewed
beer, which he much admired, having
tasted it when in England.   The dinner
was followed by music, in the perform-
ance of which the host himself took
part; and on Mr. Fairbairn's admiring
his execution on the violin, M. Gros
asked him if he played.   "A little,"
was the almost unconscious reply.
" Then you must have the goodness to
play some," and the instrument was
in a moment placed in his hands, amidst
urgent requests from all sides that he
should play.   There was no alternative;
so he proceeded to perform one of his
best tunes—" The Keel Row."   The
company listened with amazement,
until the performer's career was suddenly cut short by the host exclaiming
at the top of his voice, " Stop, stop,
Monsieur, by gar that be *home-brewed
music!*"

engineer being liable to be drenched with water every time that he descended the shaft to regulate the working of the pumps; but, thanks to a stout constitution, he bore through these exposures without injury, though others sank under them. At this period he had the advantage of occasional days of leisure, to which he was entitled by reason of his nightwork; and during such leisure he usually applied himself to reading and study.

It was about this time that William Fairbairn made the acquaintance of George Stephenson, while the latter was employed in working the ballast-engine at Willington Quay. He greatly admired George as a workman, and was accustomed in the summer evenings to go over to the Quay occasionally and take charge of George's engine, to enable him to earn a few shillings extra by heaving ballast out of the collier vessels. Stephenson's zeal in the pursuit of mechanical knowledge probably was not without its influence in stimulating William Fairbairn himself to carry on so diligently the work of self-culture. But little could the latter have dreamt, while serving his apprenticeship at Percy Main, that his friend George Stephenson, the brakesman, should yet be recognised as among the greatest engineers of his age, and that he himself should have the opportunity, in his capacity of President of the Institute of Mechanical Engineers at Newcastle, of making public acknowledgment of the opportunities for education which he had enjoyed in that neighbourhood in his early years.*

---

* "Although not a native of Newcastle," he then said, "he owed almost everything to Newcastle. He got the rudiments of his education there, such as it was; and that was (something like that of his revered predecessor George Stephenson) at a colliery. He was brought up as an engineer at the Percy Main Colliery. He was there seven years; and if it had not been for the opportunities he then enjoyed, together with the use of the library at North Shields, he believed he would not have been there to address them. Being self-taught, but with some little ambition, and a determination to improve himself, he was now enabled to stand before them with some pretensions to mechanical knowledge, and the persuasion that he had been a useful contributor to practical science and objects connected with mechanical engineering."—*Meeting of the Institute of Mechanical Engineers at Newcastle-on-Tyne*, 1858.

Having finished his five years' apprenticeship at Percy Main, by which time he had reached his twenty-first year, William Fairbairn shortly after determined to go forth into the world in search of experience. At Newcastle he found employment as a millwright for a few weeks, during which he worked at the erection of a sawmill in the Close. From thence he went to Bedlington at an advanced wage. He remained there for six months, during which he was so fortunate as to make the acquaintance of Miss Mar, who five years after, when his wanderings had ceased, became his wife. On the completion of the job on which he had been employed, our engineer prepared to make another change. Work was difficult to be had in the North, and, joined by a comrade, he resolved to try his fortune in London. Adopting the cheapest route, he took passage by a Shields collier, in which he sailed for the Thames on the 11th of December, 1811. It was then war-time, and the vessel was very short-handed, the crew consisting only of three old men and three boys, with the skipper and mate; so that the vessel was no sooner fairly at sea than both the passenger youths had to lend a hand in working her, and this continued for the greater part of the voyage. The weather was very rough, and in consequence of the captain's anxiety to avoid privateers he hugged the shore too close, and when navigating the inside passage of the Swin, between Yarmouth and the Nore, the vessel very narrowly escaped shipwreck. After beating about along shore, the captain half drunk the greater part of the time, the vessel at last reached the Thames with loss of spars and an anchor, after a tedious voyage of fourteen days.

On arriving off Blackwall the captain went ashore ostensibly in search of the Coal Exchange, taking our young engineer with him. The former was still under the influence of drink; and though he failed to reach the Exchange that night, he succeeded in reaching a public house in Wapping, beyond which he could not be got. At ten o'clock the two started on their return to the ship; but

the captain took the opportunity of the darkness to separate from his companion, and did not reach the ship until
next morning. It afterwards came out that he had been
taken up and lodged in the watch-house. The youth,
left alone in the streets of the strange city, felt himself in
an awkward dilemma. He asked the next watchman he
met to recommend him to a lodging, on which the man
took him to a house in New Gravel Lane, where he succeeded in finding accommodation. What was his horror
next morning to learn that a whole family—the William-
sons—had been murdered in the very next house during
the night! Making the best of his way back to the ship,
he found that his comrade, who had suffered dreadfully
from sea-sickness during the voyage, had nearly recovered,
and was able to accompany him into the City in search of
work. They had between them a sum of only about eight
pounds, so that it was necessary for them to take immediate steps to obtain employment.

They thought themselves fortunate in getting the promise of a job from Mr. Rennie, the celebrated engineer,
whose works were situated at the south end of Blackfriars
Bridge. Mr. Rennie sent the two young men to his foreman, with the request that he should set them to work.
The foreman referred them to the secretary of the Millwrights' Society, the shop being filled with Union men,
who set their shoulders together to exclude those of their
own grade, however skilled, who could not produce evidence that they had complied with the rules of the trade.
Describing his first experience of London Unionists, nearly
half a century later, before an assembly of working men at
Derby, Mr. Fairbairn said, " When I first entered London,
a young man from the country had no chance whatever of
success, in consequence of the trade guilds and unions. I
had no difficulty in finding employment, but before I could
begin work I had to run the gauntlet of the trade societies;
and after dancing attendance for nearly six weeks, with
very little money in my pocket, and having to ' box Harry '

all the time, I was ultimately declared illegitimate, and sent adrift to seek my fortune elsewhere. There were then three millwright societies in London : one called the Old Society, another the New Society, and a third the Independent Society. These societies were not founded for the protection of the trade, but for the maintenance of high wages, and for the exclusion of all those who could not assert their claims to work in London and other corporate towns. Laws of a most arbitrary character were enforced, and they were governed by cliques of self-appointed officers, who never failed to take care of their own interests." *

Their first application for leave to work in London having thus disastrously ended, the two youths determined to try their fortune in the country, and with aching hearts they started next morning before daylight. Their hopes had been suddenly crushed, their slender funds were nearly exhausted, and they scarce knew where to turn. But they set their faces bravely northward, and pushed along the high road, through slush and snow, as far as Hertford, which they reached after nearly eight hours' walking, on the moderate fare during their journey of a penny roll and a pint of ale each. Though wet to the skin, they immediately sought out a master millwright, and applied for work. He said he had no job vacant at present; but, seeing their sorry plight, he had compassion upon them, and said, " Though I cannot give you employment, you seem to be two nice lads ;" and he concluded by offering Fairbairn a half-crown. But his proud spirit revolted at taking money which he had not earned ; and he declined the proffered gift with thanks, saying he was sorry they could not have work. He then turned away from the door, on which his companion, mortified by his refusal to accept the half-crown at a time when they were reduced almost to their last penny, broke out in bitter remonstrances and regrets. Weary, wet, and disheartened,

---

* *Useful Information for Engineers*, 2nd series, 1860, p. 211.

the two turned into Hertford churchyard, and rested for a while upon a tombstone, Fairbairn's companion relieving himself by a good cry, and occasional angry outbursts of " Why didn't you take the half-crown?"   " Come, come, man!" said Fairbairn, " it's of no use crying; cheer up; let's try another road; something must soon cast up." They rose, and set out again, but when they reached the bridge, the dispirited youth again broke down; and, leaning his back against the parapet, said, " I winna gang a bit further; let's get back to London."   Against this Fairbairn remonstrated, saying " It's of no use lamenting; we must try what we can do here; if the worst comes to the worst, we can 'list; you are a strong chap—they'll soon take you; and as for me, I'll join too; I think I could fight a bit."   After this council of war, the pair determined to find lodgings in the town for the night, and begin their search for work anew on the morrow.

Next day, when passing along one of the back streets of Hertford, they came to a wheelwright's shop, where they made the usual enquiries.   The wheelwright said that he did not think there was any job to be had in the town; but if the two young men pushed on to Cheshunt, he thought they might find work at a windmill which was under contract to be finished in three weeks, and where the millwright wanted hands.   Here was a glimpse of hope at last; and the strength and spirits of both revived in an instant.   They set out immediately; walked the seven miles to Cheshunt; succeeded in obtaining the expected employment; worked at the job a fortnight; and entered London again with nearly three pounds in their pockets.

Our young millwright at length succeeded in obtaining regular employment in the metropolis at good wages.   He worked first at Grundy's Patent Ropery at Shadwell, and afterwards at Mr. Penn's of Greenwich, gaining much valuable insight, and sedulously improving his mind by study in his leisure hours.   Among the acquaintances he then made was an enthusiastic projector of the name of

Hall, who had taken out one patent for making hemp from bean-stalks, and contemplated taking out another for effecting spade tillage by steam. The young engineer was invited to make the requisite model, which he did, and it cost him both time and money, which the out-at-elbows projector was unable to repay; and all that came of the project was the exhibition of the model at the Society of Arts and before the Board of Agriculture, in whose collection it is probably still to be found. Another more successful machine constructed by Mr. Fairbairn about the same time was a sausage-chopping machine, which he contrived and made for a pork-butcher for 33l. It was the first order he had ever had on his own account; and, as the machine when made did its work admirably, he was naturally very proud of it. The machine was provided with a fly-wheel and double crank, with connecting rods which worked a cross head. It contained a dozen knives crossing each other at right angles in such a way as to enable them to mince or divide the meat on a revolving block. Another part of the apparatus accomplished the filling of the sausages in a very expert manner, to the entire satisfaction of the pork-butcher.

As work was scarce in London at the time, and our engineer was bent on gathering further experience in his trade, he determined to make a tour in the South of England and South Wales; and set out from London in April 1813 with 7l. in his pocket. After visiting Bath and Frome, he settled to work for six weeks at Bathgate; after which he travelled by Bradford and Trowbridge— always on foot—to Bristol. From thence he travelled through South Wales, spending a few days each at Newport, Llandaff, and Cardiff, where he took ship for Dublin. By the time he reached Ireland his means were all but exhausted, only three-halfpence remaining in his pocket; but, being young, hopeful, skilful, and industrious, he was light of heart, and looked cheerfully forward. The next day he succeeded in finding employment at Mr.

Robinson's, of the Phœnix Foundry, where he was put to work at once upon a set of patterns for some nail-machinery. Mr. Robinson was a man of spirit and enterprise, and, seeing the quantities of English machine-made nails imported into Ireland, he was desirous of giving Irish industry the benefit of the manufacture. The construction of the nail-making machinery occupied Mr. Fairbairn the entire summer; and on its completion he set sail in the month of October for Liverpool. It may be added, that, notwithstanding the expense incurred by Mr. Robinson in setting up the new nail-machinery, his workmen threatened him with a strike if he ventured to use it. As he could not brave the opposition of the Unionists, then all-powerful in Dublin, the machinery was never set to work; the nail-making trade left Ireland, never to return; and the Irish market was thenceforward supplied entirely with English-made nails. The Dublin iron-manufacture was ruined in the same way; not through any local disadvantages, but solely by the prohibitory regulations enforced by the workmen of the Trades' Unions.

Arrived at Liverpool, after a voyage of two days—which was then considered a fair passage—our engineer proceeded to Manchester, which had already become the principal centre of manufacturing operations in the North of England. As we have already seen in the memoirs of Nasmyth, Roberts, and Whitworth, Manchester offered great attractions for highly-skilled mechanics; and it was as fortunate for Manchester as for William Fairbairn himself that he settled down there as a working millwright in the year 1814, bringing with him no capital, but an abundance of energy, skill, and practical experience in his trade. Afterwards describing the characteristics of the millwright of that time, Mr. Fairbairn said—" In those days a good millwright was a man of large resources; he was generally well educated, and could draw out his own designs and work at the lathe; he had a knowledge of mill machinery, pumps, and cranes, and could turn his

hand to the bench or the forge with equal adroitness and
facility.   If hard pressed, as was frequently the case in
country places far from towns, he could devise for himself
expedients which enabled him to meet special requirements, and to complete his work without assistance.   This
was the class of men with whom I associated in early
life—proud of their calling, fertile in resources, and aware
of their value in a country where the industrial arts were
rapidly developing."*

When William Fairbairn entered Manchester he was
twenty-four years of age; and his hat still " covered his
family."   But, being now pretty well satiated with his
" wanderschaft,"—as German tradesmen term their stage
of travelling in search of trade experience,—he desired to
settle, and, if fortune favoured him, to marry the object of
his affections, to whom his heart still faithfully turned
during all his wanderings.   He succeeded in finding employment with Mr. Adam Parkinson, remaining with him
for two years, working as a millwright, at good wages.
Out of his earnings he saved sufficient to furnish a two-
roomed cottage comfortably; and there we find him fairly
installed with his wife by the end of 1816.   As in the
case of most men of a thoughtful turn, marriage served not
only to settle our engineer, but to stimulate him to more
energetic action.   He now began to aim at taking a higher
position, and entertained the ambition of beginning business on his own account.   One of his first efforts in this
direction was the preparation of the design of a cast-iron
bridge over the Irwell, at Blackfriars, for which a prize
was offered.   The attempt was unsuccessful, and a stone
bridge was eventually decided on; but the effort made
was creditable, and proved the beginning of many designs.
The first job he executed on his own account was the
erection of an iron conservatory and hothouse for Mr. J.
Hulme, of Clayton, near Manchester; and he induced one

---

* Lecture at Derby—*Useful Information for Engineers*, 2nd series, p. 212.

of his shopmates, James Lillie, to join him in the undertaking. This proved the beginning of a business connection
which lasted for a period of fifteen years, and laid the
foundation of a partnership, the reputation of which, in
connection with mill-work and the construction of iron
machinery generally, eventually became known all over
the civilized world.

Although the patterns for the conservatory were all
made, and the castings were begun, the work was not proceeded with, in consequence of the notice given by a Birmingham firm that the plan after which it was proposed to
construct it was an infringement of their patent. The
young firm were consequently under the necessity of looking about them for other employment. And to be prepared
for executing orders, they proceeded in the year 1817 to
hire a small shed at a rent of 12s. a week, in which they
set up a lathe of their own making, capable of turning
shafts of from 3 to 6 inches diameter; and they hired a
strong Irishman to drive the wheel and assist at the heavy
work. Their first job was the erection of a cullender, and
their next a calico-polishing machine; but orders came in
slowly, and James Lillie began to despair of success. His
more hopeful partner strenuously urged him to perseverance, and so buoyed him up with hopes of orders, that
he determined to go on a little longer. They then issued
cards among the manufacturers, and made a tour of the
principal firms, offering their services and soliciting work.

Amongst others, Mr. Fairbairn called upon the Messrs.
Adam and George Murray, the large cotton-spinners, taking
with him the designs of his iron bridge. Mr. Adam Murray
received him kindly, heard his explanations, and invited
him to call on the following day with his partner. The
manufacturer must have been favourably impressed by this
interview, for next day, when Fairbairn and Lillie called,
he took them over his mill, and asked whether they felt themselves competent to renew with horizontal cross-shafts the
whole of the work by which the mule-spinning machinery

was turned. This was a formidable enterprise for a young
firm without capital and almost without plant to undertake ; but they had confidence in themselves, and boldly
replied that they were willing and able to execute the
work. On this, Mr. Murray said he would call and see
them at their own workshop, to satisfy himself that they
possessed the means of undertaking such an order. This
proposal was by no means encouraging to the partners,
who feared that when Mr. Murray spied " the nakedness of
the land " in that quarter, he might repent him of his generous intentions. He paid his promised visit, and it is probable that he was more favourably impressed by the individual merits of the partners than by the excellence of
their machine-tools—of which they had only one, the lathe
which they had just made and set up ; nevertheless he
gave them the order, and they began with glad hearts and
willing hands and minds to execute this their first contract.
It may be sufficient to state that by working late and
early—from 5 in the morning until 9 at night for a considerable period—they succeeded in completing the alterations within the time specified, and to Mr. Murray's entire
satisfaction. The practical skill of the young men being
thus proved, and their anxiety to execute the work entrusted to them to the best of their ability having excited
the admiration of their employer, he took the opportunity
of recommending them to his friends in the trade, and
amongst others to Mr. John Kennedy, of the firm of
MacConnel and Kennedy, then the largest spinners in the
kingdom.

The Cotton Trade had by this time sprung into great
importance, and was increasing with extraordinary rapidity. Population and wealth were pouring into South
Lancashire, and industry and enterprise were everywhere
on foot. The foundations were being laid of a system of
manufacturing in iron, machinery, and textile fabrics of
nearly all kinds, the like of which has perhaps never been
surpassed in any country. It was a race of industry, in

which the prizes were won by the swift, the strong, and
the skilled. For the most part, the early Lancashire
manufacturers started very nearly equal in point of worldly
circumstances, men originally of the smallest means often
coming to the front — workmen, weavers, mechanics,
pedlers, farmers, or labourers—in course of time rearing
immense manufacturing concerns by sheer force of industry, energy, and personal ability. The description
given by one of the largest employers in Lancashire, of
the capital with which he started, might apply to many
of them : " When I married," said he, " my wife had a
spinning-wheel, and I had a loom—that was the beginning
of our fortune." As an illustration of the rapid rise of
Manchester men from small beginnings, the following
outline of John Kennedy's career, intimately connected as
he was with the subject of our memoir—may not be
without interest in this place.

John Kennedy was one of five young men of nearly the
same age, who came from the same neighbourhood in
Scotland, and eventually settled in Manchester as cotton-
spinners about the end of last century. The others were
his brother James, his partner James MacConnel, and
the brothers Murray, above referred to—Mr. Fairbairn's
first extensive employers. John Kennedy's parents were
respectable peasants, possessed of a little bit of ground at
Knocknalling, in the stewartry of Kirkcudbright, on which
they contrived to live, and that was all. John was one
of a family of five sons and two daughters, and the father
dying early, the responsibility and the toil of bringing up
these children devolved upon the mother. She was a
strict disciplinarian, and early impressed upon the minds
of her boys that they had their own way to make in the
world. One of the first things she made them think about
was, the learning of some useful trade for the purpose of
securing an independent living ; " for," said she, " if you
have gotten mechanical skill and intelligence, and are
honest and trustworthy, you will always find employment

and be ready to avail yourselves of opportunities for advancing yourselves in life." Though the mother desired to give her sons the benefits of school education, there was but little of that commodity to be had in the remote district of Knocknalling. The parish-school was six miles distant, and the teaching given in it was of a very inferior sort—usually administered by students, probationers for the ministry, or by half-fledged dominies, themselves more needing instruction than able to impart it. The Kennedys could only attend the school during a few months in summer-time, so that what they had acquired by the end of one season was often forgotten by the beginning of the next. They learnt, however, to read the Testament, say their catechism, and write their own names.

As the children grew up, they each longed for the time to come when they could be put to a trade. The family were poorly clad ; stockings and shoes were luxuries rarely indulged in ; and Mr. Kennedy used in after-life to tell his grandchildren of a certain Sunday which he remembered shortly after his father died, when he was setting out for Dalry church, and had borrowed his brother Alexander's stockings, his brother ran after him and cried, " See that you keep out of the dirt, for mind you have got my stockings on ! " John indulged in many day-dreams about the world that lay beyond the valley and the mountains which surrounded the place of his birth. Though a mere boy, the natural objects, eternally unchangeable, which daily met his eyes—the profound silence of the scene, broken only by the bleating of a solitary sheep, or the crowing of a distant cock, or the thrasher beating out with his flail the scanty grain of the black oats spread upon a skin in the open air, or the streamlets leaping from the rocky clefts, or the distant church-bell sounding up the valley on Sundays — all bred in his mind a profound melancholy and feeling of loneliness, and he used to think to himself, " What can I do to see and know something of the world beyond this ? " The greatest pleasure he ex-

perienced during that period was when packmen came round
with their stores of clothing and hardware, and displayed
them for sale; he eagerly listened to all that such visitors
had to tell of the ongoings of the world beyond the valley.

The people of the Knocknalling district were very poor.
The greater part of them were unable to support the
younger members, whose custom it was to move off elsewhere in search of a living when they arrived at working
years,—some to America, some to the West Indies, and
some to the manufacturing districts of the south. Whole
families took their departure in this way, and the few
friendships which Kennedy formed amongst those of his
own age were thus suddenly snapped, and only a great blank
remained. But he too could follow their example, and
enter upon that wider world in which so many others had
ventured and succeeded. As early as eight years of age,
his mother still impressing upon her boys the necessity of
learning to work, John gathered courage to say to her that
he wished to leave home and apprentice himself to some
handicraft business. Having seen some carpenters working in the neighbourhood, with good clothes on their
backs, and hearing the men's characters well spoken of,
he thought it would be a fine thing to be a carpenter too,
particularly as the occupation would enable him to move
from place to place and see the world. He was as yet,
however, of too tender an age to set out on the journey of
life; but when he was about eleven years old, Adam
Murray, one of his most intimate acquaintances, having
gone off to serve an apprenticeship in Lancashire with
Mr. Cannan of Chowbent, himself a native of the district,
the event again awakened in him a strong desire to mi-
grate from Knocknalling. Others had gone after Murray,
James MacConnel and two or three more; and at length,
at about fourteen years of age, Kennedy himself left his
native home for Lancashire.

About the time that he set out, Paul Jones was ravaging
the coasts of Galloway, and producing general consterna-

tion throughout the district. Great excitement also prevailed through the occurrence of the Gordon riots in
London, which extended into remote country places; and
Kennedy remembered being nearly frightened out of his
wits on one occasion by a poor dominie whose school he
attended, who preached to his boys about the horrors that
were coming upon the land through the introduction of
Popery. The boy set out for England on the 2nd of
February, 1784, mounted upon a Galloway, his little pack-
age of clothes and necessaries strapped behind him. As
he passed along the glen, recognising each familiar spot,
his heart was in his mouth, and he dared scarcely trust
himself to look back. The ground was covered with snow,
and nature quite frozen up. He had the company of his
brother Alexander as far as the town of New Galloway,
where he slept the first night. The next day, accompanied
by one of his future masters, Mr. James Smith, a partner
of Mr. Cannan's, who had originally entered his service as
a workman, they started on ponyback for Dumfries. After
a long day's ride, they entered the town in the evening,
and amongst the things which excited the boy's surprise
were the few street-lamps of the town, and a waggon with
four horses and four wheels. In his remote valley carts
were as yet unknown, and even in Dumfries itself they
were comparative rarities; the common means of transport
in the district being what were called " tumbling cars."
The day after, they reached Longtown, and slept there;
the boy noting *another* lamp. The next stage was to Carlisle, where Mr. Smith, whose firm had supplied a carding
engine and spinning-jenny to a small manufacturer in the
town, went to " gate " and trim them. One was put up
in a small house, the other in a small room; and the sight
of these machines was John Kennedy's first introduction
to cotton-spinning. While going up the inn-stairs he was
amazed and not a little alarmed at seeing two men in
armour—he had heard of the battles between the Scots
and English—and believed these to be some of the fighting

men; though they proved to be but effigies.   Five more
days were occupied in travelling southward, the resting-
places being at Penrith, Kendal, Preston, and Chorley, the
two travellers arriving at Chowbent on Sunday the 8th of
February, 1784.   Mr. Cannan seems to have collected about
him a little colony of Scotsmen, mostly from the same
neighbourhood, and in the evening there was quite an
assembly of them at the "Bear's Paw," where Kennedy put
up, to hear the tidings from their native county brought
by the last new comer.   On the following morning the
boy began his apprenticeship as a carpenter with the firm
of Cannan and Smith, serving seven years for his meat and
clothing.   He applied himself to his trade, and became
a good, steady workman.   He was thoughtful and self-
improving, always endeavouring to acquire knowledge of
new arts and to obtain insight into new machines.   "Even
in early life," said he, in the account of his career addressed to his children, "I felt a strong desire to know
what others knew, and was always ready to communicate
what little I knew myself; and by admitting at once my
want of education, I found that I often made friends of
those on whom I had no claims beyond what an ardent
desire for knowledge could give me."

His apprenticeship over, John Kennedy commenced
business * in a small way in Manchester in 1791, in conjunction with two other workmen, Sandford and MacConnel.
Their business was machine-making and mule-spinning,

---

* One of the reasons which induced
Kennedy thus early to begin the business of mule-spinning has been related
as follows.   While employed as apprentice at Chowbent, he happened to
sleep over the master's apartment;
and late one evening, on the latter
returning from market, his wife asked
his success.   "I've sold the eightys,"
said he, "at a guinea a pound."
"What," exclaimed the mistress, in
a loud voice, "sold the eightys for
only a guinea a pound! I never heard
of such a thing."   The apprentice
could not help overhearing the remark,
and it set him a-thinking.   He knew
the price of cotton and the price of
labour, and concluded there must be a
very large margin of profit.   So soon
as he was out of his time, therefore,
he determined that he should become
a cotton spinner.

Kennedy taking the direction of the machine department.
The firm at first put up their mules for spinning in any
convenient garrets they could hire at a low rental. After
some time, they took part of a small factory in Canal Street,
and carried on their business on a larger scale. Kennedy
and MacConnel afterwards occupied a little factory in the
same street,—since removed to give place to Fairbairn's
large machine works. The progress of the firm was steady
and even rapid, and they went on building mills and
extending their business—Mr. Kennedy, as he advanced
in life, gathering honour, wealth, and troops of friends.
Notwithstanding the defects of his early education, he
was one of the few men of his class who became distinguished for his literary labours in connexion principally
with the cotton trade. Towards the close of his life, he
prepared several papers of great interest for the Literary
and Philosophical Society of Manchester, which are to be
found printed in their Proceedings; one of these, on the
Invention of the Mule by Samuel Crompton, was for a
long time the only record which the public possessed of
the merits and claims of that distinguished inventor. His
knowledge of the history of the cotton manufacture in its
various stages, and of mechanical inventions generally, was
most extensive and accurate. Among his friends he numbered James Watt, who placed his son in his establishment
for the purpose of acquiring knowledge and experience
of his profession. At a much later period he numbered
George Stephenson among his friends, having been one
of the first directors of the Liverpool and Manchester
Railway, and one of the three judges (selected because of
his sound judgment and proved impartiality, as well as his
knowledge of mechanical engineering) to adjudicate on
the celebrated competition of locomotives at Rainhill. By
these successive steps did this poor Scotch boy become one
of the leading men of Manchester, closing his long and
useful life in 1855 at an advanced age, his mental faculties
remaining clear and unclouded to the last. His departure

from life was happy and tranquil—so easy that it was for a time doubtful whether he was dead or asleep.

To return to Mr. Fairbairn's career, and his progress as a millwright and engineer in Manchester. When he and his partner undertook the extensive alterations in Mr. Murray's factory, both were in a great measure unacquainted with the working of cotton-mills, having until then been occupied principally with corn-mills, and printing and bleaching works; so that an entirely new field was now opened to their united exertions. Sedulously improving their opportunities, the young partners not only thoroughly mastered the practical details of cotton-mill work, but they were very shortly enabled to introduce a series of improvements of the greatest importance in this branch of our national manufactures. Bringing their vigorous practical minds to bear on the subject, they at once saw that the gearing of even the best mills was of a very clumsy and imperfect character. They found the machinery driven by large square cast-iron shafts, on which huge wooden drums, some of them as much as four feet in diameter, revolved at the rate of about forty revolutions a minute; and the couplings were so badly fitted that they might be heard creaking and groaning a long way off. The speeds of the driving-shafts were mostly got up by a series of straps and counter drums, which not only crowded the rooms, but seriously obstructed the light where most required for conducting the delicate operations of the different machines. Another serious defect lay in the construction of the shafts, and in the mode of fixing the couplings, which were constantly giving way, so that a week seldom passed without one or more breaks-down. The repairs were usually made on Sundays, which were the millwrights' hardest working days, to their own serious moral detriment; but when trade was good, every consideration was made to give way to the uninterrupted running of the mills during the rest of the week.

It occurred to Mr. Fairbairn that the defective arrangements thus briefly described, might be remedied by the introduction of lighter shafts driven at double or treble the velocity, smaller drums to drive the machinery, and the use of wrought-iron wherever practicable, because of its greater lightness and strength compared with wood. He also provided for the simplification of the hangers and fixings by which the shafting was supported, and introduced the "half-lap coupling" so well known to millwrights and engineers. His partner entered fully into his views; and the opportunity shortly presented itself of carrying them into effect in the large new mill erected in 1818, for the firm of MacConnel and Kennedy. The machinery of that concern proved a great improvement on all that had preceded it; and, to Messrs. Fairbairn and Lillie's new system of gearing Mr. Kennedy added an original invention of his own in a system of double speeds, with the object of giving an increased quantity of twist in the finer descriptions of mule yarn.

The satisfactory execution of this important work at once placed the firm of Fairbairn and Lillie in the very front rank of engineering millwrights. Mr. Kennedy's good word was of itself a passport to fame and business, and as he was more than satisfied with the manner in which his mill machinery had been planned and executed, he sounded their praises in all quarters. Orders poured in upon them so rapidly, that they had difficulty in keeping pace with the demands of the trade. They then removed from their original shed to larger premises in Mather-street, where they erected additional lathes and other tool-machines, and eventually a steam-engine. They afterwards added a large cellar under an adjoining factory to their premises; and from time to time provided new means of turning out work with increased efficiency and despatch. In due course of time the firm erected a factory of their own, fitted with the most improved machinery for turning out millwork; and they went on from one contract to another, until their reputation as engineers became widely

celebrated.   In 1826-7, they supplied the water-wheels for
the extensive cotton-mills belonging to Kirkman Finlay
and Company, at Catrine Bank in Ayrshire.   These
wheels are even at this day regarded as among the most
perfect hydraulic machines in Europe.   About the same
time they supplied the mill gearing and water-machinery
for Messrs. Escher and Company's large works at Zurich,
among the largest cotton manufactories on the continent.

In the mean while the industry of Manchester and the
neighbourhood, through which the firm had risen and prospered, was not neglected, but had the full benefit of the
various improvements which they were introducing in mill
machinery.   In the course of a few years an entire revolution
was effected in the gearing.   Ponderous masses of timber
and cast-iron, with their enormous bearings and couplings,
gave place to slender rods of wrought-iron and light frames
or hooks by which they were suspended.   In like manner,
lighter yet stronger wheels and pulleys were introduced,
the whole arrangements were improved, and, the workmanship being greatly more accurate, friction was avoided,
while the speed was increased from about 40 to upwards of
300 revolutions a minute.   The fly-wheel of the engine
was also converted into a first motion by the formation of
teeth on its periphery, by which a considerable saving was
effected both in cost and power.

These great improvements formed quite an era in the
history of mill machinery; and exercised the most important influence on the development of the cotton, flax,
silk, and other branches of manufacture.   Mr. Fairbairn
says the system introduced by his firm was at first strongly
condemned by leading engineers, and it was with difficulty
that he could overcome the force of their opposition; nor
was it until a wheel of thirty tons weight for a pair of
engines of 100-horse power each was erected and set to
work, that their prognostications of failure entirely ceased.
From that time the principles introduced by Mr. Fairbairn

have been adopted wherever steam is employed as a motive power in mills.

Mr. Fairbairn and his partner had a hard uphill battle to fight while these improvements were being introduced; but energy and perseverance, guided by sound judgment, secured their usual reward, and the firm became known as one of the most thriving and enterprising in Manchester. Long years after, when addressing an assembly of working men, Mr. Fairbairn, while urging the necessity of labour and application as the only sure means of self-improvement, said, " I can tell you from experience, that there is no labour so sweet, none so consolatory, as that which is founded upon an honest, straightforward, and honourable ambition." The history of any prosperous business, however, so closely resembles every other, and its details are usually of so monotonous a character, that it is unnecessary for us to pursue this part of the subject; and we will content ourselves with briefly indicating the several further improvements introduced by Mr. Fairbairn in the mechanics of construction in the course of his long and useful career.

His improvements in water-wheels were of great value, especially as regarded the new form of bucket which he introduced with the object of facilitating the escape of the air as the water entered the bucket above, and its readmission as the water emptied itself out below. This arrangement enabled the water to act upon the wheel with the maximum of effect in all states of the river; and it so generally recommended itself, that it very soon became adopted in most water-mills both at home and abroad.*

His labours were not, however, confined to his own particular calling as a mill engineer, but were shortly directed

---

* The subject will be found fully treated in Mr. Fairbairn's own work, *A Treatise on Mills and Mill-Work,* embodying the results of his large experience.

to other equally important branches of the constructive art. Thus he was among the first to direct his attention to iron ship building as a special branch of business. In 1829, Mr. Houston, of Johnstown, near Paisley, launched a light boat on the Ardrossan Canal for the purpose of ascertaining the speed at which it could be towed by horses with two or three persons on board. To the surprise of Mr. Houston and the other gentlemen present, it was found that the labour the horses had to perform in towing the boat was much greater at six or seven, than at nine miles an hour. This anomaly was very puzzling to the experimenters, and at the request of the Council of the Forth and Clyde Canal, Mr. Fairbairn, who had already become extensively known as a scientific mechanic, was requested to visit Scotland and institute a series of experiments with light boats to determine the law of traction, and clear up, if possible, the apparent anomalies in Mr. Houston's experiments. This he did accordingly, and the results of his experiments were afterwards published. The trials extended over a series of years, and were conducted at a cost of several thousand pounds. The first experiments were made with vessels of wood, but they eventually led to the construction of iron vessels upon a large scale and on an entirely new principle of construction, with angle iron ribs and wrought-iron sheathing plates. The results proved most valuable, and had the effect of specially directing the attention of naval engineers to the employment of iron in ship building.

Mr. Fairbairn himself fully recognised the value of the experiments, and proceeded to construct an iron vessel at his works at Manchester, in 1831, which went to sea the same year. Its success was such as to induce him to begin iron shipbuilding on a large scale, at the same time as the Messrs. Laird did at Birkenhead; and in 1835, Mr. Fairbairn established extensive works at Millwall, on the Thames,—afterwards occupied by Mr. Scott Russell, in whose yard the " Great Eastern " steamship was erected,—

where in the course of some fourteen years he built upwards
of a hundred and twenty iron ships, some of them above
2000 tons burden.   It was in fact the first great iron ship-
building yard in Britain, and led the way in a branch of
business which has since become of first-rate magnitude
and importance.   Mr. Fairbairn was a most laborious ex-
perimenter in iron, and investigated in great detail the
subject of its strength, the value of different kinds of
riveted joints compared with the solid plate, and the
distribution of the material throughout the structure, as
well as the form of the vessel itself.   It would indeed be
difficult to over-estimate the value of his investigations on
these points in the earlier stages of this now highly important branch of the national industry.

To facilitate the manufacture of his iron-sided ships,
Mr. Fairbairn, about the year 1839, invented a machine
for riveting boiler plates by steam-power.   The usual
method by which this process had before been executed
was by hand-hammers, worked by men placed at each side
of the plate to be riveted, acting simultaneously on both
sides of the bolt.   But this process was tedious and expensive, as well as clumsy and imperfect; and some more
rapid and precise method of fixing the plates firmly
together was urgently wanted.   Mr. Fairbairn's machine
completely supplied the want.   By its means the rivet was
driven into its place, and firmly fastened there by a couple
of strokes of a hammer impelled by steam.   Aided by
the Jacquard punching-machine of Roberts, the riveting
of plates of the largest size has thus become one of the
simplest operations in iron-manufacturing.

The thorough knowledge which Mr. Fairbairn possessed
of the strength of wrought-iron in the form of the hollow
beam (which a wrought-iron ship really is) naturally led
to his being consulted by the late Robert Stephenson as to
the structures by means of which it was proposed to span the
estuary of the Conway and the Straits of Menai; and the
result was the Conway and Britannia Tubular Bridges, the

history of which we have fully described elsewhere.* There is no reason to doubt that by far the largest share of the merit of working out the practical details of those structures, and thus realizing Robert Stephenson's magnificent idea of the tubular bridge, belongs to Mr. Fairbairn.

In all matters connected with the qualities and strength of iron, he came to be regarded as a first-rate authority, and his advice was often sought and highly valued. The elaborate experiments instituted by him as to the strength of iron of all kinds have formed the subject of various papers which he has read before the British Association, the Royal Society, and the Literary and Philosophical Society of Manchester. His practical inquries as to the strength of boilers have led to his being frequently called upon to investigate the causes of boiler explosions, on which subject he has published many elaborate reports. The study of this subject led him to elucidate the law according to which the density of steam varies throughout an extensive range of pressures and atmospheres,—in singular confirmation of what had before been provisionally calculated from the mechanical theory of heat. His discovery of the true method of preventing the tendency of tubes to collapse, by dividing the flues of long boilers into short lengths by means of stiffening rings, arising out of the same investigation, was one of the valuable results of his minute study of the subject; and is calculated to be of essential value in the manufacturing districts by diminishing the chances of boiler explosions, and saving the lamentable loss of life which has during the last twenty years been occasioned by the malconstruction of boilers. Among Mr. Fairbairn's most recent inquiries are those conducted by him at the instance of the British Government relative to the construction of iron-plated ships, his report of which

---

* *Lives of the Engineers*, vol. iii. 416-40. See also *An Account of the Construction of the Britannia and* *Conway Tubular Bridges*. By William Fairbairn, C.E. 1849.

has not yet been made public, most probably for weighty political reasons.

We might also refer to the practical improvements which Mr. Fairbairn has been instrumental in introducing in the construction of buildings of various kinds by the use of iron. He has himself erected numerous iron structures, and pointed out the road which other manufacturers have readily followed. " I am one of those," said he, in his ' Lecture on the Progress of Engineering,' " who have great faith in iron walls and iron beams; and although I have both spoken and written much on the subject, I cannot too forcibly recommend it to public attention. It is now twenty years since I constructed an iron house, with the machinery of a corn-mill, for Halil Pasha, then Seraskier of the Turkish army at Constantinople. I believe it was the first iron house built in this country; and it was constructed at the works at Millwall, London, in 1839." *

Since then iron structures of all kinds have been erected : iron lighthouses, iron-and-crystal palaces, iron churches, and iron bridges. Iron roads have long been worked by iron locomotives; and before many years have passed a telegraph of iron wire will probably be found circling the globe. We now use iron roofs, iron bedsteads, iron ropes, and iron

---

* *Useful Information for Engineers*, 2nd series, 225. The mere list of Mr. Fairbairn's writings would occupy considerable space; for, notwithstanding his great labours as an engineer, he has also been an industrious writer. His papers on Iron, read at different times before the British Association, the Royal Society, and the Literary and Philosophical Institution of Manchester, are of great value. The treatise on " Iron " in the *Encyclopædia Britannica* is from his pen, and he has contributed a highly interesting paper to Dr. Scoffern's *Useful Metals and their Alloys* on the Application of Iron to the purposes of Ordnance, Machinery, Bridges, and House and Ship Building. Another valuable but less-known contribution to Iron literature is his Report on Machinery in General, published in the *Reports on the Paris Universal Exhibition of* 1855. The experiments conducted by Mr. Fairbairn for the purpose of proving the excellent properties of iron for shipbuilding—the account of which was published in the *Transactions of the Royal Society*— eventually led to his further experiments to determine the strength and form of the Britannia and Conway Tubular Bridges, plate-girders, and other constructions, the result of which was to establish quite a new era in the history of bridge as well as ship building.

pavement; and even the famous "wooden walls of England" are rapidly becoming reconstructed of iron. In short, we are in the midst of what Mr. Worsaae has characterized as the Age of Iron.

At the celebration of the opening of the North Wales Railway at Bangor, almost within sight of his iron bridge across the Straits of Menai, Robert Stephenson said, "We are daily producing from the bowels of the earth a raw material, in its crude state apparently of no worth, but which, when converted into a locomotive engine, flies over bridges of the same material, with a speed exceeding that of the bird, advancing wealth and comfort throughout the country. Such are the powers of that all-civilizing instrument, Iron."

Iron indeed plays a highly important part in modern civilization. Out of it are formed alike the sword and the ploughshare, the cannon and the printing-press; and while civilization continues partial and half-developed, as it still is, our liberties and our industry must necessarily in a great measure depend for their protection upon the excellence of our weapons of war as well as on the superiority of our instruments of peace. Hence the skill and ingenuity displayed in the invention of rifled guns and artillery, and iron-sided ships and batteries, the fabrication of which would be impossible but for the extraordinary development of the iron-manufacture, and the marvellous power and precision of our tool-making machines, as described in preceding chapters.

"Our strength, wealth, and commerce," said Mr. Cobden in the course of a recent debate in the House of Commons, "grow out of the skilled labour of the men working in metals. They are at the foundation of our manufacturing greatness; and in case you were attacked, they would at once be available, with their hard hands and skilled brains, to manufacture your muskets and your cannon, your shot and your shell. What has given us our Armstrongs, Whitworths, and Fairbairns, but the free industry of this country? If you can build three times more steam-engines than any other country, and have threefold the force of mechanics, to whom and to what do you owe that, but to the men who have trained them, and to those principles of commerce out of which the wealth of the country has grown? We who have some hand in doing that, are not ignorant that we have been and are increasing the strength of the country in proportion as we are raising up skilled artisans." *

The reader who has followed us up to this point will have observed that handicraft labour was the first stage of the development of human power, and that machinery has been its last and highest. The uncivilized man began with a stone for a hammer, and a splinter of flint for a chisel, each stage of his progress being marked by an improvement in his tools. Every machine calculated to save labour or increase production was a substantial addition to his power over the material resources of nature, enabling him to subjugate them more effectually to his wants and uses; and every extension of machinery has served to introduce new classes of the population to the enjoyment of its benefits. In early times the products of skilled industry were for the most part luxuries intended for the few, whereas now the most exquisite tools and engines are employed in producing articles of ordinary consumption for the great mass of the community. Machines with millions of fingers work for millions of purchasers—for the poor as well as the rich; and while the machinery thus used enriches its owners, it no less enriches the public with its products.

Much of the progress to which we have adverted has been the result of the skill and industry of our own time. "Indeed," says Mr. Fairbairn, "the mechanical operations of the present day could not have been accomplished at any cost thirty years ago; and what was then considered

---

* House of Commons Debate, 7th July, 1862.

impossible is now performed with an exactitude that never fails to accomplish the end in view." For this we are mainly indebted to the almost creative power of modern machine-tools, and the facilities which they present for the production and reproduction of other machines. We also owe much to the mechanical agencies employed to drive them. Early inventors yoked wind and water to sails and wheels, and made them work machinery of various kinds; but modern inventors have availed themselves of the far more swift and powerful, yet docile force of steam, which has now laid upon it the heaviest share of the burden of toil, and indeed become the universal drudge. Coal, water, and a little oil, are all that the steam-engine, with its bowels of iron and heart of fire, needs to enable it to go on working night and day, without rest or sleep. Yoked to machinery of almost infinite variety, the results of vast ingenuity and labour, the Steam-engine pumps water, drives spindles, thrashes corn, prints books, hammers iron, ploughs land, saws timber, drives piles, impels ships, works railways, excavates docks; and, in a word, asserts an almost unbounded supremacy over the materials which enter into the daily use of mankind, for clothing, for labour, for defence, for household purposes, for locomotion, for food, or for instruction.

INDEX.

THE END.